The Unbearable
Wholeness of Being

The Unbearable
Wholeness of Being

God, Evolution, and the Power of Love

ILIA DELIO, OSF

ORBIS BOOKS

Maryknoll, New York 10545

Fourteenth printing, March 2023

Library of Congress Cataloging-in-Publication Data

Delio, Ilia.
 The unbearable wholeness of being : God, evolution and the power of love / Ilia Delio.
  p. cm.
 Includes bibliographical references and index.
 ISBN 978–1–62698–029–7 (pbk.)
 1. God (Christianity)—Omnipresence. 2. Evolution—Religious aspects—Catholic Church. 3. Christianity—Philosophy. 4. Spirituality—Catholic Church. 5. Love—Religious aspects—Christianity. I. Title.
BT132.D45 2013
231—dc23

                   2012042399

It is the attraction of the whole that has set everything in motion in me, has animated and given organic form to everything. It is because I feel the whole and love it passionately that I believe in the primacy of being . . . nothing in the world is intelligible except in and starting from the whole.

—TEILHARD DE CHARDIN
Science and Christ

At the center of our being is a point of nothingness that is untouched by sin and by illusion, a point of pure truth, a point or spark which belongs entirely to God, which is never at our disposal, from which God disposes our lives, which is inaccessible to the fantasies of our mind or the brutalities of our own will. . . . It is like a pure diamond, blazing with the invisible light of heaven. It is in everybody, and if we could see it we would see these billions of points of light coming together in the face and blaze of a sun that would make all the darkness and cruelty of life vanish completely.

—THOMAS MERTON
Conjectures of a Guilty Bystander

Contents

Acknowledgments   xi

Introduction   xiii

1. The Decentered Human   1

The Humpty Dumpty Earth   2
The Church and Science   5
Goodbye, God   7
The Mechanistic Universe   10
Death of the Human Person   13

2. Wholeness in Nature   17

Unfolding Life   22
Quantum Wholeness   24
Implicate Order   27
Systems Biology   30
Nature's Symphony   31
Holons and Holarchy   34

3. Love, Sex, and the Cosmos   37

Love and Omega   40
Love as a Cosmological Force   43
Cosmic Personalization   46
Altruism   51

4. Birthing a New God   57

Tillich and the Ultimate Depth of Being   62
Panikkar's Cosmotheandric Invariant   65
Teilhard de Chardin and Omega   67
Trinity—Creation   69

5. Love and Suffering   73

Kenosis and Creation   77
God's Vulnerable Love   81
Crucified Love   85
God Within   89

6. Sacred Secularity   93

Christian Secularity   98
A Worldly God   103
Mystic Oneness   105
Beyond World Religions   108
A New Religious Consciousness?   110

7. Christian Love   115

The Cosmic Person   120
Christogenesis   121
The Novelty of Jesus   127
Dying to Love   131

8. Love, Learning, and the Desire for Power   137

What Must I Know?   142
The Role of Thought in Evolution   145
The Catholic Intellectual Tradition   149
Education as Wholemaking   151

9. Technology and Noogenesis   155

Transhumanism   156
InfoPhilia   159
Technology and Ecology: Competing Myths?   163
Entering the Noosphere   168
Ultrahumanity   172
Evolution, Religion, and Technology   174

10. Contemplative Evolution   177

Conscious Love   179
Love and Worship   182
Transformation   188
Cosmic Personalization   192
Hope and Future Life   196

Conclusion/Unfinished   201

Select Bibliography   209

Index   215

Acknowledgments

I would like to thank Orbis Books for supporting my work and, in particular, my dear friend and advocate, Mike Leach. I am especially grateful to Sr. Madeline Duckett, RSM, who traveled from Australia to join me for eight weeks of discussion on Christianity, evolution, and emerging wholeness. Madeline read the book chapter by chapter, offering suggestions and insightful ways of engaging the material. Thanks too to Sr. Dorothy Mc-Cormack, OSF, who read several chapters and offered editorial changes. I am grateful for the patience and understanding of my community, the Franciscan Sisters of Washington, DC, as well as its support. A sincere thank you goes to my colleagues at Woodstock Theological Center, Georgetown University, for their support and encouragement as well. I have benefited from our Ignatian-Lonergan Seminars and continue to find our conversations deeply enriching. I would like to dedicate this book to my colleague Fr. John Haughey, SJ, who opened up for me a new lens on the virtue of catholicity. John never ceases to amaze me on how to live into our questions.

Introduction

In her keynote presentation at the 2009 annual conference of the Catholic Theological Society of America, Carmelite scholar Connie Fitzgerald spoke eloquently on the theme of impasse, dark night, and the purification of memory, a theme she has explored over the last several decades through the mystical writings of John of the Cross. Impasse is the space between what was and what can be, frozen or impassible by factors of fear, distrust, anger, darkness, and the many layers of memory. It is the space in which we find ourselves today, as Fitzgerald writes:

> Although my exploration raises its own disturbing questions, I hope it will offer a significant contribution to theological reflection at a time when polarization, suspicion, denouncement, investigation, silencing, alienation, anger, cynicism and sadness divide our Church, and when our country is rocked by economic meltdown precipitated by years of wrongdoing and greed, our earth menaced with extinction, the religions of the world plagued with extremism and age-old distrust that fuel war and terrorism, the people of the world abused with violence, slavery and deprivation too great to measure. We are encumbered by old assumptions, burdened by memories that limit our horizons and, therefore, unfree to see God coming to us from the future.[1]

Fitzgerald provides a profound analysis of the purification of memory, whereby in silent prayer, the "prayer of no experience,"

---

[1] Constance Fitzgerald, OCD, "From Impasse to Prophetic Hope: Crisis of Memory," CTSA Proceedings 64 (2009): 21–42.

a new dispossessed self can emerge that "realizes more fully our relational evolution and synergistic existence in the universe."[2]

Although her study is a complex interaction of culture, psychology, and spirituality, I think the impasse Fitzgerald skillfully articulates has been developing since the Late Middle Ages, when astronomers discovered that the earth orbits around the sun, marking the birth of modern science and philosophy. It was then that modernity's impasse was born. The human person became decentered from a stable universe, insignificant in the face of modern science, while God became remote and distant. The image of a blissful Garden of Eden recounted in scripture became less a constructive image of divine-human relatedness than a fallacy of misplaced concreteness. Science and technology gained prominence as guides for the human quest.

The impasse in which we find ourselves in today, the inability of ecclesial and cultural systems to cooperate for the welfare of humankind, bears the lack of a fundamental meta-narrative. We have no overarching story that unites us and instills hope and courage. The rise of postmodernity signaled an end to meta-narratives. The postmodern age of religious and cultural pluralism invited a multiplicity of narratives as the operative norm of human community. At the center of the postmodern milieu, marked by ambivalence and relevance, is the individual whose autonomy cannot be disturbed. You are you and I am I and if each of us follows our own story, the world machine will keep on humming.[3] But we have been inattentive to the cosmology that holds our lives together. How do our individual and communal stories shape our lives in the larger order of things? What

---

[2] Ibid., 22.

[3] *Postmodernism* is a complex term that describes the contemporary philosophical and cultural milieu. Coined in the 1930s, the term is used to describe the historical transition from modernity to a period beyond modernity, namely, postmodernity. Whereas modernity emphasized objective, logical thinking and a universal morality and law, postmodernity claims that all knowledge is derived from the self who interprets reality. Thus, there is no single, universal world view. Postmodernism celebrates the local and particular at the expense of the universal, and it emphasizes a respect for difference. For an introduction to postmodernism, see Stanley J. Grenz, *A Primer on Postmodernism* (Grand Rapids, MI: Eerdmans, 1996), 39–56.

holds us together despite our differences? We need a larger story that can include diversity and difference, and in which our local stories can thrive.

Stories create meaningful lives; they provide cohesiveness and direction. For centuries Christianity told a grand narrative of God, creation, and humanity that held such power and conviction that virtually all systems were based on it. We believed everything in the Bible to be historically true. Now, modern biblical scholarship discloses that stories of the Old and New Testaments were prayerfully created for the purpose of community, rather than as historical narratives. Yet, the stories of the Bible are deeply embedded in our religious consciousness and have provided images and symbols to define our relationship with God. In the Middle Ages theologians such as Thomas Aquinas and Bonaventure elaborated a system of Christian thought based on the Bible, the church fathers, medieval cosmology, and philosophy. Core Christian doctrine was formed against the backdrop of the concentric, static, and hierarchical Ptolemaic universe. To this day all our core doctrines are fitted to this universe even though, as early as the sixteenth century, modern science began to describe a new universe that departed from the static, Ptolemaic one. The inability to engage a new religious story, however, has confined us to the old one. The impasse we find ourselves in is centuries old, and until we can purify our memory, as Fitzgerald suggests, we are heading down a dangerous path.

The church has had trouble embracing the prophets of a new age, especially those announcing new stories and new ways to think about God and God's saving plan in Christ. In the mid–twentieth century a voice cried out in the desert declaring that a new (and exciting) story had arisen, although no one of institutional rank listened to him. Pierre Teilhard de Chardin was a Jesuit scientist and one of the most profound spiritual writers of the twentieth century. A paleontologist by training and a specialist in the Eocene Period (fifty-six to thirty-four million years ago), he was engaged in some of the most significant evolutionary discoveries of human origins. As he searched for artifacts to piece together the human story, he spent long periods of time in the desert (mostly in China), which enabled him to reflect deeply on his Christian faith and the significance of his faith in view of evolution. Like the desert fathers of old, Teilhard was removed from the noise of modern life and pondered deeply the meaning of Christianity in an age of evolution. His unique blend of science, Jesuit spirituality, and profound spiritual-mystical insight produced a body of writings that has yet to be explored fully. He grasped and sought to articulate the import of evolution not only for science but for modern culture. He wrote without the rigor of academic theology, that is, without a particular method of theology or a defined philosophical framework. His writings, therefore, are not systematically organized and have not attracted the serious scholarly attention they deserve. Rather, his work has been interpreted largely as poetic and spiritual. He was censored by Rome because he rejected original sin in light of evolution; as a result he was prohibited from publishing his writings during his lifetime. Thus he never benefited from peer review. Despite refinement of his ideas, his insights are remarkable and prophetic. Teilhard is the new Elijah, calling forth a new path of salvation in the twenty-first century. In this book he is my principal guide.

Evolution is a controversial word. It does not do well in public polls where 46 percent of the population believes that Adam and Eve actually existed and were created fully formed by God. The idea of evolution arose in the seventeenth century, in a non-biological context, and came to prominence in the nineteenth century with Charles Darwin's *Origin of the Species*. The controversy over teaching evolution in public schools has brought to light the degree of polarization with regard to evolution in the United States. While scientific materialists maintain that evolution is self-explanatory and self-sufficient to address life's deepest questions, religious fundamentalists fear that evolution opposes the work of God by contradicting scripture and crushing the dignity of the human person. Yet, evolution kindles the dawn of postmodernity because it marks the break from a closed, static world of law and order to an open world of change and play. Evolution is less a mechanism than a process—a constellation of law, chance, spontaneity, and deep time. Evolution tells us that nature is not a closed, causal system of events but a complex series of fluid, dynamic, interlocking, and communicative relationships. From a scientific perspective evolution provides a framework for understanding nature's intricate mechanisms. Although I am not using *evolution* in a scientific manner, I am using the concept as a paradigm based on modern science to understand the meaning and purpose of Christian life today. In this respect I follow the path of Teilhard de Chardin but widen his thought in dialogue with twentieth-century thinkers. In my view, evolution *is* the story, the meta-narrative of our age. It is not only a scientific explanation for physical reality; it is, rather, the overarching description of reality, the cosmological framework for all contemporary thought. While scientists continue to understand how evolution works for physical systems, it is important to understand how evolution works for religious systems as well, since physical reality and spiritual reality are intertwined. I am particularly interested in the relationship between Christianity and evolution, and the import of this relationship for the forward movement of Christian life. To understand this relationship I am taking an integral approach to theology (or what I call integral theology) that includes theology, spirituality, philosophy, technology, and history.

The Catholic Church has taken an ambivalent stance toward evolution. On one hand, it recognizes it as a theory of science and, on the other, says that it is a theory or a constellation of theories that science has yet to understand fully. Contrary to popular opinion, the Catholic Church is not opposed to science and, in fact, for centuries has strongly supported scientific endeavors. In his 1987 message to the director of the Vatican Observatory, Pope John Paul II stated that "science can purify religion from error and superstition; religion can purify science from idolatry and false absolutes. Each can draw the other into a wider world, a world in which both can flourish."[4] In his address to the Pontifical Academy of Sciences in 1996 the pope said that there was no opposition between evolution and the doctrine of faith according to *Humani generis,* but "almost half a century after the publication of the encyclical, new knowledge has led to the recognition of the theory of evolution as more than a hypothesis." However, he added that evolution pertains only to the material body; theories of evolution "which consider the spirit as emerging from the forces of living matter or as a mere *epiphenomenon* of this matter, are incompatible with the

---

[4] Pope John Paul II, "Letter to Rev. George V. Coyne, S.J., Director of the Vatican Observatory," in *Science and Theology: The New Consonance,* ed. Ted Peters (Boulder, CO: Westview Press, 1999), 157.

truth about man. Nor are they able to ground the dignity of the person."[5] While John Paul supported evolution to some extent, it is unclear what he understood by the term *evolution*, since it is virtually impossible, from a scientific perspective, to separate matter and spirit.

More recently, Pope Benedict XVI has modified the church's support of evolution, saying that "we are not the causal and meaningless products of evolution."[6] Unlike John Paul's openness to evolution, Benedict states that the theory of evolution is not yet a complete and scientifically verified theory.[7] He has expressed caution with regard to evolution, noting its ideological offspring of national-socialism, communism, and economic social-Darwinism. In his encyclical *Spe salvi* he writes, "Science can contribute greatly to making the world and mankind more human. Yet it can also destroy mankind and the world unless it is steered by forces that lie outside it" (para. 25). In short, the church recognizes evolution as a possible scientific explanation of biological life but does not accept it as *the* explanation of all life.[8] Hence, evolution is not considered in its philosophical implications and is not integral to the development of theology or doctrine.

Despite the common question, "Do you believe in evolution?" evolution is not a belief, as if one may or may not accept evolution. For most scientists evolution is simply the way

---

[5] Pope John Paul II, "Message to the Pontifical Academy of Sciences, October 22, 1996," paras. 4–5.

[6] Pope Benedict XVI, "Homily, April 24, 2005."

[7] Melissa Eddy, "Pope Says Evolution Can't Be Proven," available on the usatoday.com website.

[8] One has only to note paragraph 36 of Pope Pius XII's encyclical *Humani generis*, which is still the church's current position on evolution; it holds that the body may come about through evolution but the soul is created immediately by God: "For these reasons the Teaching Authority of the Church does not forbid that, in conformity with the present state of human sciences and sacred theology, research and discussions, on the part of men experienced in both fields, take place with regard to the doctrine of evolution, in as far as it inquires into the origin of the human body as coming from pre-existent and living matter—for the Catholic faith obliges us to hold that souls are immediately created by God" (para. 36).

biological, physical, and chemical systems work. By this I mean there is implicit trust that nature has within itself the means and mechanisms to change, given sufficient time. Carter Phipps indicates that evolution is a process that affects everything from biology to politics, economics, psychology, and ecology. He points out that evolution is not a superficial idea but "a matter of evidence, painstaking work, and breathtaking science."[9] The area where it is least influential is theology, and this is due, in part, to the misconception that God and evolution have little in common. Theologians continue to talk about God and explore theological questions as if evolution is irrelevant or marginal to our understanding of God. However, if evolution is the story of the cosmos, that is, the order of physical reality, then evolution is essential to our understanding of God and God's relationship to the world. Raimon Panikkar said that when theology is divorced from cosmology, we no longer have a living God but an idea of God. God becomes a thought that can be accepted or rejected rather than the experience of divine ultimacy. Because theology has not developed in tandem with science (or science in tandem with theology) since the Middle Ages, we have an enormous gap between the transcendent dimension of human existence (the religious dimension) and the meaning of physical reality as science understands it (the material dimension). This gap underlies our global problems today, from the environmental crisis to economic disparity and the denigration of women.

Theology is a function of cosmology; knowledge of the sciences is *fundamental* to the task of theology. I am not suggesting that science provides the basis for theology. Theology emerges from religious experience and revelation, not from scientific proof. Religious experience can engage in dialogue with the world at large only if it makes use of concepts drawn from the culture around it. It seems today that the relation between faith and science results in a fragile sort of theology, for it is tied to a scientific view that is itself subject to change. But we too easily forget where earlier theological world-images came from. Zachary Hayes states that "we have forgotten many of

---

[9] Carter Phipps, *Evolutionaries: Unlocking the Spiritual and Cultural Potential of Science's Greatest Idea* (New York: Harper, 2012), 7.

the details of the world as conceived by earlier theologies (for example, the medieval concept of the planetary spheres)." As a result, we are often unaware of the extent to which such secular views have shaped our familiar religious language. He goes on to say: "If Augustine was able to speak theologically in a world conditioned by neo-Platonism, and if an Aquinas was able to construct a theology using Aristotelian categories to speak to a world wrestling with the Aristotelian world view, is it possible for contemporary theology to do a similar thing, taking a world view from the sciences?"[10]

Both John Paul II and Pope Benedict XVI said that Thomism does not and should not exhaust the liberty of Christian thought, although few alternatives are embraced. In order for a more adequate philosophy to emerge from our present understanding of reality, theologians would do well to overcome the inherited hellenic complex or at least translate the best of it into a contemporary theological framework. By *hellenic complex* I mean the Greek architecture of metaphysics (God as the transcendent One, the flow of created reality from the One, and the return of all created things to the One) and Aristotelian concepts of form and matter. Leslie Dewart noted almost fifty years ago that Greek philosophical thought has become inadequate for the continued life and development of the Christian faith.[11] Although evolution dehellenizes Christianity and frees it from its medieval construct, we have yet to accept change in nature as integral to life in God or, even more so, in regard to the nature of God.

Chapter 1 explores the roots of resistance to evolution, beginning in the Middle Ages, when the discovery of heliocentrism (the orbiting of the earth around the sun) uprooted the human person from the geocentric (earth-centered) cosmos. As the human person became displaced from the center of the cosmos, God was replaced by nature's laws. Teilhard said that evolution imparts a new identity to the human person; we are the arrow of evolution and the direction of its future, but we have yet to

---

[10] Zachary Hayes, OFM, *A Window to the Divine: Creation Theology* (Quincy, IL: Franciscan Press, 1997), 41, 87.

[11] Leslie Dewart, *Christianity and Revolution* (New York: Herder, 1963), 286.

understand what this means both for the human person and the centrality of God.

To deepen understanding of our new role in the cosmos is to plumb evolution as a movement of convergence and complexity. Stephen L. Talbott's article "The Unbearable Wholeness of Beings," opened me up to the magnificent interdependence of living systems.[12] His article reminded me of what I had known from my graduate studies in biology (but forgotten in the ensuing years)—that biological processes, for example, those of a living cell, do not operate like clockwork but like artful, choreographed rhythms. The whole is made up of interrelated little wholes. When examined closely, all parts of the cell reveal a dynamic integration of components. Chapter 2 examines the fluid nature of biological organisms, which in some sense mimics the intrinsic relationality of the subatomic world. Physicist David Bohm speaks of an underlying order despite quantum randomness and unpredictably, which he called implicate order. Ken Wilber states that we are wholes within wholes, and the evolution of life is toward integral wholeness. Wholeness in the natural world is explored as the basis for wholeness in the human species through the evolution of love and consciousness.

There is a relationship among wholeness, complexity, and consciousness that I attempt to break open in this book, but in no way can I claim to understand this triad fully. Teilhard spoke of evolution as the emergence of consciousness and complexity. As entities become more complex in nature, consciousness increases or develops. I understand consciousness as the mindfulness or awareness that underscores, in some way, evolution's direction. The question of consciousness belongs to philosophy, and Teilhard himself sought to articulate a new philosophy based on the energy of love. Chapter 3 expounds Teilhard's ontology of love and thus a radical shift from the world of being as substance to a world of love-energy and consciousness.

The nature of love as personal, attractive, and unitive spoke to Teilhard of a new understanding of reality, one more consonant with the dynamic impulse of evolution. A new understanding of reality evokes a new understanding of God, which I take up in

---

[12] Stephen L. Talbott, "The Unbearable Wholeness of Beings," *The New Atlantis* 29 (Fall 2010).

Chapter 4. Here I include my other dialogue partners, Raimon Panikkar and Paul Tillich. Panikkar's Gifford Lectures, *The Rhythm of Being*, have illuminated a new understanding of God and cosmos in a way that complements the insights of Teilhard. Although Panikkar came to his insights from an interreligious (Christian-Hindu) perspective and Tillich from modern culture, their new insights on God and world are consonant with evolution and with what Richard Kearney calls "anatheism," a new God rising up from the old God. What Teilhard shows is that this new God is much more at home in evolution, a God who delights in the messiness of the world rather than the Greek metaphysics of order and structure. He brings together creation and incarnation in a way that illuminates the meaning of Jesus Christ in evolution. Chapters 5 and 6 focus on creation and incarnation, Chapter 5 by taking a closer look at love and suffering and Chapter 6 by exploring God and secularity. In its root meaning, Christianity is a thoroughly secular religion, and Teilhard sought to expound the secular as the divine milieu.

My aim is to elucidate Christian life in an evolutionary world. Do we grasp what we are about, or are we merely reciting old formulas? Is Christian life rote catechesis or an engaged life of the Spirit? Chapter 7 focuses on Christ in evolution or what Teilhard called "Christogenesis," literally, the birthing of Christ. Although he was not directly influenced by the notion of the primacy of Christ (he discovered Franciscan theologian Duns Scotus late in life), his insights are consonant with those of Scotus. Basically, Teilhard realized (like Scotus) that Christ is not ordained to creation; rather, creation is patterned on the Christ. From a religious perspective, Big Bang evolution is about the emergence of Christ. We are so wired to think about Christ *only* in relation to Jesus that it seems scandalous to consider anything further. The significance of Jesus' life, however, came to consciousness in the gathering of the early Christians who bestowed on Jesus the title *Christos,* which is Greek for "messiah" or "anointed one." Christian life finds its meaning in Jesus as the Christ, and evolution imparts new meaning to the Christ, not only for Christians but for all cosmic life. These ideas are expounded in light of a cosmic christic universe.

We are reaching a fork in the road; two paths are diverging on planet earth, and the one we choose will make all the difference

for the life of the planet. Shall we continue our medieval religious practices in a medieval paradigm and mechanistic culture and undergo extinction? Or shall we wake up to this dynamic, evolutionary universe and the rise of consciousness toward integral wholeness? The two most significant factors that affect culture are religion and education. While there is much good that takes place at universities today, and there is a new attentiveness to environmental sustainability on many campuses, still the whole process of higher education points to a fragile future. The university is a "multiversity" of sub-specialized disciplines that does not promote an ecology of the mind but a mechanized system of information that conditions the mind to grasp a particular aspect of some discipline, for example, theology or ecology. If evolution is about increasing wholeness/complexity, modern education is about parceling out the whole into specialized fragments. Chapter 8 takes up this discussion in order to ask, does the Catholic intellectual tradition have anything to offer a world that seeks greater wholeness and unity? Here I focus on the recent work of my colleague John Haughey, SJ, whose insights on catholicity are consonant with an evolutionary epistemology, as Teilhard described it. Thinking is essential to the forward movement of evolution, and thinking is a form of love. Hence, the relationship among love, knowledge, and evolution is examined.

Chapter 9 is a brief look at what happens to us when love is absent from the knowing process. The result is silicon chips and robots. With our religious heads in the clouds of heaven and our hearts wandering in search of love, computer technology has swiftly inundated our daily lives. Transhumanism is a philosophical and cultural movement that seeks to enhance or perfect human beings beyond our biological limits. Our cell phones and computers are our best friends, and the cyber world offers us the ability to remake ourselves into whatever we want to be. If religion guided our lives in the past, technology promises to guide our lives into a new, posthuman future. Technology is ambivalent; it can be a blessing or a curse. The problem is not technology itself but the values, including the religious values of salvation and immortality, we are projecting onto our technologies. This chapter takes up the discussion of technology as a religious development and briefly examines how the cyber dreams of engineers may be competing not only with our theological aims but our desire for ecological sustainability. Teilhard saw that computer technology could lead us to a new level of consciousness, what he called the noosphere, where we could be more united and more unified in love. This deepening of humanity through a new level of global consciousness is essential for the forward movement of evolution into a sustainable future. The rise of ultrahumanity is a deepening of love, a consciousness of "interbeing," an awareness that we are one, large, interweaving body of life in formation. This new stage of integral consciousness has implications for world religions and the emergence of Christ in evolution, which I discuss. What Teilhard realized is that we must harness our energies for the forward movement of love, and computer technology can facilitate the gathering of our human energies.

Love is the fundamental energy of evolution. Beginning with Big Bang cosmology through quantum reality and biological formation, love shows itself as explicit God-consciousness in the person of Jesus and the continuation of Christ in evolution. This Love is God-Omega, the love that generates new life and urges cosmic life toward greater unity in love. What Teilhard reminds us is that evolution is the openness of life to the future. We are an unfinished species, corporately and personally, grounded in an infinite depth of Love; thus openness of our lives to love and what this means in terms of creatively reinventing ourselves as persons in evolution is the challenge ahead of us. Divine Love is the heart of an evolutionary universe, and this love is a constant birthing; it is the emergence of Christ in whom all peoples, religions, cultures, trees, flowers, stars, sun, and moon are gathered in one body of being-in-love. The God of evolution is a God of "newness" because God is a dynamic communion of Persons in love, becoming ever more deeply in love through the generation of the Word and Spirit. Evolution thrives not on "rugged individualism" but on communal interdependence. God is the dynamism of love that gathers being together into greater unity and consciousness. The doctrinal name for this reality is Trinity, but as Karl Rahner once quipped, Christians could drop the doctrine of the Trinity and it would make no difference to their religious practice. Yet, Trinity is what cosmic christification is about. Chapter 10 examines the role Christians play in this birthing process of God, a particular way of love that shows itself in action. Teilhard grasped the dynamism of Christian life within the wider process of Christogenesis, and he illumined a new way for the church to lead evolution into the next level of cosmic life.

Love is a consciousness of belonging to another, of being part of a whole. To love is to be on the way toward integral wholeness, to live with an openness of mind and heart, to encounter the other—not as stranger—but as another part of oneself. When we enter into the heart of love, that integral wholeness of love that is God, we enter into the field of relatedness and come to see that we are wholes within wholes. This is the consciousness we need today, an integral wholeness of love that is open to new life; a being-at-home in love that can evolve. By centering itself on the fundamental energy of love, Christianity (and all religions) can find new meaning and purpose by allowing modern science to challenge its stories and, at the same time, to offer the world of scientific reductionism a creative vision for the world. To do so, we need to pull back, pray, and reflect in our inner worlds who and what we want to be in our outer worlds. "The Christian of the future will be a mystic or will not be at all," Rahner remarked.[13] We need to discover the inner desert of the heart, that "still point" of love within us that empowers us to do new things. This center of love is God, the inner power who seeks to evolve, to become more conscious and unified: "Divine Love which moves the sun and the other stars."[14] Our challenge today is to trust the power of love at the heart of life, to let ourselves be seized by love, to create and invent ways for love to evolve into a global wholeness of unity, compassion, justice, and peacemaking. As a process of evolution, the universe is incomplete, and we humans are incomplete. We can change, grow, and become something new. We have the power to do so, but do we have the will? We need a religious imagination that ignites our energies to move beyond mediocrity and fear, one that anticipates a new future of planet life.

---

[13] Karl Rahner, "The Spirituality of the Church of the Future," in *Concern for the Church,* trans. Edward Quinn, vol. 20, Theological Investigations (New York: Crossroad, 1981), 149.

[14] Dante Aligheri, "Canto XXXIII," in *The Divine Comedy: 3 Paradiso,* trans. Dorothy Sayters and Barbara Reynolds (New York: Penguin Books, 1962), 347.

Our failure to be enkindled is because our image of God is old. Evolution discloses a new God, an immanent-transcendent fullness of love that inspires us to create anew, a new earth with a new God rising from within. The Gospels tell us of God's faithful presence. We are invited to trust, surrender, and believe that this world can be different, that justice and forgiveness are possible for the earth community. God's love is ever new, always with us yet ever before us. To live in this love is to be committed to the whole, to live in the whole, to think the whole, to love the whole, to be "turned to the whole." Evolution is "wholemaking" in action, the rise of consciousness that realizes self-separateness is an illusion. This book is a way to move from what is partial and fragmenting to what promises to be more whole and full.

Chapter One

The Decentered Human

Science sprang not from Greek philosophers or the Brahmin-Buddhist-Taoist East but from the heart of the Christian West. Historically, the foundations of modern science are found in the Judeo-Christian tradition, beginning with the Old Testament and its emphasis on an orderly, rational, and contingent world. Patristic writers such as Saint Augustine encouraged study of the natural world. Creation bore the footprints *(vestigia)* of God, and understanding the natural world *(scientia)* could help deepen one's faith. From the ancient Greeks up to the Middle Ages, the model of the universe was the geocentric, Ptolemaic universe, where the immobile earth was center of the cosmos, and the sun, stars, and planets circled around the earth. This perfectly ordered system was guided by the forces of the crystalline heavens. The universe was a world machine where everything was ordered, one to another, each thing having its proper location, arrangement, and purpose in this world. Things were ordered not only *within* creation, but everything in creation was oriented and directed toward a *telos*, a final goal.[1] Dante's picture of the world as a series of concentric spheres—heaven the largest—followed by the planets' crystalline spheres down through our earth's concentric "elements" and the seven circles of hell gave everything and everyone a proper place in the medieval scheme of things.

---

[1] Ilia Delio, *A Franciscan View of Creation: Learning to Live in a Sacramental World*, ed. Elise Saggau, vol. 2, Heritage Series, ed. Joseph P. Chinnici (New York: Franciscan Institute, 2003), 24.

Most people accepted this hierarchical structure without question because it represented the way the world really is. Society mirrored the hierarchy that supposedly existed in the heavens.

In the center of this three-tiered universe was the solid, stable, unmoving earth, completely at rest. Medieval writers such as Thomas and Bonaventure said that the whole cosmic order was created by God to reflect God's power, wisdom, and goodness. Bonaventure wrote that the congruent relation between God and creation rendered creation like a mirror reflecting the footprints of the Trinity on each created being. Creation was likened to a beautiful song that flowed in the most excellent of harmonies. Just as everything emanates from God, everything is to return to God. The intimate relationship between God and nature led Thomas Aquinas to state that a mistake about creation could lead to a mistake about God.

The human person stood in the center of creation, a personal union of matter and spirit, the noble image of God, participating in the glory of God.[2] A world that manifested the glory of God but did not include some creature able to revel in that glory would make little sense; hence the human person was central to this world view.[3] God freely created a glorious universe and called forth within the universe human persons endowed with the freedom to participate in the divine artistic splendor. The human person was created on the sixth day so that every thing could be ordered to the human, who was ordained by God to have dominion over creation (Gn 1). As the most noble of all creatures, whose Godlike identity and central position gave purpose and direction to human life, the human person was to lead creation back to God.

The Humpty Dumpty Earth

The medieval Ptolemaic world view lasted until the end of the Middle Ages, when astronomers discovered that the earth

---

[2] Ibid., 23.

[3] Zachary Hayes, "Bonaventure: Mystery of the Triune God," in *The History of Franciscan Theology*, ed. Kenan Osborne (St. Bonaventure, NY: The Franciscan Institute, 1994), 64.

was not stationary and the center of the cosmos but rather was circling around the sun. When Nicholas of Cusa and later Nicholas Copernicus proposed a sun-centered universe—heliocentrism—the church was not ready for the major upheaval of a moving earth. Once the center of the cosmos and the home of the book of Genesis, the earth was abandoned for a new cosmic center. The stable center of God's throne was pushed over by the astronomer's telescope, and the consequences were enormous.

If the earth moved around the sun, then the human person was no longer center of a stable earth but simply part of a spinning planet. How could this finding be reconciled with the Genesis account in which the human person was created on the sixth day, after which God rested? How would sin and salvation be understood? Galileo argued that the Bible and the natural world both come from God and are meant to be in harmony. His "Dialogue on the Great World Systems" (1632) compared the Ptolemaic and Copernican systems, giving preference to the latter. The older cosmology set the eternal celestial realm in opposition to the terrestrial scene of change and decay; the gradual "hierarchy of being" approached perfection as it approached the Divine. But the new cosmology erased the distinction between corruptible and incorruptible and applied uniform natural categories to the whole universe. The church was not happy with Galileo's explanation because the uniqueness of the human person and God's particular concern for the human person seemed in danger. Robert Cardinal Bellarmine issued a statement in 1616 saying that "the doctrine attributed to Copernicus, that the Earth moves around the Sun, and that the Sun is stationary in the center of the world and does not move from east to west, is contrary to the Holy Scriptures and therefore cannot be defended or held."[4] Wisely, Cardinal Baronius remarked that the Bible teaches "how to go to heaven, not how the heavens go."[5] The mobility or stability of either the earth or sun is neither a matter of faith nor contrary to morals. But fear was high. Once

---

[4] In N. Max Wildiers, *The Theologian and His Universe: Theology and Cosmology from the Middle Ages to the Present* (New York: Seabury Press, 1982), 98n30.

[5] In Kenneth Woodward, "How the Heavens Go," *Newsweek* (July 20, 1998), 52.

the theory of heliocentrism became the law of the planets, the church found itself in a vulnerable position with regard to science because God was on trial.

From the patristic to the Middle Ages, theology and cosmology were united. Theology, known as the Queen of the Sciences, governed the harmonious relationship between heaven and earth. Like philosophy, theology was not a particular science; rather it was related to the whole. Cosmology was part of theology as long as the cosmos was believed to be God's creation.[6] The rise of heliocentrism changed this God-world relationship. From this point on, we might say, the *concept* of God arose apart from the cosmos; that is, a scholastic formula of God developed from the logic of the schoolmen rather than from reading the book of nature. It was only a matter of time for the concept of God to become detached from earth, a God without a cosmos, subject to death. Raimon Panikkar writes:

> God is always God for a World, and if the conception of the World has changed so radically in our times, there is little wonder that the ancient notions of God do not appear convincing. To believe that one might retain a traditional idea of God while changing the underlying cosmology implies giving up the traditional notion of God and substituting an abstraction for it, a *Deus otiosus*. One cannot go on simply repeating "God creator of the world," if the word "world" has changed its meaning since that phrase was first uttered—and the word "creator," as well.[7]

The medieval synthesis was a congruent relationship among God, world (macrocosm), and human (microcosm). Creation flowed from God and returned to God through the human person. Heliocentrism disrupted this relational harmony by relegating the human person to the margins of a spinning planet. The displacement of the human person from the center was also the displacement of God, who became more distant and abstract.

---

[6] Raimon Panikkar, *The Rhythm of Being: The Gifford Lectures* (Maryknoll, NY: Orbis Books, 2010), 186.
[7] Ibid.

The Church and Science

While the church opposed heliocentrism, it did not oppose the study of nature; indeed, the roots of modern science emerge from Christianity. At the University of Oxford, for example, Aristotle's philosophy of nature, combined with the light metaphysics of Pseudo-Dionysius, gave rise to new theories on light.[8] The bishop of Lincoln, Robert Grosseteste, was one of the first Scholastics to understand fully Aristotle's vision of the dual path of scientific reasoning: generalizing from particular observations into a universal law, and then back again from universal laws to prediction of particulars. While this path became important to modern science, he also subordinated the sciences to mathematics, which he considered the highest of all sciences and the basis for all others. Observing the properties of light, Grosseteste believed that light was the "first form" of all things and the source of all generation and motion (approximating what we know as biology and physics today). Since light could be reduced to lines and points and fully explained in the realm of mathematics, mathematics was the highest order of the sciences.

Grosseteste would have found the Big Bang theory remarkably consonant with his own discoveries. In his *De Luce* he begins with God's creation of a single point of light from which, through expansion and extension, the entire physical order came into existence. To initiate the process of creation from that single point of primordial light, Grosseteste used the image of an expanding sphere of light that diffuses in every direction instantaneously so long as no opaque matter stands in the way. He believed that the mathematical nature of the universe followed most directly from its being made of light. The expansion of light replicating itself infinitely in all directions was the basis of the created world.[9]

---

[8] R. K. French and Andrew Cunningham, *Before Science: The Invention of the Friars' Natural Philosophy* (Brookfield, VT: Scolar Press, 1996), 230.

[9] See Daniel Horan, "Light and Love: Robert Grosseteste and Duns Scotus on the How and Why of Creation," *Cord* 57, no. 3 (2007): 246–47.

Grosseteste's scientific program was continued by a younger Englishman, Roger Bacon (c. 1216–92). An admirer of Grosseteste (but probably not his student), Bacon was inspired by the scholar's mastery of mathematical sciences. Not much is known of Bacon except that he studied at Oxford and Paris and taught in the faculty of arts at Paris, where he lectured on Aristotle's books on natural philosophy. He joined the Franciscan Order and spent his life in study and writing. Evidently, he was a difficult person to live with. He wrote that Richard of Cornwall was "an absolute fool," Alexander of Hales was "ignorant of natural philosophy and metaphysics," and Thomas Aquinas full of "puerile vanity and voluminous superfluidity."[10] Despite the fact that Roger did not suffer others easily, he is known as the father of experimental science. Following Grosseteste's philosophy of light and influenced by the Islamic mathematician and philosopher Alhazen, Bacon helped develop mathematical analysis of light and vision that eventually led to the understanding of optics.

Bacon distinguished natural scientific argument from moral and religious mystical intuition. His aim was to provide a *method for science*, one analogous to the use of logic to test validity in arguments. This new method consisted of a combination of mathematics and detailed experiential descriptions of discrete phenomena in nature. He advocated the skillful mathematical use of instruments for an experimental science. He was a forerunner of critical realism, distinguishing real universals from mental universals. For Bacon, there are not Platonic universals in a separate world; rather, real universals are found only in and with individual things. Matter and form constitute things and are the causes of individuation.

Although some may see Bacon as a modern out of step with his age, others describe him as an eccentric schoolman who was wildly religious. He was certain that scientific knowledge would someday give humans mastery over nature; he envisioned the technical world of the future, including submarines, automobiles, airplanes, and other inventions that have become part of daily

---

[10] Kenan B. Osborne, *The Franciscan Intellectual Tradition: Tracing Its Origin and Identifying Its Central Components*, vol. 1, Heritage Series, ed. Joseph P. Chinnici (New York: Franciscan Institute, 2003), 46.

life.[11] However, for Bacon, scientific knowledge was in the service of theology, the purpose of which was to help prepare for the second coming of Christ.

Goodbye, God

The flourishing of the human in the Renaissance and the rise of the Enlightenment gave the human a new mastery over nature. Philosopher Nick Bostrom writes: "The otherworldliness and stale Scholastic philosophy that dominated Europe during the Middle Ages gave way to a renewed intellectual vigor in the Renaissance. . . . Renaissance humanism encouraged people to rely on their own observations and their own judgment rather than to defer in every matter to religious authorities."[12] Francis Bacon wrote that science aimed "to improve the living conditions of human beings."[13] The rise of modern science and its discoveries freed human beings from the constraints of religious authority; now they could use their intellect to create a new world. With the collapse of the Ptolemaic universe and the rise of heliocentrism, the need for a creator God seemed to be no longer necessary, since what was once attributed to God could now be explained largely by science. As the Marquis de Laplace purportedly replied to the emperor's question on the place of God in his system, "I have no need for such a hypothesis."[14] It was not an outright denial of God but a denial of supernatural intervention in natural systems. In his "Exposition du système

---

[11] Richard E. Rubenstein, *Aristotle's Children: How Christians, Muslims, and Jews Rediscovered Ancient Wisdom and Illuminated the Middle Ages* (New York: Harcourt Books, 2003), 188–89.

[12] Nick Bostrom, "A History of Transhumanist Thought," *Journal of Evolution and Technology* 14, no. 1 (April 2005): 2.

[13] Ibid.

[14] According to Charles Gillispie, this account of Laplace's exchange with Napoleon presented a "strangely transformed" (*étrangement transformée*) or garbled version of what had actually happened. It was not God that Laplace had treated as a hypothesis, but merely his intervention at a determinate point. See Charles Coulston Gillispie, *Pierre-Simon Laplace, 1749–1827* (Princeton, NJ: Princeton University Press, 1997), 5.

du monde" (explanation of a world system), published in 1796, Laplace hypothesized that the cosmos had begun as nebular gas, concentrated and contracted by gravity—an account of creation at direct odds with theological tradition. Mechanisms within nature and the development of mathematics could now explain the workings of nature without relying on God as the explanation of physical action.[15]

The new cosmology wrought by heliocentrism had set the eternal celestial realm in opposition to the terrestrial scene of change and decay, challenging the immutability of God and dissolving the hierarchy of being. The spinning earth demoted the human person from the stable center of the universe to an elliptical orbit so that human uniqueness and God's particular concern for human life seemed in danger. The displacement of the human person from the centered earth disconnected the human from creation; the human person no longer experienced the world as God's creation. Dislocated from the *axis mundi*, the human person renounced the harmony of transcendence and immanence. What the human person lost, most essentially, was a sense of the integrated whole. The relationship among self, God, and cosmos was undone by the simultaneous rise of heliocentrism and the church's resistance to it.[16]

Philosopher Mark Taylor identifies the decisive turning point in human development through the work of René Descartes, who tried to reconcile the picture of a mechanical world with belief in God. Cartesian philosophy, he states, reversed the Copernican revolution. "Whereas Copernicus had displaced the human from the center of the universe by discovering that the earth circles

---

[15] K. Lee Lerner, "A Mechanistic Universe," available on the omnilogos .com website.

[16] It is interesting to note that Teilhard de Chardin also identified human decentering following the rise of heliocentrism. In *Activation of Energy* he wrote: "Starting with the Copernican revolution, man has continually, as the centuries unfold, felt more and more 'de-centered': decentered first of all in the universe, by astronomy; then de-centered in the living world, by biology; and now de-centered in the innermost core of his own self, by psychology." See Pierre Teilhard de Chardin, *Activation of Energy*, trans. René Hague (New York: Harcourt Brace Jovanovich, 1971), 187.

the sun, Descartes insisted that everything revolves around the human."[17] Martin Heidegger said that with the rise of modern science, "the objective became swallowed up into the immanence of subjectivity."[18] Descartes overcame the doubt and anxiety created by modern science by collapsing truth into self-certainty, the *ego cogito*. He sought to rescue God from the clutches of a changing world by searching for true and certain knowledge in the human person as thinking self; basic certainty was no longer centered on God but on self. His famous "I think, therefore I am" drew a strong line of separation between matter and spirit and shifted the certainty of knowledge from God to the individual.

In the medieval synthesis God was the source of unity, but in the Enlightenment the power to unify was to be found in the self-thinking subject. This "turn to the subject" imposed a burden on each person to make sense of the world individually and unify it by rational thought alone. With this inward turn of consciousness, objectivity came to be constituted by and to exist *for the sake of* subjectivity. Friedrich Nietzsche saw the direction of this trajectory as the death of God. Divine power lost control of creation as the human person became self-determining, gaining mastery over that which exists as a whole. The human person lost a sense of transcendence in creation and created new gods to fill the need for worship. Unable to bear the weight of unity (that is, holding the many together), the human person surrendered personal autonomy to science and technology, power, violence, and money. The rise of the self-thinking subject became a substitute for the transcendent self of the ultimate whole, according to Ken Wilber.[19] That is, the whole, the cosmos, was replaced by the feeling of being a separate, thinking individual. Descartes's *cogito* became a substitute for the cosmos. Instead of being one with the cosmos, the human could now possess the cosmos; instead of being one with God, the human could now play God. Cartesian subjectivity came to define the modern age. Wilber writes:

---

[17] Mark Taylor, *After God* (Chicago: University of Chicago Press, 2007), 44.

[18] In ibid., 44n3.

[19] Ken Wilber, *Up from Eden: A Transpersonal View of Human Evolution* (Wheaton, IL: Quest Books, 1996), 16.

> Because man wants real transcendence above all else, but because he will not accept the necessary death of his separate-self sense, he goes about seeking transcendence in ways that actually prevent it and force symbolic substitutes. And these substitutes come in all varieties: sex, food, money, fame, knowledge, power—all are ultimately substitute gratifications, simple substitutes for true release in Wholeness.[20]

The combination of heliocentrism and Cartesian dualism created a radical disconnect among God, human, and cosmos that found an orderly structure in Newton's world.

The Mechanistic Universe

At the dawn of the eighteenth century the theologies of Judaism, Christianity, and Islam argued the existence of an unchanging, immutable God who ruled a static universe. For most theologians Newtonian physics and the general shift toward a mechanistic explanation of the natural world initially offered not a threat, but the promise of a deeper understanding of the inner workings of a cosmos linked directly to the very mind and nature of God. During the course of the eighteenth century, however, a major conceptual rift developed between science and theology. As growing scientific disregard for knowledge based upon divine revelation—and increasing reliance upon natural theology (the belief that God can be known solely through human reason and experience, without divine revelation or scripture)—made experimentation the determinant authority in science. This marked a critical period in the development of scientific thought. Over the course of the century, advances in astronomy led to greater understanding of the workings of the solar system, sending sweeping changes across the theological, political, and social landscapes. Using equations based on Newton's laws, mathematicians of this era were able to develop the symbolism and formulas needed to advance the study of dynamics (the study of motion). An important consequence of these advancements al-

---

[20] Ibid.

lowed astronomers and mathematicians to calculate and describe the real and apparent motions of astronomical bodies (celestial mechanics) as well as to propose the dynamics related to the formation of the solar system.

In 1687, English physicist Sir Isaac Newton (1642–1727) published *Philosophiae naturalis principia mathematica* (mathematical principles of natural philosophy), which dominated the intellectual landscape of physical science throughout the eighteenth century. Newton was, without question, the culminating figure in the scientific revolution of the sixteenth and seventeenth centuries—and the leading advocate of the mechanistic vision of the physical world initially posited by French mathematician René Descartes (1596–1650). Within his lifetime Newton developed the science of mechanics and saw the widespread acceptance of a mechanistic universe (one that operates with mathematical precision and predictable phenomena) among philosophers and scientists. Newton's laws—and his theory of a clockwork universe in which God established creation and the cosmos as a perfect machine governed by the laws of physics—viewed matter as passive, moved and controlled by "active principles." The *Principia,* which formulated Newton's laws of gravitation, provided the first comprehensive and mathematically consistent explanation for the behavior of astronomical objects. Within a century of Newton's *Principia* the concept of a mechanistic universe led to the quantification of celestial dynamics, which, in turn, spurred a dramatic increase in the observation, cataloging, and quantification of celestial phenomena. As natural theology developed, scientists and philosophers debated conflicting cosmologies that argued the existence and need for a supernatural God who acted as "prime mover" and guiding force behind a clockwork universe.

Newton rejected mainstream concepts of Christianity but found God manifest in the order and beauty of the universe. He argued that God set the cosmos in motion, and to account for small differences between predicted and observed results, actively intervened from time to time to reset or "restore" the mechanism. The rise of natural theology took the form of deism, a belief in a divine Creator, a "clockmaker," who created and wound the timepiece that is the universe but had no further role in operating it; deism rejected revelation, prophecy, scripture, embracing nature and reason instead. The movement gained support within scientific communities as increasingly detailed evidence regarding the scope and scale of the universe showed no direct evidence of an active Creator.

If Galileo, Descartes, and Newton sowed, even inadvertently, the seeds of dispute between modern science and theology, eighteenth-century society provided the soil in which they bloomed. Not only did the facts of science challenge conventional theology, especially Western Christianity, but the very nature of scientific reason, evidence, and truth (epistemology) was anathema. Deterministic interpretations of Newtonian physics stripped God of personality and sovereign action, defining God only as the force associated with first movement—the original Creator of a mechanistic universe.[21] But this universe came to define all aspects of cosmic life, including Christian life. Barbara Brown Taylor recounts how we eventually structured Christian life according to Newton's world:

> Believing that Newton told us the truth about how the world works, we modeled our institutions on atomistic principles. You are you and I am I. If each of us will do our parts, then the big machine should keep on humming. . . . Our "God view" came to resemble our worldview. In this century, even much of our practical theology has also become mechanical and atomistic. Walk into many churches and you will hear God described as a being who behaves almost as predictably as Newton's universe. Say you believe in God and you will be saved. Sin against God and you will be condemned. Say you are sorry and you will be forgiven. Obey the law and you will be blessed.[22]

As science developed between the seventeenth and twentieth centuries, the human person was not part of the cosmic story. In Newton's world the sovereign, omnipotent God governed the world from above and the cosmos ran like a machine according to internal laws and mechanisms. While the cosmos assumed a

---

[21] Lerner, "A Mechanistic Universe."

[22] Barbara Brown Taylor, *The Luminous Web: Essays on Science and Religion* (Cambridge, MA: Cowley Publications, 2000), 54.

new world picture through modern science, religion remained tied to the medieval cosmos. The marriage of Greek metaphysics to Christianity gave rise to a system of God, humanity, and creation that was too neat and orderly to be disrupted. Christian doctrine was inscribed within the framework of a perfect, immutable, hierarchical, and anthropocentric order.

Death of the Human Person

Cosmology was part of theology as long as the cosmos was believed to be God's creation, but as modern science began to understand the laws of the universe, there was no need for a doctrine of creation. The Bible spoke of the human person as image of God, but in the new science of cosmic life the human person had no defined role. God became the remote clockmaker, and the cosmos assumed a mechanistic explanation according to internal laws and order. The traditional criticism of the scientific paradigm is that it leaves no place for God, to which the scientist responds that there is no need for one. But in truth, the new scientific paradigm left no place for the human person. The great absentee in the scientific description of nature to this day is the human person. Panikkar writes: "Gods there are aplenty, the form of black holes, galaxies, and infinities, etc. . . . Matter and energy are all-pervasive, as are time and space. Only man does not come into the picture. Man cannot be located among the data. Man is in a certain way the obstacle to pure information."[23] Some scientists came to believe that humans are simply products of the laws of nature. Nobel Prize winner Jacques Monod has said that nature has no purpose or goal, and neither do humans: "The ancient covenant is in pieces; man at last knows that he is alone in the universe's unfeeling immensity, out of which he emerged only by chance. His destiny is nowhere spelled out, nor is his duty. The kingdom above or the darkness below: it is for him to choose."[24] In Panikkar's view, modern science and technology did not dispense with God; they dispensed with the

---

[23] Panikkar, *The Rhythm of Being*, 400.
[24] Jacques Monod, "The Ethic of Knowledge and the Socialist Ideal," available on the marxists.org website.

human person as image of God. The displacement of the earth from a stable center caused a dislocation of the human person from the center of creation. The decentering of the human person was also the decentering of God.

Although many scholars note the rise of atheism with modern science, I think the root of atheism was in the rise of heliocentrism and the displacement of the human person from the center of the cosmos to the periphery of a spinning planet. Once the earth was identified as moving, the human person lost stability and purpose in nature, and nature was stripped of its divine character. Modern atheism is less about the death of God than the death of the human person as human, that is, the absence of the human person from the cosmos story as significant to that story.

The decentering of the human person has given rise to inexorable desire, but the results have been disastrous: war, economic injustice, environmental crisis, and corrupt political power. By not being "at home" in the cosmos, the human person has not been "at home" as human. The rise of nihilism and alienation attributed to the death of God more aptly reflects the death of the human person as *human*. The centered, relational human person of the Middle Ages mutated into the peripheral, functional individual of the Enlightenment, divorced from nature.

This divorce was enhanced by the rise of the printing press and the Reformation. With the printed page, Walter Ong states, people forgot to think of words as primarily oral events, and hence as necessarily powered. Words became "out there" on a flat surface. "Such 'things' are not actions but are, in a radical sense dead, though subject to dynamic resurrection."[25] The subjective control of the word-event became the subjective control of nature itself. The Reformation followed on the heels of the revolutionary printed word. Martin Luther's emphasis on *sola scriptura,* while certainly not intending to divorce itself from nature, led to radical anthropocentrism and a preoccupation with sin and grace. Luther was deeply concerned with the problems of righteousness and justification. Redemption is a free gift of grace disposed freely by God and not merited by human action.

---

[25] Walter Ong, *Orality and Literacy: The Technologizing of the Word* (London: Methuen, 1982), 32–33.

Luther's fixation on sin and salvation reflected an "age of anxiety" symbolized by the "wrath of God" and intensified by images of hell and purgatory that drove people to find ways to ease the tension. This anxiety grew out of insecurity and uncertainty that resulted from dissolution of the social structure, ecclesiastical order, and theological synthesis that had developed in the High Middle Ages.[26] It intensified following the bubonic plague or Black Death, which decimated Europe and created a new apocalyptic mentality.[27] Technology became more prominent as the anticipated end of the world evoked the need for spiritual preparedness. Creation became a background for the drama of salvation, and all but humans were excluded from the realm of grace.[28]

The widening gap between theology and cosmology relegated religion to a set of abstract, speculative ideas on fixed principles, while science opened up to a world of dynamic change. The Newtonian revolution toppled the crystalline spheres and replaced them with a physics of ordinary matter governed by mathematical laws rather than divine command. A religion built on stability and immutability could not be prepared for a cosmic order based on change. But change was on the horizon. The rise of evolution in the nineteenth century would do for the world of biology what Newton's laws did for the world of physics—mark the dawn of a new age.

---

[26] Taylor, *After God*, 48, 49.

[27] Thomas Berry, "Traditional Religion in the Modern World," in *Sacred Universe: Earth, Spirituality, and Religion in the Twenty-First Century*, ed. Mary Evelyn Tucker (New York: Columbia University Press, 2009), 4; Thomas Berry, "Christianity and Ecology," in *The Christian Future and the Fate of Earth*, ed. Mary Evelyn Tucker and John Grim (Maryknoll, NY: Orbis Books, 2009), 61–62, 93.

[28] Lynn White, "The Historic Roots of Our Ecological Crisis," *Science* 155 (March 10, 1967): 1205; Colin Grant, "Why Should Theology Be Unnatural?" *Modern Theology* 23, no. 1 (January 2007): 91.

Chapter Two

Wholeness in Nature

The breakup of the medieval synthesis and the rise of the mechanistic universe spawned new scientific discoveries and perhaps the greatest of these for the modern era is evolution. What makes the world in which we live specifically modern—what distinguishes it from past worlds—is evolution, a word that now defines almost all of science as a history of systems. The term *evolution* arose in the area of biology, although Francisco Ayala writes, "Contrary to popular opinion, neither the term nor the idea of biological evolution began with Charles Darwin. . . . It first appeared in the English language in 1647 in a nonbiological connection, and it became widely used in English for all sorts of progressions from simpler beginnings."[1] The theory of biological evolution was made famous by Charles Darwin in *On the Origin of Species*, even though he "did not use the term 'evolution' which did not have its current meaning, but referred to the evolution of organisms by the phrase 'common descent with modification' and similar expressions."[2] Darwin sought to show that natural life unfolds through "a process that promotes or maintains adaptation and thus gives the appearance of purpose or design."[3] As a process, evolution means that nature does not

---

[1] Francisco J. Ayala, "Biological Evolution," in *An Evolving Dialogue: Theological and Scientific Perspectives on Evolution*, ed. James B. Miller (T&T Clark, 2001), 10.
[2] Ibid., 27.
[3] Ibid., 13.

operate only according to fixed laws but also to the dynamic interplay of law, chance, and deep time.

The discovery of this process has come to explain more than biology alone and can be thought of as a broad set of principles and patterns that generates novelty, change, and development over time. The interplay of forces creates a dynamic process of unfolding life, pointing to the fact that nature is incomplete; there are no fixed essences. However, nature is consistently oriented toward new and complex life. Evolution is a movement toward more complex life forms, in which, at critical points in the evolutionary process, qualitative differences emerge: "There is only one real evolution, the evolution of convergence, because it alone is positive and creative."[4] The foundation of things is not so much a ground of being sustaining its existence from beneath as it is a power of attraction toward *what lies ahead.*

Nature is characterized by genuinely new and dynamic physical reality. Philip Clayton defines emergence as "the theory that cosmic evolution repeatedly includes unpredictable, irreducible, and novel appearances."[5] He writes: "Emergent properties are those that arise out of some subsystem but are not reducible to that system. Emergence is about *more than but not altogether other than. . . .* The world exhibits a recurrent pattern of novelty and irreducibility."[6] With emergence, something is constituted from components in such a way that it has new properties that are not reducible to the properties of the components. The mark of emergence is *irreducible novelty,* which pertains not only to the properties of the new emerging entity but to the entity itself as new.[7] Evolution is a process marked by novelty, creativity, and

---

[4] Pierre Teilhard de Chardin, *Christianity and Evolution,* trans. René Hague (New York: Harcourt, 1971), 87.

[5] Philip Clayton, *Mind and Emergence: From Quantum to Consciousness* (New York: Oxford University Press, 2006), 39. Although evolution is marked by novelty in nature, it *does not* mean naive optimism, which I find frequently articulated by those unfamiliar with science. A more thorough explanation of evolution would include aspects of devolution, mutations, and punctuated equilibrium over long periods of developmental processes.

[6] Ibid.

[7] Ibid.

future; new entities rise up out of the old as elements become more complex and converge.

Jesuit scientist Pierre Teilhard de Chardin, one of the most original thinkers of the twentieth century, said that evolution is more than a theory or a hypothesis. It is a general condition to which all theories, systems, and hypotheses must bow, and which they must satisfy if they are to be thinkable and true. Scientists may argue about the way things happen, but the fact that evolution exists and applies equally to life as a whole and to every living creature is now a fundamental basis for doing science. Evolution is not background to the human story; it *is* the human story. It is neither theory nor fact but a "dimension" to which all thinking in whatever area must conform.[8] Teilhard wrote:

> For many, evolution still means only transformism, and transformism itself is an old Darwinian hypothesis as localized and obsolete as the Laplacean concept of the solar system or the Wegnerean theory of continental drift. They truly are blind who do not see the scope of a movement whose orbit, infinitely transcending that of the natural sciences, has successively overtaken and invaded the surrounding fields of chemistry, physics, sociology, and even mathematics and history of religions. Drawn along together by a single fundamental current, one after the other all the domains of human knowledge have set off toward the study of some kind of development. . . . Evolution is a general condition, which all theories, all hypotheses, all systems must submit to and satisfy from now on in order to be conceivable and true.[9]

In 1940 Teilhard completed his most important work, *The Human Phenomenon*, in which he described the fourfold sequence of the evolution of galaxies, earth, life, and consciousness. The human person is not a ready-made fact but the outflow of billions of years of evolution, beginning with cosmogenesis and

---

[8] Robert G. North, *Teilhard and the Creation of the Soul* (Milwaukee, WI: Bruce, 1967), 49.

[9] Pierre Teilhard de Chardin, *The Human Phenomenon*, trans. Sarah Appleton-Weber (Brighton: Sussex Academic Press, 1999), 152.

the billions of years that led to biogenesis. Thomas King writes: "Throughout the ages life has constructed organisms of ever greater complexity, and with this increased complexity the organism has also shown an increase in consciousness, that is, an increase of intention, of acting with a goal."[10] Teilhard saw evolution of the human person as part of the whole natural process of creativity and generativity. The human person is not the great exception to evolution but rather its recapitulation. What the ancients called the soul or the core of personhood emerges through a process of centro-genesis whereby convergence and complexity give rise to greater consciousness. Convergent evolution is directed toward a projected point of maximum human organization and consciousness, which is the Omega point. The human person is not a chance arrival but an integral element of the physical world. Teilhard described human distinction in three ways: (1) The extreme physical complexity (apparent in the brain) marks the human person as the most highly synthesized form of matter known to us in the universe; (2) in light of this complexity, the human is the most perfectly and deeply centered of all cosmic particles within the field of our experience; and (3) the high degree of mental development (reflection, thought) places the human person above all other conscious beings known to us.[11] The human person is integrally part of evolution in that we rise from the process but in reflecting on the process we stand apart from it. Teilhard defines reflection as "the power acquired by a consciousness of turning in on itself and taking possession of itself as an object endowed with its own particular consistency and value; no longer only to know something—but to know *itself*; no longer only to know, but to know that it knows."[12] He quotes a phrase of Julian Huxley, "We are *nothing else than evolution become conscious of itself.*"[13] To this idea he adds, "Until it is established in this perspective, the modern mind (because and insofar as it is modern) will always be restless.

---

[10] Thomas M. King, *Teilhard's Mysticism of Knowing* (New York: Seabury Press, 1981), 33.

[11] Pierre Teilhard de Chardin, *The Future of Man*, trans. Norman Denny (New York: Harper and Row, 1964), 90.

[12] Teilhard de Chardin, *The Human Phenomenon*, 110.

[13] Ibid., 154.

. . . Reflecting in the consciousness of each one of us, evolution is becoming aware of itself."[14] Thus the human person emerges from the evolutionary process and is integral to evolution. The person is "the point of emergence in nature, at which this deep cosmic evolution culminates and declares itself."[15] Hence, the human person is not a random event but the arrow of evolution.

To realize that humans are part of a larger process that involves long spans of developmental time brings a massive change to all of our knowledge and beliefs. Evolution is the term that describes cosmological as well as biological movement toward greater unity and complexity. Teilhard described evolution as a "biological ascent," a movement toward more complex life forms; at critical points in the evolutionary process, qualitative differences emerge. Complexity refers to the quality of a thing based on the number and organization of the elements that compose it. For example, the atom is more complex than the electron, and a living cell more complex than the highest chemical nuclei of which it is composed; the difference depends not only on the number and diversity of the elements but on the correlation of the links formed among them. "It is not therefore a matter of simple multiplicity but of organized multiplicity: not simple complication but centered complication."[16] At some point evolution reaches a reflexive state that generates the idea of evolution, namely, the human person.

---

[14] Ibid.

[15] Pierre Teilhard de Chardin, *Human Energy*, trans. J. M. Cohen (New York: Harcourt Brace Jovanovich, 1969), 23. Teilhard's position on human evolution put him at odds with church teaching, primarily because he rejected the idea of original sin in light of evolution. However, in the 1950 encyclical *Humani generis*, Pope Pius XII stated that evolution may explain how the physical body of the human person is formed, but that *the soul is created immediately by God*: "The Teaching Authority of the Church does not forbid that, in conformity with the present state of human sciences and sacred theology, research and discussions, on the part of men experienced in both fields, take place with regard to the doctrine of evolution, in as far as it inquires into the origin of the human body as coming from pre-existent and living matter—for the Catholic faith obliges us to hold that souls are immediately created by God" (para. 36).

[16] Teilhard de Chardin, *The Future of Man*, 105.

Unfolding Life

The dynamic, unfolding process of life—evolution—now defines every area of cosmic life, which includes the infinitely large (cosmos), the infinitely small (quantum reality), and the infinitely complex (Homo sapiens). There is a wholeness in nature that the term *mechanism* obscures and the term *process* captures. Nature is not a series of little mechanisms but more of a waltz or flowing movement. Whether on the level of the infinitely large or the infinitely small, there is an inestimable wholeness that continues to unfold or evolve in nature.

The first major discovery that unraveled Newton's world was made by Albert Einstein in 1905. For three hundred years Newton's vision of time and space as absolute was the sacred dogma of scientific cosmology. Space, for Newton, was an empty stage on which the drama of physics was played out, an emptiness constant everywhere and at all times. Time too was constant. No matter where one stood in the universe, time flowed at the same rate. Einstein's short, revolutionary paper swept away in a single stroke absolute space and time. Space is not an empty stage, and time does not flow at a fixed rate. Rather, space and time form a single dimension, each relative to the other. As Adam Frank writes, "Space and time could shrink or expand depending on the relative motion of the observers who measured them."[17] According to Frank, "The new universe was a *hyperspace,* a world with an extra dimension. . . . In relativity every object becomes four-dimensional as it extends through time."[18] We do not live in a three-dimensional universe but a multidimensional universe;

---

[17] Adam Frank, *The Constant Fire: Beyond the Science vs. Religion Debate* (Berkeley and Los Angeles: University of California Press, 2009), 146; Simon Singh, *Big Bang: The Origin of the Universe* (New York: HarperCollins, 2004), 120–28. For a succinct description of the new cosmology, see Brian Swimme and Thomas Berry, *The Universe Story: From the Primordial Flaring Forth to the Ecozoic Era—A Celebration of the Unfolding of the Cosmos* (New York: HarperOne, 1994); Judy Cannato, *Radical Amazement: Contemplative Lessons from Black Holes, Supernovas, and Other Wonders of the Universe* (Notre Dame, IN: Sorin Books, 2006).

[18] Frank, *Constant Fire,* 147.

some scientists suggest that the universe may have up to eleven dimensions. Cosmic wholeness is very strange.

Einstein's creative insight eventually yielded to a new understanding of gravity, which, for Newton, was "the force between massive objects that pulled them toward each other."[19] The elastic nature of space-time impelled Einstein to think of gravity not as a substance but as a curvature of space-time by matter. It not only stretches or shrinks distances (depending on their direction with respect to the gravitational field) but also appears to slow down or "dilate" the flow of time. In other words, gravity acts to structure space. We now understand the universe in terms of the Hot Big Bang model. The four key aspects of the model are expansion of the universe; nucleosynthesis of the light elements; origin of the cosmic background radiation; and formation of galaxies and large-scale structure.[20] According to Big Bang cosmology, the universe is about 13.7 billion years old, with a future of billions of years before us. Some scientists estimate the span of the universe is at about one hundred trillion years, although the sun will die out in approximately nine billion years. It is a large universe, stretching light years in diameter, only one of the many universes that occupy space.

Our own galaxy, the Milky Way, is a mid-size galaxy consisting of at least 200 billion stars, and stretching about 100,000 light years in diameter. The galaxies are often grouped into clusters—some having as many as two thousand galaxies. We are one of billions of galaxies. After 300,000 years of expansion and cooling, negatively charged electrons were moving slowly enough to get caught by positively charged protons. Each capture created a new atom of hydrogen. Once the process started, the universe rapidly made the transition from a mix of free photons and electrons to a vast gas of electronically neutral atomic hydrogen. As the eons passed, a vast cosmic network of form emerged from these humble beginnings. Galaxies appeared first. Then clusters of galaxies were swept together by their mutual gravitational pull. . . . Gravity alone constructed a cosmic architecture that is filamentary and beautiful. . . . [But] the universe is also composed

---

[19] Ibid., 147.
[20] David Alles, "The Evolution of the Universe," available on the fire .biol.wwu.edu website.

of tremendous quantities of something that emits no light. This is known as *dark matter*, and it constitutes the majority of mass in the universe. It is dark matter that sculpts the large-scale structure. Frank writes: "The visible galaxies we see strewn across space are nothing more than strings of luminous flotsam drifting on an invisible sea of dark matter."[21] The continuous expansion of the universe is due to the predominance of a repulsive cosmic force that is associated with dark energy. Scientists speculate that dark energy comprises about 73 percent of the total mass-energy of the universe and accelerates expansion of the universe. Dark matter, on the other hand, prevents the universe from collapsing in on itself. The recent discovery of the Higgs Boson particle may provide new insight on dark energy and dark matter. What we now know is that the universe is expanding and will expand indefinitely into the future.

Quantum Wholeness

While cosmic wholeness is difficult to identify in light of the complexity of the large size of the universe, the wholeness of nature becomes more readily apparent on the level of quantum physics. In Newton's time, particles were visualized as discrete entities forming atoms and molecules, and electromagnetic radiation was conceived as wave motion involving changing electric and magnetic fields. The conventional visualization of the physical world was changed by Einstein's special theory of relativity, which showed that matter was itself a form of energy. According to science, the mass of a body is a measure of its energy content. Mass and energy are not identical but equivalent. Einstein's famous equation $E = mc^2$ showed that the energy *(E)* of a physical system is numerically equal to the product of its mass *(m)* and the speed of light *(c)* squared; matter can be converted into energy and energy into matter. In the real world matter is "disappearing" all the time. Whenever matter interacts and binds with other matter, matter "disappears" (which is also the case for matter/antimatter interaction); whenever matter "falls apart" (as in alpha and beta decay), matter is "created." The

---

[21] Frank, *Constant Fire*, 152–55.

"invisible" world of energy has a direct and solid connection to the "concrete" world of matter. For all practical purposes, energy is the "real world."

Quantum physics is the study of the behavior of matter and energy at the molecular, atomic, nuclear, and microscopic levels. The word *quantum* comes from the Latin meaning "how much" and refers to the discrete units of matter and energy that are predicted by and observed in quantum physics. The birth of quantum physics began with Einstein's theory of relativity. French physicist Louis De Broglie was excited by this theory and proposed that light waves could behave as particles—for instance, electrons—and particles could behave like waves. In the famous double-slit experiment an electron will seem to pass through two separate openings simultaneously. However, only one of those two behaviors, wave or particle, can be observed at any moment. This wave-particle duality, also known as complementarity, became the basis of quantum physics. Quantum objects manifest both wave-like and particle-like behaviors.[22]

According to the Newtonian world view, everything is one vast machine or mechanism made up of matter and energy, like a giant clock with discrete parts. This machine is entirely deterministic, running according to internal laws of nature; everything happens in a three-dimensional space. In the quantum world view, the universe is a vast unified sea of possibility, with matter and energy as two facets of the same universal process. The discovery of relativity and the mysterious nature of matter and energy has led scientists to conclude that matter is not composed of basic building blocks but rather comprises complicated webs of relations in which the observer constitutes the final link in the chain of observational processes. The properties of an atomic object can be understood only in terms of the object's interaction with the observer. Physicist Fritjof Capra writes:

> Careful analysis of the process of observation in atomic physics has shown that the subatomic particles have no meaning as isolated entities, but can only be understood as

---

[22] For a discussion on the double-slit experiment, see Jack Geis, *Physics, Metaphysics, and God* (Bloomington, IN: AuthorHouse, 2003); Shan Gao, *God Does Play Dice with the Universe* (Suffolk: Abramis, 2008).

interconnections between the preparation of an experiment and the subsequent measurement. Quantum theory thus reveals a basic oneness of the universe. It shows that we cannot decompose the world into independently existing smallest units. As we penetrate into matter, nature does not show us any isolated "basic building blocks," but rather appears as a complicated web of relations between the various parts of the whole.[23]

Albert Einstein had problems with quantum physics, especially with the uncertain nature of events and the strange interaction among particles. In 1935 Einstein and two postdoctoral students, Boris Podolsky and Nathan Rosen, performed a thought experiment based on insights from quantum physics to see if particles could affect one another at a distance without interacting.[24] Generally referred to as the EPR experiment—EPR being the first initials of their surnames—their work quickly became a centerpiece in the debate over the interpretation of quantum theory. The experiment centers on a quantum particle split in half, with the halves heading off in opposite directions; one half is spinning in one direction, and the other half is spinning in the opposite direction. The total spin must be zero by the conversation of the spin at the point at which the parent split. If the particles are separated by distance, measurement of particle A as "up" will influence the measurement of particle B as "down." The measurement on A does not merely reveal an already established state of B: it actually *produces* that state, which renders the particles entangled. The object of the experiment was to show that measurements performed on spatially separated parts of a quantum system can apparently have an instantaneous influence on one another. This effect is now known as *nonlocal behavior* (or *quantum weirdness* or *spooky action at a distance*). Physicist

---

[23] Fritjof Capra, *The Tao of Physics*, 4th ed. (Boston: Shambhala, 2000). On quantum theory see Geis, *Physics, Metaphysics, and God*; Nick Herbert, *Quantum Reality: Beyond the New Physics* (New York: Anchor Press, 1985), 18.

[24] A thought experiment considers a theory in order to think through its possible consequences. There need not be any intention of actually carrying out the experiment; in fact, it may not be possible to do so.

Erwin Schrödinger writes: "If two separated bodies, each by it-self known maximally, enter a situation in which they influence each other, and separate again, then there occurs regularly that which I have just called *entanglement* of our knowledge of the two bodies."[25] Quantum entanglement is nonlocal interaction or unmediated action at a distance, without crossing space, without decay, and without delay.[26]

The idea of quantum entanglement was a speculative theory until physicist John Bell provided mathematical proof. According to Bell's theorem, all reality must be nonlocal. The term *nonlocal* means that the atom's measured attributes are determined not just by events happening at the actual measurement site but by events arbitrarily distant, including events outside the light cone, that is, events so far away that to reach the measurement site their influence must travel faster than light. In other words, if an atom's momentum is measured, its true momentum is disturbed not only by the momentum meter itself but by a vast array of distant events—events that are happening right now in other cities, in other countries, and possibly in other galaxies. According to Bell, the act of measurement is not a private act but rather a public event in whose details large portions of the universe instantly participate.[27]

Implicate Order

Einstein's original intention in performing the EPR experiment was to show the difficulty with quantum theory. The idea of nonlocal action at a distance requires a connection that travels faster than light, an idea which conflicted with relativity theory. However, David Bohm and his colleagues did not see a problem with quantum entanglement but considered it an alternate view

---

[25] Erwin Schrödinger, "The Present Situation in Quantum Mechanics: A Translation of Schrödinger's 'Cat Paradox Paper,'" trans. John D. Trimmer, available on the tu-harburg.de website.

[26] Arthur Fine, "The Einstein-Podolsky-Rosen Argument in Quantum Theory," available on the plato.stanford.edu website; Herbert, *Quantum Reality*, 199–210.

[27] Herbert, *Quantum Reality*, xiv.

of reality. They interpreted the nonlocal effects as pointing to something new in reality that could not be attributed to causal connections. Bohm attributed the strange phenomenon of non-locality to hidden variables; he developed the idea of holomovement or implicate order as his primary explanation.[28] Rather than starting with the parts and explaining the whole in terms of the parts, Bohm started with a notion of undivided wholeness and derived the parts as abstractions from the whole. He called this unbroken order "implicate order," indicating an enfolding of events. Implicate order is a way of looking at reality not merely in terms of external interactions between things, but in terms of the internal (enfolded) relationships among things. As human beings and societies we seem separate, but in our roots we are part of an indivisible whole and share in the same cosmic process. The term *holomovement* describes the unbroken and undivided totality of implicate order. Movement is what is primary; what may appear to be permanent structures are only relatively autonomous sub-entities that emerge out of the whole of flowing movement and then dissolve back into it an unceasing process of becoming. Each relatively autonomous and stable structure is to be understood not as an independent and permanent existent but as a product that has been formed in the whole flowing movement and that will ultimately dissolve back into this movement. How it forms and maintains itself depends on its place function within the whole.[29]

Bohm's theory of implicate order is based on several important ideas. First, being is intrinsically relational and exists as unbroken wholeness in a system. Whereas classical physics is based on parts making up wholes, Bohm took relationships between parts as primary. Each part is connected with every other part at the quantum level. Thus, the whole is the basic reality; primacy belongs to the whole. The second aspect of Bohm's implicate order is that systems are in movement or what Bohm calls "holomovement." Kevin Sharpe explains: "The holomovement

---

[28] David Bohm, *Wholess and the Implicate Order* (New York: Routledge, 1995). For a summary of Bohm's ideas, see Kevin J. Sharpe, "Relating the Physics and Metaphysics of David Bohm," available on the ksharpe.com website.

[29] Ibid.

model for reality comes from the properties of a holographic image of an object. . . . Any portion of the holographic plate (the hologram) contains information on the whole object."[30] Third, because reality is marked by relationality and movement, it has endless depth. Hence, Bohm directs us to think in terms of wholeness, relationality, and depth. What we know of reality does not exhaust it; properties and qualities will always be beyond us. Bohm provides a clear account of how a "particle" conception of matter not only causes harm to the sciences, but also to the way we think and live, and thus to our very society and its future evolution. He writes:

> The notion that all these fragments are separately existent is evidently an illusion, and this illusion cannot do other than lead to endless conflict and confusion. Indeed, the attempt to live according to the notion that the fragments are really separate is, in essence, what has led to the growing series of extremely urgent crises that is confronting us today. Thus, as is now well known, this way of life has brought about pollution, destruction of the balance of nature, over-population, world-wide economic and political disorder and the creation of an overall environment that is neither physically nor mentally healthy for most of the people who live in it. Individually there has developed a widespread feeling of helplessness and despair, in the face of what seems to be an overwhelming mass of disparate social forces, going beyond the control and even the comprehension of the human beings who are caught up in it.[31]

Quantum physics has yet to be reconciled with Einstein's theory of special relativity, but it is clear that our understanding of matter and form has radically changed. Our view of reality has been deconstructed from its Greek Aristotelian categories of matter and form and defined as an interconnected web and flow of information. On the macro level the laws of Newtonian mechanics still apply, but the fundamental stuff of reality,

---

[30] Ibid.
[31] Bohm, *Wholeness and the Implicate Order*, 1–2.

according to quantum physics, is radically different from what Newton envisaged.

Systems Biology

In the twentieth century Austrian biologist Ludwig von Bertalanffy challenged biology as mechanistic, homeostatic (steady state) systems and emphasized that real systems are open to, and interact with, their environments. Whereas Newtonian mechanics was a science of forces and trajectories, evolution—which relied on change, growth, and development—required a new science of complexity. The first formulation of this new science was classical thermodynamics, with its celebrated "second law," the law of the dissipation of energy. According to the second law of thermodynamics, there is a trend in physical phenomena from order to disorder. Any isolated or "closed" physical system will proceed spontaneously in the direction of ever-increasing disorder.[32] According to the laws of thermodynamics, the entire world machine is running down and will eventually grind to a halt. But evolution says that the living world is unfolding toward increasing order and complexity. Bertalanffy took a bold step by saying that living organisms cannot be described by classical thermodynamics because they are open systems. By "open systems" he meant that systems feed on a continual flux of matter and energy from their environment; "the organism is not a static system closed to the outside and always containing the identical components; it is an open system . . . in which material continually enters from, and leaves into, the outside environment."[33] He set out to replace the mechanistic foundations of science with a holistic vision and developed the theory of general systems, a science of "wholeness" that up to the twentieth century was considered a vague, hazy concept. Bertalanffy sought to establish a science of general systems based on solid biological principles.

Surprisingly, German philosopher Immanuel Kant recognized wholeness in nature long before modern biologists discovered

---

[32] Fritjof Capra, *The Web of Life: A New Scientific Understanding of Living Systems* (New York: Doubleday, 1996), 47.

[33] Ibid., 48n29.

open systems. An organized being is not a mere machine with only motive power, he indicated, but one with formative power. This formative power cannot be explained by the capacity of movement alone, that is, by mechanism, but by *something deep within nature itself.*[34] Kant's insights on the natural world were prophetic. He suggested that (1) In living organisms order is internally emergent rather than externally imposed. (2) The relation between parts and whole is thoroughly interactive—the whole simultaneously emerges from the interplay of parts and acts back on these parts to constitute their differential identities. (3) The whole is an integrative relational structure—it is, in other words, the interplay of parts. (4) While the whole provides a certain stability, it is not a fixed form but a dynamic pattern that changes constantly. (5) This relational structure provides the parameters of constraint within which parts continue to develop. Since the whole is refigured as parts change, whole and part are codependent and coevolve.[35]

Nature's Symphony

The discovery of systems biology led scientists to ask whether systems organize. Humbert Maturana and Francisco Varela wrote that "living systems are machines that cannot be shown by pointing to their components. Rather, one must show their organization in a manner such that the way in which all their peculiar properties arise becomes obvious."[36] They distinguished between "organization" and "structure" by saying that organization of a living system is the set of relations among its components that characterize the system as belonging to a particular class. The structure of a living system is constituted by the actual relations among the physical components; structure is the physical embodiment of its organizations. They coined the term *autopoeisis* to describe "a network of production processes, in which the function of each component is to participate in the production or transformation of other components in the network. In this

---

[34] Taylor, *After God*, 315.
[35] Ibid., 315–16.
[36] Cited in ibid., 318. See also Capra, *Web of Life*, 98n50.

way the entire network continually 'makes itself.' It is produced by its components and in turn produces those components."[37] In other words, in living systems "the product of its operation is its own organization."[38]

The shift from mechanism to holism has reversed the relationship between the parts and the whole. The properties of the parts are not intrinsic properties but can be understood only within the context of the larger whole. What we call a part is merely a pattern in an inseparable web of relationships. Therefore. the shift from parts to the whole can also be seen as a shift from objects to relationships. A system is an integrated whole whose essential properties arise from the relationships among its parts. Nature is an interlocking network of systems, an "unbearable wholeness of beings," as Stephen Talbott writes. Nature is more flow than fixed. "The body," he states, "is a *formed* stream."[39] Structures, once formed as stable, do not necessarily stay that way. The cell as a whole, even an undividing cell such as a neuron, may experience a complete replacement of its contents a thousand times or more over the course of its life. Many of the body's structures are more like standing waves than once-and-for-all constructed objects. Organisms show a meaningful coordination of activities whereby a functioning and self-sustaining unity engages in flexible responses to the myriad stimuli of the environment. Nature is like a choreographed ballet or a symphony, whereby an organism is dynamically engaged in its own self-organization, pursuing its own ends amid an ever-shifting context of relationships.

Today we know that there are different living systems, all of which are integrated wholes whose essential properties have arisen from the interactions and interdependence of their parts. Over billions of years of evolution many species have formed such tightly knit communities that the whole system resembles a large, multi-creatured organism. Bees and ants, for example, are unable to survive in isolation, but in great numbers they act almost like the cells of a complex organism with a collective intelligence and capabilities for adaptation far superior to those of

---

[37] Capra, *Web of Life*, 98.

[38] Ibid., 98n52.

[39] Stephen L. Talbott, "The Unbearable Wholeness of Beings," *The New Atlantis* 29 (Fall 2010).

their individual members. Similar close coordination of activities exists among different species where higher-level cooperation and reciprocal altruism are identified. In *Cooperation Among Animals* biologist Lee Alan Dugatkin highlights numerous studies of cooperation among fish, birds, nonprimate animals, nonhuman primates, and insects. He reports, for example, on vampire bats who share food. Female vampire bats regurgitate blood meals to nest mates who otherwise would starve. The blood meal is critical for survival of the recipient; those who have given in the past are more likely to receive in the future. There is a type of reciprocal altruism where the good that is done for another can be self-serving as well. For example, smaller fish provide a service to larger fish by cleaning them of debris. Larger fish do not eat smaller fish because the smaller fish provide this benefit. In another example, various species of birds call out when predators near. Although calling out jeopardizes each caller, the cacophony of calls makes it difficult for predators to hone in on any one bird as potential prey. What these examples show is that cooperation among those of various species benefits each individually.[40]

At the turn of the twentieth century James Baldwin saw that the sustained behavior of a species or group in response to its environment is gradually assimilated into the group's genetic structures.[41] Learned behaviors cannot be directly inherited, but the initiatives of organisms can be a factor in the establishment of random genetic changes and thereby affect the direction of evolutionary change. The behavior of thriving organisms can be imitated by others and transmitted socially for a long enough period that random genetic mutations can support that beneficial behavior.[42] The Baldwin effect of evolutionary change complements what biologist Rupert Sheldrake describes as an organic model of morphogenetic fields. Sheldrake postulated that repetitive behavior creates informational fields that can

---

[40] Lee Alan Dugatkin, *Cooperation Among Animals: An Evolutionary Perspective* (New York: Oxford University Press, 1997), 113–15.

[41] James Mark Baldwin, *Development and Evolution* (New York: Macmillan, 1902).

[42] For a contemporary evaluation of the Baldwin theory, see Bruce Weber and David Depew, eds., *Evolution and Learning: The Baldwin Effect Reconsidered* (Cambridge, MA: MIT Press, 2003).

influence similar behavior in an unrelated area. He calls these informational fields "morphogenetic" fields because they are formative fields (*morphe* meaning "form") that carry information, not energy, and are available throughout time and space without any loss of intensity after they have been created. Morphogenetic fields are unseen forces that preserve the *form* of self-organizing systems, maintaining order from within; that is, morphogenetic fields direct other members of the species toward the same form or behavior or what he calls morphic resonance. According to Sheldrake these fields of habitual patterns link all within the species. The more a group has a habit or pattern—whether of knowledge, perception, or behavior—the stronger it is in the field and the more easily it replicates in other members of the species. The novelty of Baldwin's theory as well as that of Sheldrake is that creaturely agency plays a role in evolution.[43] We are more than our genes; we are our relationships.

Holons and Holarchy

The view of living systems as networks provides a novel perspective on the so-called hierarchies of nature. The interconnected levels of networks constitute a web of life wherein systems interact with other systems or networks within networks. Because reality exists in systems, every system is a supersystem; systems exist within systems, which has led to the description of holons or whole/parts. Arthur Koestler proposed the word *holon* to describe the hybrid nature of sub-wholes and parts within in vivo systems. A holon is simultaneously a whole and part.[44] From this perspective holons exist simultaneously as self-contained wholes in relation to their sub-ordinate parts, and dependent parts when considered from the inverse direction. Koestler defines a holarchy

---

[43] Thomas Jay Oord, *Defining Love: A Philosophical, Scientific, and Theological Engagement* (Grand Rapids, MI: Brazo Press, 2010), 131.

[44] For a discussion of holons, see Judy Cannato, *Radical Amazement* (Notre Dame, IN: Sorin Books, 2006), 94–102; idem, *Fields of Compassion: How the New Cosmology Is Transforming Spiritual Life* (Notre Dame, IN: Sorin Books, 2010); Ken Wilber, *A Theory of Everything* (Boston: Shambhala Publications, 2000).

as a hierarchy of self-regulating holons that functions first as autonomous wholes in supra-ordination to their parts, and secondly as dependent parts in sub-ordination to controls on higher levels, and thirdly in coordination with their local environment. Holarchy is the principle of holons or whole/parts whereby the number of levels in a holarchy describe its depth.[45] David Splangler distinguishes hierarchy from holarchy in this way: "In a hierarchy participants can be compared and evaluated on the basis of position, rank, relative power, seniority and the like. But in a holarchy each person's value comes from his or her individuality and uniqueness and the capacity to engage and interact with others to make the fruits of that uniqueness available."[46] Ken Wilber notes that evolution produces greater depth and less span; as the individual holon acquires greater depth, the span or the collective gets smaller and smaller.[47] A whole atom is part of a whole molecule; a whole molecule of part of a whole cell; a whole cell is part of a whole organism. Similarly, the human person is a whole within self and yet part of a large communal whole that is a part within a whole society. Reality is composed of neither wholes nor parts but of whole/parts—holons—or what Ken Wilber calls integral systems.[48] Although scientists are only beginning to understand the complexities of nature in terms of networks and integral systems, the idea that nature has an unbearable wholeness is irresistibly attractive in view of God.

---

[45] Mark Edwards, "A Brief History of Holons," available on the integralworld.net website.

[46] David Spangler, "A Vision of Holarchy," available on the sevenpillarshouse .org website.

[47] Wilber, *Theory of Everything*, 50.

[48] Ken Wilber, *Sex, Ecology, Spirituality: The Spirit of Evolution* (Boston: Shambhala, 2001); Ken Wilber, *The Integral Vision* (Boston: Shambhala, 2007).

Chapter Three

Love, Sex, and the Cosmos

The discovery of evolution, according to Teilhard de Chardin, is not only a new scientific discovery of nature but of nature passionately alive, throbbing, and pulsating with energy and growth. Science's preoccupation with objectivity, clarity, and reproduction of data has created a partial understanding of life. What needs illumination is its wholeness, depth, and relationality. Nature is endowed with mysterious forces of attraction that science alone cannot explain, forces that give rise to integral wholes. Brian Swimme describes the birth of a star that reflects nature's mysterious attractive force of gravity:

> Imagine a vast dark cloud of hydrogen atoms stretching through millions of miles of space. Each of these trillions upon trillions of atoms is involved in an attracting activity for all the rest, and slowly begins to move. A common center emerges, and the hydrogen atoms begin to clump together. The growing pressure from the gravitational attraction enables the hydrogen atoms to fuse into helium atoms, thus releasing their hidden energy in a vast profusion of light emanating in all directions: the core of the star ignites. All of this activity is the result of the cosmic allurement of gravitation.[1]

---

[1] Brian Swimme, *The Universe Is a Green Dragon: A Cosmic Creation Story* (Santa Fe, NM: Bear and Company, 1984), 43.

37

Gravity, electromagnetic interaction, and chemical attraction are fundamental forces of life whose mechanical details can now be described but whose very existence escapes the laws of mathematics: "We understand the details concerning the consequences of this [gravity's] attraction. We do not understand the attraction itself."[2] Our universe could have been different, operating on other laws that would have shaped it completely differently. However, our universe, which is governed by attraction and allurement and held together by gravity, is the one we live in. Without gravity, the universe would disintegrate; in fact, it would not have formed in the first place. Gravitational attraction permeates all reality, and evolution adds to this attraction the direction toward increasing complexity and consciousness in nature.[3]

Evolution, through all its stages, seems to be an immense complexification of psychic energy that, through different forms, eventually becomes more aware of itself. Something accounts for the dynamic unfolding of evolution and gives evolution its direction. Teilhard describes this "something" as the energy of consciousness. While consciousness studies have significantly advanced since Teilhard's time, and the "hard" problem of consciousness is yet to be resolved (that is, how and why we have subjective conscious experience), still his ideas are provocative within the larger scope of evolution. The human experience of consciousness means that the stuff of the universe is mysteriously held together by something more than mere materiality. Teilhard speculated on two fundamental types of energy: radial and tangential energy. Each individual element has two distinct components: a *tangential energy* making the element interdependent with all elements of the same order in the universe as itself, what we might call "bonding" energy, and a *radial energy* attracting the element in the direction of an ever more complex and centered state, toward what is ahead, which is "psychic" or conscious energy.[4] While tangential energy follows the second

---

[2] Ibid., 44.

[3] See Margaret McIntyre, *The Cosmic Pilgrim: A Spiritual Exploration of the New Story of Science and Religion* (Eugene, OR: Wipf and Stock, 2010), 28–29.

[4] Pierre Teilhard de Chardin, *The Human Phenomenon,* trans. Sarah Appleton-Weber (Brighton: Sussex Academic Press, 1999), 29–30; Harold J. Morowitz, Nicole Schmitz-Moormann, and James F. Salmon,

law of thermodynamics, dissipating into entropy, radial energy defies this second law and increases with complexity. The physical sciences observe the dissipation of energy and disintegration of matter, but they do not acknowledge the continued growth of radial energy, and thus a continual expansion and deepening of consciousness. It is this inner energy of evolving consciousness that gives evolution its qualitative direction.[5] The increase in radial energy, the energy of consciousness, led Teilhard to suggest that consciousness is the core of evolution:

> We still persist in regarding the physical as constituting the "true" phenomenon in the universe, and the psychic as a sort of epiphenomenon. However . . . if we really wish to unify the real, we should completely reverse the values— that is, we should consider the whole of thermodynamics [as an] interior energy of unification (true energy) gradually emerging, under the influence of organization, from the superficial system of action and reactions that make up the physical-chemical. In other words, there is no longer just one type of energy in the world: there are two different energies—one axial, increasing, and irreversible, and the other peripheral or tangential, constant, and reversible: and these two energies are linked together in "arrangement" but without nevertheless being able either to form a compound or directly to be transformed into one another, because they operate at different levels.[6]

These fundamental energies of nature speak of depth in nature. From the Big Bang onward there is a "withinness" and "withoutness," according to Teilhard, a growth in radial and tangential

---

SJ, "Looking Again at Teilhard, Tillich, and Haught: Teilhard's Two Energies," *Zygon: Journal of Science and Religion* 40, no. 3 (September 2005): 721–32.

[5] In some cases bonding energy may be sublated by conscious energy insofar as what seems to be dissipating (tangential) energy may be converted to radial energy and enhance it. This type of *negentropy* means that while *entropy* is increasing on one level, *energy* is increasing on a higher level.

[6] Pierre Teilhard de Chardin, *Activation of Energy*, trans. René Hague (New York: Harcourt Brace Jovanovich, 1970), 393.

energies. The universe orients itself toward intelligent, conscious, self-reflective life. Astrophysicist James Jeans writes:

> The universe begins to look more like a great thought than a great machine. Mind no longer appears as an accidental intruder into the realm of matter; we are beginning to suspect that we ought rather to hail it as the creator and governor of the realm of matter—not of course our individual minds, but the mind in which the atoms out of which our individual minds have grown exist as thoughts. . . . We discover that the universe shows evidence of a designing or controlling power that has something in common with our own individual minds.[7]

The adage "mind over matter" may no longer be true, as the new science points to "mind in matter." Evolution seems to be the unfolding of mind, and one might say that the evolution of the cosmic mind provides new ground for the return of the world soul. Teilhard points to this idea in his concept of noogenesis, or global mind, which will be discussed in Chapter 9.

Love and Omega

The direction of evolution toward increased consciousness must be seen together with the evolution of integral wholeness. The development of consciousness is *a transition from a lower to a higher state of centro-complexity*, but centricity is another way to talk about integration. As life becomes more complex and conscious, it becomes more integrally whole. What makes anything "whole"? Is there a "whole factor" or a principle of relationality? Modern science has often been reluctant to recognize in evolution anything in nature that cannot be measured, but open systems are changing the way we think about nature, that is, not as related structures but as contextual patterns of relationship. Teilhard called this unitive principle undergirding wholeness *Omega*. Omega is the most intensely personal center

---

[7] James Jeans, *The Mysterious Universe* (New York: Macmillan, 1931), 158.

that makes beings personal and centered.[8] It is both in evolution and independent of evolution, within and yet distinct from the process itself.[9] As the principle of centration that is both within and ahead, Omega emerges from the organic totality of evolution. It is operative from the beginning of evolution, acting on pre-living cosmic elements, even though they are without individualized centers, by setting them in motion from the beginning, a single impulse of energy.[10]

David Bohm speaks of a quantum potential in nature that underscores unbroken wholeness of the entire universe despite quantum fluctuations. Omega is like the quantum potential in that it subsists throughout nature as the centrating principle or the principle of integrated wholeness. It is present from the beginning of the Big Bang and is the goal of evolution, according to Teilhard. It is immanent in each emerging entity and the principle of every whole; it is the whole that makes wholeness in evolution possible. Teilhard identified this deep personal presence of centrating energy—Omega—with the ultimate depth of love we name God. Thus he breaks open a new understanding of God and matter through the energy of love. For so long we have kept love outside the limits of nature, as if it is a peculiarly human emotion that we develop. But as Philip Hefner asked, "Can we entertain the hypothesis that love is rooted in the fundamental nature of reality, including the reality we call nature?"[11]

The classical work of Anders Nygren, *Eros and Agape,* set off wide-ranging debates on love that continue to this day. Love known as *agape* is love that is unconditioned, spontaneous, or unmotivated. It is indifferent to any type of reward or reciprocity and thus opposed to what can be called self-love. *Agape* is the simple yet profound recognition of the worthiness and goodness

---

[8] Teilhard de Chardin, *Activation of Energy,* 112.

[9] In this respect Omega is like the strange attractor of chaos theory—within the system and yet different from the system's pattern of behavior. For a discussion on chaos theory, see Ilia Delio, *The Emergent Christ: Exploring the Meaning of Catholic in an Evolutionary Universe* (Maryknoll, NY: Orbis Books, 2011), 26–27.

[10] Teilhard de Chardin, *Activation of Energy,* 114, 121.

[11] Philip Hefner, *The Human Factor: Evolution, Culture, and Religion* (Minneapolis, MN: Fortress Press, 1993), 208–9.

in a person's "self-giving" or "a person's spending himself freely and carelessly for the other person," the "unconditional willing of the good."[12] *Eros*, on the other hand, speaks of desire and longing, to accumulate for ourselves what we find valuable but not to covet or desire a person at the expense of overall well-being.[13] Edward Vacek defines *eros* as "loving the beloved for our own sake."[14] Jay Oord identifies *eros* as "acting intentionally, in sympathetic response to others (including God), to promote overall well-being when affirming what is valuable, beautiful, or excellent." He states: "Whereas agape repays evil with good, *eros* affirms the good perceived and promotes it."[15] While this may be true it does not capture the heart of *eros*, which is passion or desire. *Eros* is that ineffable longing that stretches beyond oneself for the sake of oneself. This deep, aching desire is not in contrast to agape but is related to it. This longing for the other impels one to act wholeheartedly for the other.

There is a third type of love that exists between *eros* and *agape* and may be the thread between them, that is, *philia*. Vacek argues that *philia* is the goal of the good life. "In *philia*," he writes, "persons give themselves over to the relationship . . . and thereby create a good that they could not separately achieve."[16] *Philia* is love expressed in communal life or life together. It has often been "rejected or displaced in favor of an individualistic, nonmutual, and task-oriented love."[17] But it may be the most cosmic of love because it is based on mutuality, reciprocity, and cooperation—with the purpose of promoting overall well-being or to promote well-being by cooperating with others. Teilhard's notion of love spans all three types of love because it is a fundamental energy of attraction that differentiates personality. It is not simply the promotion of well-being but the deepening of

---

[12] Oord, *Defining Love: A Philosophical, Scientific, and Theological Engagement* (Grand Rapids, MI: Brazo Press, 2010), 37.

[13] Ibid., 38.

[14] Edward Collins Vacek, *Love, Human and Divine: The Heat of Christian Ethics* (Washington, DC: Georgetown University Press, 1994), 157–58.

[15] Oord, *Defining Love*, 47, 48.

[16] Vacek, *Love, Human and Divine*, 288.

[17] Ibid., 284.

being itself. Love is not an epiphenomenon, something that human nature acquires, but rather it undergirds and complements the rise of consciousness. The evolution of consciousness and the deepening of love support the rise of wholeness in nature.

Love as a Cosmological Force

For Teilhard, love is a passionate force at the heart of the Big Bang universe, the fire that breathes life into matter and unifies elements center to center; love is deeply embedded in the cosmos, a "cosmological force."[18] In his essay poem "The Eternal Feminine," he reflects on love in the voice of wisdom:

> When the world was born, I came into being. Before the centuries were made, I issued from the hand of God—half-formed, yet destined to grow in beauty from age to age, the handmaid of his work. Everything in the universe is made by union and generation—by the coming together of elements that seek out one another, melt together two by two, and are born again in a third. God instilled me into the initial multiple as a force of condensation and concentration. In me is seen that side of beings by which they are joined as one, in me the fragrance that makes them hasten together and leads them, freely and passionately, along their road of unity. Through me, all things have their movement and are made to work as one.[19]

Evolution unveils a depth of integrated wholeness that is open to more unity, centricity, and consciousness. Love is not sheer emotion or simply a dopaminergic surge in the limbic system;[20] it is

---

[18] Pierre Teilhard de Chardin, *Human Energy*, trans. J. M. Cohen (New York: Harcourt Brace Jovanovich, 1969), 72.

[19] Pierre Teilhard de Chardin, *Writings in Time of War*, trans. René Hague (New York: Harper and Row, 1968), 192.

[20] I do not want to overlook the neuroscience of love that has recently been discovered. Recent studies on the brain show that love is a complex neurobiological phenomenon, relying on trust, belief, pleasure, and reward activities within the brain, that is, limbic processes associated

much more deeply embedded in the fabric of the universe. Love is the integrated energy field, the center of all centers, the whole of every whole, that makes each whole desire more wholeness. While love-energy may not explicitly show itself on the level of the pre-living and the non-reflective, it is present inchoately as the unifying principle of wholeness as entities evolve toward greater complexity. But even among the molecules," Teilhard wrote, "love was the building power that worked against entropy and under its attraction the elements groped their way towards union."[21] Love-energy marks the history of the universe. It is present from the Big Bang onward, though indistinguishable from molecular forces. It amplifies itself by way of union because it "is the most universal, the most tremendous and the most mysterious of the cosmic forces. . . . The *physical* structure of the universe is love."[22] It draws together and unites; in uniting, it differentiates. Love is the core energy of evolution and its goal.

Teilhard grasped a profound philosophical shift in light of evolution and the fundamental energy of love. He wrote: "What

---

with emotion, aggression, sexual behavior, and, more recently, religion. Areas that are activated in response to romantic feelings are largely coextensive with those brain regions that contain high concentrations of a neuro-modulator that is associated with reward, desire, addiction, and euphoric states, namely, dopamine. Like two other modulators that are linked to romantic love, oxytocin and vasopressin, dopamine is released by the hypothalamus, a structure located deep in the brain and functioning as a link between the nervous and endocrine systems. Release of dopamine puts one in a "feel good" state, and dopamine seems to be intimately linked not only to the formation of relationships but also to sex. An increase in dopamine is coupled to a decrease in another neuro-modulator, serotonin (5–HT or 5–hydroxytryptamine), which is linked to appetite and mood. The early stages of romantic love seem to correlate as well with another substance, nerve growth factor, which has been found to be elevated in those who have recently fallen in love compared to those who are not in love or who have stable, long-lasting relationships. Moreover, the concentration of nerve growth factor appears to correlate significantly with the intensity of romantic feelings. See S. Zeki, "The Neurobiology of Love," *FEBS Letters* 581 (2007): 2575–79.

[21] In Thomas M. King, *Teilhard's Mysticism of Knowing* (New York: Seabury Press, 1981), 104–5.

[22] Teilhard de Chardin, *Human Energy,* 72.

comes first in the world for our thought is not "being" but "the union which produces this being."[23] Love-energy is intrinsically relational and as core energy undergirds relationality in the universe. Beings do not act toward a self-sufficient end in which relationship may or may not be important; rather, union is the end toward which each being directs itself. Love is the affinity of being with being in a personal, centered way, a unity toward greater wholeness that marks all cosmic life. If there was no internal propensity to unite, even at a rudimentary level—indeed in the molecule itself—it would be physically impossible for love to appear higher up, in a hominized form.

Teilhard's philosophy of love distinguishes itself from classical metaphysics where Being is the primary category of existence. To be or not to be *is not* the question. For Teilhard, union is the primary category; to be is to be united. Being is the outflow of union, and union is always toward more being. The term *being* has no real meaning unless it is considered first as union and then as being-in-union or what we might call "interbeing." Reality is woven through layers of bondedness; cosmic life is intrinsically relational. The poet Wallace Stevens wrote, "Nothing is itself taken alone. Things are because of interrelations or interactions."[24]

Teilhard's insights on love-energy as the core energy of evolution provide a new basis to understand cosmic nature. If being is intrinsically relational, then nothing exists independently or autonomously. Rather, "to be" is "to be with." Reality is "being with another" in a way open to more union and more being. Since being is existence towards another, being is relational and exists for the sake of giving. I do not exist in order that I may possess; rather I exist in order that I may give of myself, for it is in giving that I am myself. Cosmic life is intrinsically communal. Being is first a "we" before it can become an "I." There is no being who can stand up and say, "I did it alone." Rather, the universe is thoroughly relational and in the framework of love.

By reversing the relationship between being and union, Teilhard overturned classical metaphysics and unveiled a new

---

[23] Pierre Teilhard de Chardin, *Christianity and Evolution*, trans. René Hague (New York: Harcourt, 1971), 227.

[24] Wallace Stevens, *Opus Posthumous: Poems, Plays, Prose*, ed. Samuel French Morse (New York: Vintage Books, 1982), 163.

principle of reality: *hyperphysics.* Existence is for the sake of giving. Union is always toward *more being* so that evolution is directed toward the future fullness of life. Whereas metaphysics is the principle of static being, hyperphysics is the principle of more being. Metaphysics connotes "sameness" while hyperphysics connotes "more-ness"—more life, more being, more consciousness. In an evolutionary universe that is incomplete and open to the future, the principle of life is not support from above but from the future.

Through his concept of love-energy, Teilhard offers us a way out of the philosophical impasse brought about by materialism, where the properties of reality became the entire basis of empirical knowledge. Love is related to the radial energy of consciousness, so that emergent wholeness and direction are linked. Love-energy is the "beingness" of matter and underlies the intelligibility of the natural order, which means that love is the basis of all real knowledge. While philosophers render love secondary to knowledge, mystics value love as the end of all knowledge in which nothing exists alone and everything becomes.[25]

Cosmic Personalization

If love is the principal energy of life, the whole within every whole, and evolution has direction in the unfolding of consciousness, then it is not difficult to see that evolution is the movement toward greater wholeness and consciousness, that is, the rise of love. Love undergirds the union of elements center to center; as wholes unite with wholes, they differentiate and personalize through unity. This center-to-center process of development is both personal and universal. True unity does not fuse the elements it brings together: "union differentiates."[26] Hence, this

---

[25] A frequent error of Western metaphysics has been to see love and *eros* as a means to knowledge rather than as the end of all knowledge. See Max Scheler, "Love and Knowledge," in *On Feeling, Knowing, and Valuing,* ed. Harold Bershady (Chicago: University of Chicago Press, 1992), 147–65.

[26] Teilard de Chardin, *Human Phenomenon,* 186.

center-to-center union and differentiation gives rise to person-alization.[27]

Teilhard wrote in one of his essays that it is not *something* but *Someone* who is forming in evolution.[28] By "Someone" he had in mind the Christ, but we could translate this "Someone" into the most integrated, self-conscious personal wholeness of energy. In *Human Phenomenon* Teilhard writes:

> Love alone is capable of completing our beings in them-selves as it unites them, for the good reason that love alone takes them and joins them by their very depths—this is a fact of daily experience. Is not the moment when two lov-ers say they are lost in each other the moment when they come into the most complete possession of themselves? All around us at every moment does love not accomplish that magic act, reputed to be so contradictory, of "personaliz-ing" as it totalizes? And if it does this on a daily basis on a reduced scale, why could it not someday repeat it in the dimensions of the Earth?[29]

The term *cosmic personalization* suggests that the cosmos is oriented toward integral wholeness, complexification, and con-sciousness. There is something going on in evolution that is more than blind, mechanical processes of nature. In Teilhard's view, evolution is the process of cosmic personalization. By this he means that evolution is directed toward integral wholeness or personal unity in love. That is, the universe is *oriented* toward a personal, integrated field of love shown by an increase in con-sciousness and centeredness. This orientation toward wholeness in love means that *eros*, or yearning for wholeness, is at the heart of nature.

The fifth-century mystical writer Pseudo-Dionysius said that creation is an erotic outpouring, a divine ecstasy of divine goodness into all things. Teilhard too saw a deep energy at the heart of cosmic life that is evident in the human person. Sexual energy, he said, is the energy of centricity and unification. Any

---

[27]Teilhard de Chardin, *Activation of Energy*, 116.
[28]Teilhard de Chardin, *Christianity and Evolution*, 156, 184.
[29]Teilhard de Chardin, *Human Phenomenon*, 189.

explanation of the world (biological, philosophical, or religious) that does not succeed in finding an essential place for sexuality in its system "is virtually condemned."[30] The word *sex* has a Latin root, the verb *secare*. In Latin, *secare* means "to cut off," "to sever," "to amputate," "to disconnect from the whole." To be sexed, therefore, literally means to be cut off from, to be severed from, to be amputated from the whole.[31] Ronald Rolheiser uses a simple example to illustrate:

> Were you to take a chain saw and go to a tree and cut off one of its branches, you would have "sexed" that branch. This branch, could it feel and think, would wake up on the ground, severed, cut off, disconnected, a lonely little piece of wood which was once part of a great organism. It would know in its every cell that if it wants to continue living and especially if it wants to produce flowers and bear fruit, it must somehow reconnect itself to the tree.[32]

Sexuality presumes that we are part of a whole and have been separated from the whole. Hence our incompleteness makes us long for wholeness and union. Rolheiser writes: "We wake up in the world and in every cell of our being we ache, consciously and unconsciously, sensing that we are incomplete . . . aching at every level for a wholeness that, at some dark level, we know we have been separated from."[33] We are wholes longing for more wholeness and being. Teilhard asks: "What exactly are the essence and direction of 'passionate love' in a universe whose stuff is personality?"[34] While the church maintains that the purpose of sex is for procreation,[35] Teilhard writes that in evolution another

---

[30]Teilhard de Chardin, *Human Energy*, 72.

[31] Ronald Rolheiser, *The Holy Longing: The Search for a Christian Spirituality* (New York: Doubleday, 1999), 193.

[32] Ibid.

[33] Ibid., 194.

[34]Teilhard de Chardin, *Human Energy*, 73.

[35] See Congregation for the Doctrine of Faith, "Instruction *Dignitas personae* on Certain Bioethical Questions," which states: "The Church moreover holds that it is ethically unacceptable to *dissociate procreation from the integrally personal context of the conjugal act*" (para. 16).

more essential role for love has emerged, "the necessary synthesis of the two principles, male and female, in the building of the human personality."[36] In the process of cosmic personalization, persons sexually unite not solely for the purposes of reproduction but for the flowering of personality. Through the passion of union the individual emerges from isolation and enters into union with another in a way that is more spiritualized from the start than the individual personality. Sexuality is integral to a personalizing universe. As Teilhard writes:

> The cosmic role of sexuality appears in its full breadth . . . the rules appear which will guide us in the mastery of that terrifying energy, in which the power that causes the universe to converge on itself pass through us . . . the general laws of creative union contribute to the spiritual differentiation of the two beings which it brings together. The one must not absorb the other nor, still less, should the two lose themselves in the enjoyments of physical possession, which would signify a lapse into plurality and return to nothingness. . . . Love is an adventure and a conquest. It survives and develops like the universe itself only by perpetual discovery. The only right love is that between couples whose passion leads them both, one through the other, to a higher possession of their being.[37]

Love does not propagate itself for the sake of propagation but in order to accumulate the elements necessary for its personalization. That is, love attains a higher consciousness through a deeper centeredness or union of souls. Authentic sexual love (without control or manipulation) is the emergence of spirit: "Without ceasing to be physical, in order to remain physical, love will make itself more spiritual." Teilhard speaks of the "creative role of erotic attraction" not only on the level of the individual but the universe itself is erotic.[38] Passion is the true stuff of the universe; "the whole creation is groaning in the pains of new

---

[36] Teilhard de Chardin, *Human Energy*, 73.

[37] Ibid., 74–75.

[38] Ibid., 77, 82.

birth" (Rom 8:22). Every star, cell, flower, bird, and human person yearns for wholeness and completeness. Sex is not mere continuation of the species; it is the energy of love by which this universe is in the process of personalization, becoming more spiritualized, energized, and conscious:

> The fact that love is increasing instead of diminishing in the course of hominization has a very natural explanation and extension into the future. In the human individual, evolution does not close on itself, but continues further towards a more perfect concentration, linked with further differentiation, also obtained by union. . . . Hence, it is no longer strictly correct to say that the mesh of the universe is, in our experience, the thinking monad. The complete human molecule is already around us: a more synthesized element, and more spiritualized from the start, than the individual personality. It is a duality, comprising masculine and feminine together. Here the cosmic role of sexuality appears in its full breadth. And here at the same time, the rules appear which will guide us in the mastery of that terrifying energy, in which the power that causes the universe to converge on itself passes through us.[39]

There is no doubt that Cartesian dualism rendered love an interference in the mechanism of life, an obstacle to thought. By separating mind and body, the organism was reduced to a mechanism. A mechanized body is a dehumanized person "whose only currency is abstractions divorced from real life—the industrious, coolly rational, economic, prosaic mind."[40] Love has been consigned to emotion and sentiment, emptied of any real power and thus a thing for play. Modern culture's preoccupation with the physical body and the exploitation of the body as soulless matter reflects the deep human disconnect from self, neighbor,

---

[39] Ibid., 74. Teilhard emphasized that love is the maturing of personality and not a question of reproduction. Hence, the ideal of chastity is the pureness of love detached from the flesh, becoming more spiritual without ceasing to be physical (77).

[40] Ken Wilber, *Up from Eden: A Transpersonal View of Human Evolution* (Wheaton, IL: Quest Books, 1996), 225.

earth, and God. Sex has become more like a video game with the thrill of winning rather than part of the deep religious core of cosmic evolution. Teilhard indicated that mechanistic structures of relationship, mass collectivization, or radical individualism all thwart evolution and threaten to destroy personalization. This is true of married, single, and consecrated celibate life on the whole; we have no real consciousness of sexuality as integral to the flowering of personality and thus to the forward movement of evolution. Evolution continues through humanity only when there is consciousness of love as the integral wholeness of love that includes a healthy sexuality. Awareness of our desires and attention to our deepest longings must orient us toward a unified heart and consciousness. Love is more than a survival mechanism; it is the fire breathed into the fabric of the cosmos that enkindles life, rendering life more than biological function. Love turns passion into transformative power.

One might say that evolution depends on healthy sexuality. The love between persons creates a thread of passionate energy that winds around the embrace of persons and enters into the heart of the cosmos, contributing to the energetic movement of universal convergence. Love *is* what "makes the world go 'round." It is fundamental to the forward movement of evolution and cosmic personalization. It is the whole of every whole, the open, dynamic field of energy that seeks greater wholeness within every star, leaf, plant, and galaxy. By the sheer power of its energy, love draws everything into an endless depth of greater wholeness. On the level of human consciousness, the core energy of personal/sexual love must reach out to the wider realm of humanity that includes love of neighbor, friendship, and love of the stranger. Love, sex, and cosmic evolution are intertwined in a field of integral wholeness; to deny, avoid, or negate any of them is to thwart the process of deepening life.

Altruism

Life is not about the lone individual but the individual who is part of a larger whole. Every creature wants to belong to community. If love, consciousness, and integrated wholeness are at the heart of evolution and cosmic personalization, then they form the basis of selfless (altruistic) love. Even Darwin thought that there must be some reason for unselfishness to emerge first in groups of nonrelated individuals. "It seems scarcely possible that the number of people in a tribe who cooperate could be increased through natural selection, that is, by the survival of the fittest."[41] Cooperation might arise when a member of a group learns through personal experience that helping others provides personal benefits. "Each man would soon learn from experience that if he aided his fellow-men, he would commonly receive aid in return. . . . From this love motive he might acquire the habit of aiding his fellows . . . strengthening the feeling of sympathy, which gives the first impulse to benevolent actions."[42] Darwin anticipated the question of how self-sacrifice for the good of others might arise in a world of severe competition. He speculated that self-sacrifice arose first in the parent-child relationship. Parents sometimes give sacrificially to their children at a significant and sometimes even ultimate cost to themselves. From this extremely basic parental impulse to nurture children, a person retains "some degree of instinctive love and sympathy for his fellows."[43]

Edward O. Wilson calls altruism "the central theoretical problem of sociobiology." How can altruism, which by definition reduces personal fitness, possibly evolve by natural selection? In *On Human Nature* he relates human-kin altruism to the "self-sacrificing termite soldier who protects the rest of its colony, including the queen and king, its parents. As a result, the soldier's more fertile brothers and sisters flourish, and through them the altruistic genes are multiplied by a greater production of nephews and nieces."[44] The difference between man and higher animals is one of degree not of kind. Frans de Waal's work with chimpanzees, rhesus monkeys, and baboons suggests moral continuities between humans and nonhumans. De Waal states, "A chimpanzee stroking or patting a victim of attack or sharing her

---

[41] Charles Darwin, *The Descent of Man, and Selection in Relation to Sex*, reprinted in *From So Simple a Beginning: The Four Great Books of Charles Darwin*, ed. E. O. Wilson (New York: W. W. Norton, 2005), 870.

[42] Ibid.

[43] Ibid., 825.

[44] Edward O. Wilson, *On Human Nature*, 25th anniv. ed. (Cambridge, MA: Harvard University Press, 2004), 153.

food with a hungry companion shows attitudes that are hard to distinguish from those of a person picking up a crying child or doing volunteer work at a soup kitchen. The biggest step in the evolution of human morality was the move from interpersonal relations to a focus on the greater good. "In apes we can see the beginnings of this when they smooth relations between others. Females may bring males together after a fight between them, thus brokering reconciliation, and high-ranking males often stop fights among others in an evenhanded manner, thus promoting peace in the group."[45] Some primates exhibit moral behavior that mirrors compassion, writes Tijn Touber. Bonobos, for example, "share food, show a strong sense of right and wrong and exhibit feelings of shame, guilt, sympathy and concern." Touber tells the story of a three-year-old boy "who fell 18 feet into the primate enclosure at Chicago's Brookfield Zoo. A gorilla named Binti Jua picked up the child and carried him to safety. She sat down on a log and rocked the boy on her lap, patting him a few times on his back, before taking him to waiting zoo staff. Her show of sympathy, captured on video and shown around the world, touched many hearts."[46]

Richard Dawkins sees incompatibility between gene-centered evolution and self-sacrificial love: "We are survival machines . . . robot vehicles blindly programmed to preserve the selfish molecules known as genes." He continues by saying that "a predominant quality to be expected in a successful gene is ruthless selfishness. This gene selfishness will usually give rise to selfishness in individual behavior. . . . Universal love and the welfare of the species as a whole are concepts that simply do not make evolutionary sense."[47] But as Holmes Rolston rightly notes, genes are not moral agents, they cannot be selfish, and they cannot be altruistic, but they can transmit information. Genes have more of an eye on the species than on the individual:

---

[45] Frans de Waal, *Primates and Philosophers: How Morality Evolved*, ed. Josiah Ober and Stephen Macedo (Princeton, NJ: Princeton University Press, 2006), 54.

[46] Tijn Touber, "Do Primates Feel Compassion?" available on the care2.com website.

[47] Richard Dawkins, *The Selfish Gene* (London: Granada, 1978), x, 2.

The solitary organism living in the present is born to lose; all that can be transmitted from past to future is its kind. Though selection operates on individuals, since it is always an individual that copes, selection is for the kind of coping that succeeds in copying, that is re-producing, producing again the kind, distributing the information coded in the gene more widely. Survival (of the species) is through making *others* (altruism, even if similar others), who share the same valuable information. Survival is of the better transmitter of whatever is of generic value in self into others, descendants. Survival of the fittest turns out to be survival of the senders.[48]

If wholeness is at the heart of life, then behavior itself will ultimately depend on love if a species is to survive. The over-emphasis on genes or the neurochemical basis of love obscures the nature of love as Omega, the integrated center of wholeness in which every whole has its meaning. Although the primacy of love-energy in nature seems to contradict nature's relentless survival of the fittest and sometimes violent means of self-assertion, love is not an object to measure or even a completely positive force. Where there is love there is suffering, because love is always aimed toward greater wholeness, that is, more being. In a world of limits the drive toward more being will always encounter resistance. Teilhard said that at every level of evolution, evil forms and reforms implacably in us and around us. This is relentlessly imposed by the play of large numbers at the heart of a multitude undergoing organization. Death will continue to be an indispensable condition not only as the replacement of one individual by another in the phyletic system but also as the essential lever in the mechanism and upsurge of life. As we continue to evolve toward greater consciousness and complexity, we will continue to labor. Suffering and failure, tears and blood are byproducts (often precious, moreover, and re-utilizable) begotten by the evolution of consciousness itself. Yet love is creative because the nature of wholeness is open and dynamic. Love is not

---

[48] Holmes Rolston, "Kenosis and Nature," in *The Work of Love: Creation as Kenosis*, ed. John Polkinghorne (Grand Rapids, MI: Eerdmans, 2001), 57.

a mechanistic force or lawful determinant but rather a creative power that unites. It is not a measurable particle but life-giving energy. Love draws together even in the face of resistance. If energy is the fire of life, then love is the energy of all life. Evolution rests on the power of love because what ignites the core of being is ultimately unitive and transformative.

Chapter Four

Birthing a New God

A mechanistic view of reality makes it easy to parcel out God, humans, and other creatures. Each has its part to play in the whole clockwork system, the *machina mundi*. But cosmic evolution is an entirely different story. The most fundamental levels of nature are more like quantum fuzziness on the background of an evolutionary Etch-a-Sketch. Out of a long history of cosmic cataclysms and mass extinctions, we humans emerge. We are born out of stardust, cousins of daffodils and bonobos; we are the conscious voice of a fragile earth. "We are up to our neck in debt," David Toolan wrote. "Where would we be without star factories? Without blue-green algae? Without rain forests? Without the mitochondria in our cells?"[1] We humans are the most recent arrival on the evolutionary scene, a scant 140,000-year-old existence in a 13.7 billion-year-old universe. So why do we think this story is all about us? Who or what is the subject of the new cosmos story?

We talk about evolution as if it is a process outside ourselves, something that we can study or ponder. As children of Descartes we continue to make the cosmos story an object of our thought rather than seeing ourselves as part of the whole. Because we do not see ourselves as part of something larger than ourselves, we have no consciousness of wholeness; hence, the absence of God from the whole. The subject matter of the new cosmos

---

[1] David Toolan, *At Home in the Cosmos* (Maryknoll, NY: Orbis Books, 2003), 218.

story is neither the cosmos nor the human, Panikkar states, but the cosmos inhabited by God *and* human, who is a constitutive member of reality. "The very name of God is a cosmological notion. . . . Theology without cosmology is a mere abstraction of a non-existing God, and a cosmology without theology is just a mirage."[2] If the new cosmos story is indeed a love story, then we can no longer tell this story as if divinity and humanity are opposed to each other. It is not merely evolution of Homo sapiens who, at advanced levels of consciousness, express a need for religious myth and ritual; there is something much more fundamental going on in the universe. Teilhard writes, "Religion, born of the earth's need for the disclosing of a god, is related to and co-extensive with, not the individual man but the whole of mankind."[3] That is, religion belongs fundamentally to the cosmos, not to the human person alone. There is no cosmos without God and no God without cosmos. The divine is never alone or by itself because it has no "self"; it is a dimension of the Whole.[4] A Westerner's immediate cry is "pantheism!" The word *pantheism* is derived from the Greek *pan*, meaning "all," and the Greek *theos*, meaning "God." It is the view that everything is part of God and God is part of everything; God and nature are identical. This is *not* what Panikkar is saying. Rather, the very existence of the cosmos points to One who is not cosmos but whose existence renders the cosmos its existence. This is God, the name above every other name because it is the name of the whole. God is the whole of every whole. God is not created being, and created being is not God, but God is one with created/cosmic being and created/cosmic being is one with God. Panentheism means that God is in the cosmos and the cosmos is in God, but God is more than the cosmos by the nature of being God. Panikkar describes this panentheistic God as the "cosmotheandric invariant."

It is amazing how some of the most educated people still think of God as a prime mover or an apathetic deity who watches us from a distance. The recent discovery of the Higgs Boson

---

[2] Raimon Panikkar, *The Rhythm of Being: The Gifford Lectures* (Maryknoll, NY: Orbis Books, 2010), 187–88.

[3] Pierre Teilhard de Chardin, *Christianity and Evolution*, trans. René Hague (New York: Harcourt, 1971), 119.

[4] Ibid., 190.

particle, for example, led some scientists to suggest that we no longer need to invoke God as prime mover. A concept of God that can be rejected, such as prime mover, is a concept empty of God. God is not an idea but the living wholeness of reality, seen not by the physical eye of the scientist but by the gaze of the mystic, the inner eye of love. One of the most insightful twentieth-century theologians, Paul Tillich, identifies the problem of misunderstanding God when he writes:

> A God whose existence or nonexistence you can argue is a thing beside others within the universe of existing things. . . . It is regrettable that scientists believe that they have refuted religion when they rightly have shown that there is no evidence whatsoever for the assumption that such a being exists. Actually, they not only have refuted religion, but they have done it a considerable service. They have forced it to reconsider and to restate the meaning of the tremendous word *God.* Unfortunately, many theologians make the same mistake. They begin their message with the assertion that there is a highest being called God, whose authoritative revelations they have received. They are more dangerous for religion than the so-called atheistic scientists. They take the first step on the road which inescapably leads to what is called atheism. Theologians who make of God a highest being who has given some people information about Himself, provoke inescapably the resistance of those who are told they must subject themselves to the authority of this information.[5]

God is not a timeless being without relation to anything in time; nor is God apathetic to the fate of the cosmos. God belongs to the cosmos, and when this relationship is aborted theology becomes a mere abstraction of a nonexistent God.[6] When the relationship between God and cosmos is aborted, we wind up with religious atheism and acosmism (that is, a cosmos without God and God without cosmos). From the moment we say God

---

[5] Paul Tillich, *Theology of Culture* (New York: Oxford University Press, 1959), 4–5.
[6] Panikkar, *The Rhythm of Being*, 188.

is Being, it is clear that in a certain sense, God alone is. This was Western philosophy's problem with God.

The age of Newtonian science and the rise of modernity fashioned God into a distant deity governing the world from above. In the twentieth century two world wars caused such utter destruction that people felt abandoned by God; their cries for mercy seemed to fall on deaf ears. Anxiety and despair took hold of the human heart, as people sought meaning amid the ashes of history. Philosophers noted that profound violence within humanity revealed the failure of religion. God became so removed from history and the cosmos that people acted as if God did not exist. Martin Heidegger named this problem of God as the beginning of ontotheology—God as Super Being. God became the great letdown, a thing among other things, and in the midst of human atrocities, the biggest failure. Friedrich Nietzsche, the son of Lutheran pastors, said that the death of God was the death of the transcendent *moral* God but, conversely, in the chaos of human evolution, God was born as "the divine artist whose creativity is beyond good and evil."[7] The discovery of evolution and quantum physics opened up a new window to the divine mystery that illuminates the role of God and human in evolution. It is not a matter of trying to fit the old God into the new cosmos; rather, it is the birth of a new God.

Heidegger returned to the world of Being not as a conceptual argument for God but as an activity immanent in this world, a self-giving presence rather than a transcendent creator God. In his view we are "immersed in a world of finite material things that we try to control for our own individual purposes but which in the end control us because we have lost perspective on how to deal with them in meaningful ways."[8] "We accept without thinking the givenness of the world around us and most of the things within it. *It takes an 'emergency,' a break in our everyday consciousness, to become aware of what is always already*

---

[7] In Mark Taylor, *After God* (Chicago: University of Chicago Press, 2007), 122–23.

[8] Joseph A. Bracken, *Subjectivity, Objectivity, and Intersubjectivity: A New Paradigm for Religion and Science* (West Conshohocken, PA: Templeton Foundation Press, 2009), 110.

there awaiting our response" (emphasis added).[9] Integral to this awareness is a grasp of our own subjectivity. The Carmelite philosopher Edith Stein, a classmate of Heidegger, writes: "I do not exist of myself, and of myself I am nothing. Every moment I stand before nothingness, so that every moment I must be dowered anew with being. . . . This nothinged being of mine, this frail received being, is being. . . . It thirsts not only for endless continuation of its being but for full possession of being."[10] For Stein, the very existence of "I" means the "I" is not alone; the "I" experiences loneliness only when it becomes unconscious of its very existence. In the words of French philosopher and mystic Simone Weil, "Whoever says 'I' lies."[11] Heidegger's "already there" and Stein's beingness of the "I" awakened twentieth-century postmodern philosophers to a new sense of religion. The term *posttheism* is used to speak of a new presence of God, a return to God *after* God, an ordinary mysticism that lives without a why.[12] God is the systole-diastole of being—but to know this

---

[9] Ibid., 111.

[10] Cited in Brendan Purcell, *From Big Bang to Big Mystery. Human Origins in the Light of Creation and Evolution* (New York: New City Press, 2012), 315. Purcell notes that this text may be an evocative version of Edith Stein's *Finite and Eternal Being: An Attempt at an Ascent to the Meaning of Being*, trans. Kurt F. Reinhardt (Washington, DC: ICS Publications, 2002), 55–56. Stein's words read: "My own being as I know it and as I know myself in it, is null and void [*nichtig*]; I am not by myself (not a being *a se* and *per se*), and by myself I am nothing; at every moment I find myself face to face with nothingness, and from moment to moment I must be endowed and re-endowed with being. And yet this empty existence that I am is *being,* and at every moment I am in touch with the fullness of being. . . . The ego shrinks back from nothingness and desires not only an endless continuation of its own being but a full possession of being as such: It desires a being capable of embracing the totality of the ego's contents in one changeless present."

[11] Cited in Panikkar, *The Rhythm of Being*, 190.

[12] This idea comes from the German mystic Meister Eckhart, who wrote: "If anyone went on for a thousand years asking of life: 'Why are you living?' life, if it could answer, would only say, 'I live so that I may live.' That is because life lives out of its own ground and springs from its own source, and so it lives without asking why it is itself living." See Meister Eckhart, "Sermon 5b," in *Meister Eckhart: The Essential*

God we must rid ourselves of the old distant God. As Meister Eckhart boldly preached in a sermon, "Let us pray to God that we may be free of God."[13]

The greatest obstacle to religion today does not come so much from atheists but from the neo-foundationalists whose fundamental tenets of religion claim ontological certainty. These are the religious fundamentalists whose certainty of divine truths based on the inerrancy of scripture creates division. Their grip on God strips the world of the divine mystery. The only way to overcome this (paradoxical) religious atheism is to let go of God.

> God is not simply a principle of which we are the consequence, a will whose instruments we are. . . . There is sort of an impotence of God without us, and Christ attests that God would not be fully God without becoming fully man. . . . God is not above but beneath us—meaning that we do not find him as a suprasensible idea, but as another ourself which dwells in and authenticates our darkness. Transcendence no longer hangs over man; he becomes, strangely, its privileged bearer.[14]

To come to a new understanding of God in our age, a God who is the God of evolution, is to know ourselves as privileged bearers of transcendence. We look below at three twentieth-century theologians who explored new ways to understand the divine mystery—Paul Tillich, Raimon Panikkar, and Pierre Teilhard de Chardin.

Tillich and the Ultimate Depth of Being

The best way to know God, many great spiritual writers say, is to know oneself. In *The Confessions* Saint Augustine writes: "I

Sermons, Commentaries, Treatises, and Defense, trans. and intro. Edmund Colledge, OSA, and Bernard McGinn (New York: Paulist Press, 1981), 184.

[13] Ibid., 200.

[14] Merleau Ponty, *Signs*, cited in Richard Kearney, *Anatheism* (New York: Columbia University Press, 2010), 91.

was searching without while you were within . . . more inward than my inmost self and superior to my highest being,"[15] or as Eckhart said, "God is closer to me than I am to myself."[16] God is the center of our center, the most inward center and hence depth of our existence. Sigmund Freud was a Jew and an avowed atheist, so it would be alarming to suggest that he gave us new insight on God, but indeed he did so through the work of Paul Tillich. Freud insisted that belief in God represented nothing more than the projection of images from the erotic experience of the infant into a supernatural realm, but Tillich drew the obvious parallels between that process and the biblical notion of idol worship and idolatry. If every idea and image of God is a projection, it is a projection of *something*. Tillich claimed that the realm against which the divine images are projected is not itself a projection. "It is the *experienced ultimacy* of being and meaning. It is the realm of ultimate concern."[17] Freud had illuminated the pathways into the depths of human experience, and Tillich followed Freud's lead relentlessly. He increasingly spoke of religion as "the dimension of depth":

> If we enter the levels of personal existence which have been rediscovered by depth psychology, we encounter the past, the ancestors, the collective unconscious, the living substance in which all living beings participate. In our search for the "really real" we are driven from one level to another to a point where we cannot speak of level any more, where we must ask for that which is the ground of all levels, giving them their structure and their power of being.[18]

Rather than looking for the failed God of the philosophers, Tillich focused on the human passion for meaning—what gives

---

[15] Augustine, *The Confessions of St. Augustine*, trans. John K. Ryan (New York: Doubleday, 1960), 84.

[16] In Richard Woods, "Eckhart's Eye," available at whitecranejournal .com/wc01047.htm.

[17] Paul Tillich, *Systematic Theology*, vol. 1 (Chicago: University of Chicago Press, 1951), 212.

[18] Paul Tillich, *Biblical Religion and the Search for Ultimate Realty* (Chicago: University of Chicago Press, 1955), 13.

fire to our lives. Even a critical, logical, and strictly scientific analysis of the human situation reveals the presence of something unconditional within the self and the world. Rising up from human awareness of finitude is an awareness of the infinite. The background of everything that exists is another existence. God, according to Tillich, is not open to argumentation because God is not something that can be proved or disproved. God does not merely exist; rather, God *is* existence (Ex 3:14, "I Am"). Tillich writes:

> It would be a great victory for Christian apologetics if the words "God" and "existence" were very definitely separated except in the paradox of God becoming manifest under the conditions of existence. . . . God does not exist. He is being-itself beyond essence and existence. To argue that God exists is to deny him. . . . In arguments for the existence of God the world is given and God is sought. . . . But, if we derive God from the world, he cannot be that which transcends the world infinitely. He is the "missing link" . . . the uniting force between the *res cogitans* and the *res extensa,* or the end of the causal regression in answer to the question, "Where from?" (Thomas Aquinas), or the teleological intelligence directing the meaningful processes of reality—if not identical with these processes (Whitehead). In each of these cases God is "world," a missing part of that from which he is derived in terms of conclusions.[19]

By saying that "God does not exist" Tillich indicated that God is not *a* Being among beings. Rather, God is existence itself, which means God can only appear in otherness, in that which exists. According to Tillich: "God does not exist. He is being itself beyond essence and existence," except in the paradox of "God becoming manifest under conditions of existence."[20] There is no being without form. In other words, Being is not an abstract concept but the real of what exists, and everything that exists has particular form. Being, therefore, is dynamically oriented toward becoming:

---

[19] Tillich, *Systematic Theology,* 205.
[20] Ibid.

The dynamic character of being implies the tendency of everything to transcend itself and create new forms. At the same time everything tends to conserve its own form as the basis of its self-transcendence. It tends to unite identity and difference, rest and movement, conservation and change. Therefore, it is impossible to speak of being without also speaking of becoming. Becoming is just as genuine in the structure of being as is that which remains unchanged in the process of becoming.[21]

This insight is the basis of Tillich's "theonomous culture," whereby every cultural creation—a painting, a law, a political movement—has a religious meaning to be explored and a theological element to be explained. Every dynamic aspect of being is a dynamic presence of God.

Panikkar's Cosmotheandric Invariant

Panikkar's understanding of God, like Tillich's, is integrally related to created reality; there is no God without cosmos and no cosmos without God. Indeed, the very utterance of God depends on cosmos. Whereas Tillich's explorations are theological, psychological, and social, Panikkar takes an interreligious, philosophical approach to understanding God. He develops the term *cosmotheandrism* to describe a non-dualistic interbeing of divine and created realities. Being is a co-inherence of divine, cosmic, and anthropic being, mutually coexisting, so that one cannot be separated from the other. Divine being is uncreated, yet it mutually co-inheres in created being. God is not created being and created being is not God, but God is one with created/cosmic being and created/cosmic being is one with God. Panikkar's cosmotheandric being is univocal being. The term *univocity* refers to the way God's being and created being are related through the one concept of being. God does not exist outside the relational ordering of being, as if only the effects were ordered and the cause lay outside the relationship. That is, the first principle (God) does not transcend order. Rather, the essential

---

[21] Ibid., 181.

order represents the unified whole of all that is, including God. Although God's being and created being are not identical, the concept being *(ens)* stands as the foundation between the mind and reality and is the way we come to know and understand the world around us, ourselves, and God. Because of this relationship we are able to understand something of the world in which we live. Everything makes a piece, a unified whole that reveals the rationality, freedom, and creativity of God.[22] Hence "God" is the cosmotheandric depth dimension of all created reality. Rather than reducing God to one among many, the cosmotheandric invariant provides a ground to the unity of multiplicity and an empowerment whereby the many become one. Creation exists because God exists, and because God exists creation exists, that is, God and creation mutually co-inhere.

Panikkar's cosmotheandrism highlights theology's relationship to the whole. The divine is never alone or by itself because it has no "self"; it is the Whole of the Whole.[23] The divine mystery is the ultimate *AM* of everything. God is not the ontologically distinct Being who empowers created being but the very dimension of created being by which being transcends itself toward ever greater relationality, wholeness, and depth. This is the cosmotheandric experience—the undivided experience of the three pronouns simultaneously. Panikkar writes: "Without the divine we cannot say *I*; without consciousness we cannot say *Thou*; and without the World we cannot say *It*. They are pro-nouns, or rather pro-noun; they stand for the same (unnameable) noun."[24] Each pronoun is the whole noun in its pronominal way–perichoresis. Technocracy has let the human person evaporate, Panikkar claims, because we have failed to see divine being as interrelated to cosmic, anthropic being. The subject matter of the whole of the New Story is neither the cosmos nor the human but the cosmos inhabited by God and human who is a constitutive member of reality. Everything is related to everything but without monistic identity or dualistic separation.

---

[22] Mary Beth Ingham, *Scotus for Dunces: An Introduction to the Subtle Doctor* (New York: Franciscan Institute Publications, 2003), 39–42.

[23] Panikkar, *The Rhythm of Being*, 190.

[24] Ibid., 191.

Teilhard de Chardin and Omega

Tillich's divine depth of being and Panikkar's cosmotheandrism contribute to a new understanding of God that overturns the hellenization of God and is more consonant with Christianity insofar as God truly belongs to physical reality. Like Tillich and Panikkar, Teilhard saw that the God of Scholasticism, forged out of Greek philosophy, no longer speaks to the world of modern science. In *Christianity and Evolution* he sums up the problem of God:

> In the case of a world which is by nature evolutive . . . God is not conceivable (either structurally or dynamically) except in so far as he coincides with (as a sort of "formal" cause) but without being lost in, the centre of convergence of cosmogenesis. . . . Ever since Aristotle there have been almost continual attempts to construct models of God on the lines of an outside Prime Mover, acting *a retro*. Since the emergence in our consciousness of the "sense of evolution" it has become physically impossible for us to conceive or worship anything but an organic Prime-Mover God, *ab ante*. Only a God who is functionally and totally "Omega" can satisfy us. Who will at last give evolution *its own* God?[25]

While in the case of a static world the creator is structurally independent of his work, in the case of an evolutive world, the contrary is true. God is not conceivable except insofar as he coincides with evolution but without being lost in the convergence of cosmogenesis.[26] God is a "hyper-center"—that is to say, of greater *depth* than us.[27] The world is not God and God is not the world, yet God is the unlimited depth of love of all that is, a love that overflows into new life.

Teilhard did not hold to a separate doctrine of creation but saw creative union as the way God acts in evolution by uniting himself to matter:

---

[25] Teilhard de Chardin, *Christianity and Evolution*, 239–40.
[26] Ibid., 239.
[27] Pierre Teilhard de Chardin, *Toward the Future*, trans. Rene Hague (New York: Harcourt, 1975), 76.

The theory of creative union is not so much a metaphysical doctrine as a sort of empirical and pragmatic explanation of the universe. This theory came to birth out of my own personal need to reconcile, within the confines of a rigorously structured system, the views of science respecting evolution (which views are accepted here as being definitively established, at least in their essence) with an innate tendency which has driven me to *seek out the presence of God, not apart from the physical world, but rather through matter and in a certain sense in union with it.*[28]

Creation is a kenosis of divine love, a constant emptying of divine self into other. God becomes "element" and draws all things through love into the fullness of being. Thomas King writes: "Matter is the principle of otherness. In matter God and man can become other than what they are. Through matter God and man can meet. God is not found through opposition to matter (antimatter) or independent of matter (extra-matter) but through matter (trans-matter)."[29] We take hold of God in the finite; God is sensed as "rising" or "emerging" from the depths, born not in the heart of matter but *as* the heart of matter.[30] Teilhard believed that without creation, something would be absolutely lacking to God, considered in the fullness not of his being but of his act of union. Christopher Mooney explains:

The assertion that the world's movement towards unity "completes" God in some way is unusual and needs to be clarified. . . . Teilhard is doing nothing more nor less than asserting in an evolutionary context the paradox which is already contained in St. Paul: *the Pleroma of Christ cannot constitute an intrinsic completion of God himself,* but it will nonetheless in some sense be a real completion. . . . Teilhard wants to do away once and for all with the idea

---

[28] Donald P. Gray, *The One and the Many: Teilhard de Chardin's Vision of Unity* (London: Burns and Oates, 1969), 34.

[29] Thomas M. King, *Teilhard's Mysticism of Knowing* (New York: Seabury Press, 1981), 66.

[30] Ibid., 103.

that God's continuous act of creation is one of *absolute* gratuity.[31]

Teilhard opposed the idea of an absolutely gratuitous creation that makes creation independent of God or merely contingent on God.[32] This type of radical dependency between God and world diminishes the significance of the world in relation to God. Creation is not merely gift of God; it is being-in-love *with* God. It is more than an act willed out of intellect or desire. Creation is the Beloved of God and the becoming of God in love. God is in matter and matter is in God, but God is not matter and matter is not God because matter exists by what it is not—God; and God exists by what it is not—matter. God and matter need each other to be what they distinctly are. God is not the supernatural being above but the *supranatural* center of everything that exists. In other words, God and matter are not opposed to each other but are a coincidence of opposites and thus mutually affirming. Teilhard proposed that union with God "must be effected by passing through and emerging from matter."[33] He wrote in *Christianity and Evolution*, "I can be saved only by becoming one with the universe."[34] That is, we are not rescued *from* the world by divine grace; rather, we are saved or made whole in and through the world by cooperating with divine love.

Trinity—Creation

If God is at the heart of this physical, evolving cosmos, then love is the energy that makes everything precious and alive. God is the ultimate wholeness and depth of love, the inner Omega of everything from the smallest quark to the largest galaxy. Because divine love is *totally* other-centered, the whole cosmos is a theophany, a revelation of God's glory. Michael Meerson states: "God's ultimate reality cannot be located in substance (what it

---

[31] Christopher F. Mooney, SJ, *Teilhard de Chardin and the Mystery of Christ* (New York: Harper and Row, 1966), 174–75.

[32] Gray, *The One and the Many*, 127.

[33] King, *Teilhard's Mysticism of Knowing*, 66–67.

[34] Teilhard de Chardin, *Christianity and Evolution*, 128.

is in itself) but only in personhood: what God is toward another. God exists as the mystery of persons in communion. God exists in freedom and ecstasies. Only in communion can God be what God is, and only in communion can God be at all. . . . Since love produces communion among persons, love causes God to be who God is."[35] The Trinity symbolizes integrated wholeness; of "persons" in love or fully integrated energies of personal being. The revelation of God as love (Jn 4:13) means that God is the most dynamic, most relational, most unitive, and most personal love—the love of all love. The "Father" is fountain fullness of love, the divine, infinite source of love. The "Word" expresses the Father's love and the Spirit is the bond of love that breathes forth between the Artist and the Art, fountain fullness and Word. Janet Kvamme writes: "It is love that brings the persons together in unity; through the generosity of love the divinity emanates and the divine persons proceed. Love flows out from the fountain fullness of fecundity . . . originating in the One who is boundless and inexhaustible love."[36] Every created being is held in being by the breath of divine love whose infinite depth exceeds the capacity of any finite being to contain it; hence, every being stretches toward its own self-expression, its longing to love as it is loved, reaching out toward more being and more life.

This dynamic personal relatedness of infinite love means that creation is not a mere external act of God, an object on the fringe of divine power; rather, it emerges out of the innermost depths of trinitarian life.[37] Evolution is the process by which Trinity becomes cosmos, and cosmos becomes christified; that is, love unto love becomes more personal and unitive. The drama of creation is the drama of trinitarian life. Denis Edwards writes, "The begetting of the Word is an eternal act of letting go, of divine kenosis, of creating space for the other." Elsewhere he writes: "God does not create discrete individual beings through a series

---

[35] Michael Aksionov Meerson, *The Trinity of Love in Modern Russian Theology* (Quincy, IL: Franciscan Press, 1998), 4.

[36] Janet Kvamme, "The *Fontalis Plenitudo* in Bonaventure as a Symbol for His Metaphysics" (PhD diss., Fordham University, 2000), 170, 175.

[37] Ilia Delio, *Simply Bonaventure: An Introduction to His Life, Thought, and Writings* (New York: New City Press, 2001), 54.

of interventions, but rather God creates in one divine act that embraces the whole process. It is this one divine act that enables what is radically new to emerge in creation being."[38] Trinity is not merely the condition for evolution but the dynamic, flowing movement of evolution—Love poured into Word continuously breathed anew in Spirit. Evolution is Trinity enfolding space-time, not only in this visible universe but in all universes where there is the capacity for love.

The fecund relationality of God renders creation neither chance nor necessity; it is God's destiny.[39] God does what God is—what is true to God's nature and thus what is divine—love. Because God is love, God is entirely free, and in this freedom God is entirely Godself.[40] God loves the world with the very same love which God *is*. God is not divine substance governing creation but the radical subject of everything that exists, the depth and wholeness of nature itself that reveals itself in its hiddenness. God's love fills up each being as "this" (and not "that"), but the limits of any being cannot contain God; thus, the excess of God's love spills over as "transcendence," more than any being can grasp. Transcendence is the fecundity of love and the "yearning" dimension of everything that exists. The excess of love draws each element and creature toward greater union and more being. God, therefore, can never be behind creation, as if God does something then steps away to observe it from a distance. Rather God-Omega-Love is the power of everything that exists and, as the excess of love, the future who holds open in the present moment the radical possibilities of love.

God's love is divine, dynamic energy, always seeking more relationship, more unity, and being in love. Since love is the core energy of evolution and God is love, God is the core of evolution, the unstoppable urge of cosmic reality for more life. In this respect evolution has a religious core, a deep, inherent drive toward ultimate wholeness. God is divine love spilling over the limits of being that seeks to become more being in love; God is

---

[38] Denis Edwards, *The God of Evolution: A Trinitarian Theology* (Mahwah, NJ: Paulist Press, 1999), 30–31, 76.

[39] Jürgen Moltmann, *God in Creation: A New Theology of Creation and the Spirit of God* (Minneapolis, MN: Fortress Press, 1983), 83.

[40] Ibid., 76.

the unstoppable urge of evolutionary transcendence. As the love-center Omega, God is in evolution because love seeks more unity and being in love. Although we can say, with Teilhard, that God is rising from within evolution to become the God of evolution, God is also the transcendence of love. God is up ahead as the future of evolution because God is the fullness of love and all that can be in love. Hence, God is the One who is and who is coming to be.[41]

---

[41] Evolution is not only the universe coming to be but it is *God* who is *coming to be* insofar as God arises with the development of consciousness. See Teilhard de Chardin, *Christianity and Evolution*, 171–72; cf. Teilhard de Chardin, *Human Energy*, trans. J. M. Cohen (New York: Harcourt Brace Jovanovich, 1969), 43–47, where he writes: "From universal evolution God emerges in our minds greater and more necessary than even. . . . The birth and progress of the idea of God on earth are intimately bound up with the phenomenon of hominization."

Chapter Five

Love and Suffering

We think of religion as something institutional, static, and ritualistic, but the meaning of religion, "to bind back" (from the Latin *ligare*), connotes dynamism and transcendence, an active yearning for ultimacy. This yearning is the "suffering" of incompletion, the desire to be "bound back" to something more whole and transcendent; it is within everything that exists but comes to explicit consciousness in the human person. Religion is the transcendent dimension of being's desire for ultimate wholeness. In some respect every aspect of evolution bears a religious dimension because everything yearns for more life. Religion is more than the institution of cult and worship; religion is the heart of evolution.

While evolution is nature's means of unfolding life, *creation* is the term for nature's relationship with God. We used to think of creation as an event of the past, something that God did and governed from above. However, the new physics of love-energy and the discovery of evolution give new meaning to God and creation. Evolution opens a new window to the divine mystery. Rather than God as cause of creation, Teilhard perceived God as the One who is emerging through the process of complexity-consciousness. The Dominican mystic Meister Eckhart said that "God is the newest thing there is, the youngest thing there is. God is the beginning and if we are united to God we become new again."[1] The idea of newness

---

[1] *Meditations with Meister Eckhart*, intro. and trans. Matthew Fox (Santa Fe, NM: Bear and Company, 1983), 32.

of God overturns our traditional understanding of God as the most eternal (and hence unchanging) thing there is. God is not the prime mover of a static cosmos but the dynamism of love swelling up in space-time through the process of evolution and the rise of consciousness.

For centuries we have said "God is love," and yet we have made God into something static and fixed. A fixed something cannot be dynamic love because love, by its nature, goes out to another to be for the other. The name *God* points to that in which being and act are one and the same; if the act of God is dynamic evolution wherein change is integral to developing life, then God too must be God in relation to change. To say "God is love" is to say that the name God refers to the divine energy of love that is dynamic, relational, personal, and unitive; hence, God is most dynamic, relational, personal, and unitive. God does what God is—love. Rather than seeing God as a separate being over the world, we can say that love-energy is the stuff of existence; divine love-energy and created love-energy exist in mutual complementarity. Thus, where there is energy of attraction, union, generativity, and life, there is God.

Evolution and quantum physics help us realize that God creates us less as subjects of divine will than out of the freedom of divine love. Creation actively takes place in the present moment as divine love expresses itself in finite being open to more being and love. Hence, the term *creation* points to that which is always coming to be; it is being-held-in-love or being that longs for more being-in-love. This longing is a type of suffering in the sense that what exists is not yet filled; creation lacks what it still needs to be complete. Creation, therefore, is not so much a past event as a present becoming that is oriented toward new being up ahead. While the old God-world relationship meant two distinct realities of God *and* world, the new cosmotheandrism means that God and world belong to the same whole; they are mutually related without being identical. God does not exist apart from creation, as if God lives in a place called heaven and watches over another place called earth. Nor is creation the amusement of a lonely deity. Rather, creation is integral to the very nature of God as love. God is eternally committed to creation, or, as Karl Rahner wrote, "the fate of God is in and with the world."[2] "WorLd," we might say, is the divine Word expressed in love. Divine transcendence is the fecundity of love, whereby being desires more being and love seeks more love. There is an ultimacy at the heart of being itself, an allurement or attraction that is more than any being can possess. This ultimacy of love is God.

Love is generative and divine love longs to become more visible in the fruitful flowering of life. We can imagine the universe as a cosmic womb wherein God is seeking to come to birth through suffering, death, and new life. Mary, the mother of Jesus, is a symbol of the cosmos as *theotokos* or God-bearer. Mary said yes, and God's birthing was disclosed as the history of evolution and its future. Through the icon of Mary we see that creation is the place where God becomes God. A world giving birth to God is a reversal of classic Neoplatonic spirituality that has dominated Christian spirituality for centuries. The third-century pagan philosopher Plotinus developed a metaphysical scheme whereby everything flows from the One and returns to the One. This scheme was also found in the work of Origen of Alexandria, the first Christian theologian whose thought highly influenced generations of Christian thinkers. Rather than seeing God as the source of multiplicity, evolution helps us envision God as the goal of multiplicity; the One flows from the many. Because evolution is dynamic, unfolding love-energy, God rises up in evolution, as love unifies and complexifies. Plotinus's spirituality undergirds a flight from the world, whereas Teilhard's evolutionary theology calls for an embrace of the world. Teilhard writes of creative union as an act of gradual unification of multiplicity; the world is in process of being created. Multiplicity is dependent on unity and on some final unity that does not need any principle beyond itself to unify it, since it is the "already One." This One is God, the love-energy center of every center. As love grows into greater consciousness and unity in evolution, so too God emerges as Omega and the future of evolving life. Teilhard spoke of the *evolutive* God who rises up from the world in order to be God

---

[2] Karl Rahner, *Theological Investigations*, vol. 21 (Baltimore: Helicon Press, 1988), 191.

for the world.[3] God, therefore, is not so much the beginning of evolution as its direction. Even in human relations the truth of love is revealed at the end of a long, loving relationship, not at the beginning. Sin is resistance to love. It is the "essential reaction of the finite to the creative act" and the "reverse side of all creation."[4] Without sin, Teilhard claimed, there is no creative union; that is, the incompleteness of reality and the resistance to relatedness are stimuli for creative union. There is suffering in holding the tension of desire for completion, on the one hand, and resistance to our relatedness, on the other. Yet through this tension God unfolds in evolution or what Teilhard calls theogenesis, in which two phases can be distinguished:

> In the first [phase], God posits himself in his trinitarian structure ("fontal" being reflecting itself, self-sufficient, upon itself): Trinitization. In the second phase, he envelops himself in participated being, by evolutive unification of pure multiple ("positive non-being") born (in a state of absolute potency) by antithesis to pre-posited trinitarian unity: Creation.[5]

God is the name of personal divine love emerging in evolution, as consciousness complexifies and persons unite: "Where two or more are gathered in my name, there am I in the midst of them" (Mt 18:20). Evolution reveals a newness to God because love is always expressing itself in new patterns of relationships. Rather than a static theology of a God-world relationship, Teilhard reframes the God-world relationship from the point of evolution. The dynamic fountain fullness of divine love means forever the newness of world; God is ever newness in love, and thus the world is ever new as well. The Greek philosopher Heraclitus once said that "you cannot step into the same river twice," meaning

---

[3] Pierre Teilhard de Chardin, *Activation of Energy*, trans. René Hague (New York: Harcourt Brace Jovanovich, 1971), 262.

[4] David Grumett, "Teilhard de Chardin's Evolutionary Natural Theology," *Zygon* 42, no. 2 (June 2007): 525.

[5] Teilhard de Chardin, *Christianity and Evolution*, trans. René Hague (New York: Harcourt, 1971), 178n4.

change is inherent to life; every act bears an essential newness. Evolution is not repetition of the old world or a cyclic return to the beginning but an ever newness of life born out of the ever newness of love. Divine love is not a river of stagnant water but a fountain fullness of overflowing love, love that is forever awakening to new life. God is ever newness in love and the power of everything new in love.

Kenosis and Creation

Anyone who has ever loved knows that love does not live in the abstract; in fact, when it is abstract, in word only, one is suspect of the lover. Love is embodied act, expressed in physical reality. To be itself, love must be for another. Because God is love and love is relational, the name God points to otherness and relationality. If otherness is integral to godliness, then creation is more than divine will; rather, creation gives expression to divine love. Paul Fiddes states that God does not "need" the world in the sense that there is some intrinsic necessity in his nature, binding his free choice; but he does need the world in the sense that he has freely chosen to be in need.[6] Fiddes writes:

> There seems to be something profoundly unsatisfactory about this notion of God's choosing to love the world in such a way that we can say "he need not have done so" or "he could have done otherwise." It does not seem to touch the core of the meaning of love, which must be more than willing the good of another as one alternative among other possibilities.[7]

---

[6] Paul S. Fiddes, "Creation Out of Love," in *The Work of Love: Creation as Kenosis,* ed. John Polkinghorne (Grand Rapids, MI: Eerdmans, 2001), 74.

[7] Ibid., 71. Process theologians, beginning with Whitehead, maintain that God and the world have always coexisted because the absolute factor of the creative process requires both God and other actualities as necessary component parts. It is for this reason that process thinkers do not hold a literal *creation ex nihilo* because God creates by work-

God would not be perfect love if God could choose otherwise. God's "need" of creation is not due to a lack in God; rather, it expresses the absolute freedom of God as love and thus the freedom to be totally for another. God's act of creation is God's freedom to love, God's relatedness. God is totally for, with, and in the other. Instead of thinking of God as prime mover and supernatural Being, what if we were to think of God in terms of wholeness, depth, and relationality? God, who is divine love, is expressed in wholly other creation by which creation becomes "holy" and something other than divine Love. This pouring out of divine love into wholly other matter is the christification of the universe. Hence, there is no divine love without creative union, and no creative union without Christ. Franciscan theologian Duns Scotus (1265–1308) asserts that Christ is first in God's intention to love because from all eternity God willed to share love in one predestined to grace and glory.[8] Christ is not an individual person; rather, Christ is the cosmic Person, the whole creation with humanity as its growing tip (in this part of the universe and in other parts of the universe where there is intelligible life), oriented toward unity in love. Evolution is directed toward the Christ because it is grounded in a personal center of love.

Teilhard's faith in Christ led him to posit Christ as the "centrating principle," the "pleroma," and the "Omega point" where the individual and collective adventure of humanity finds its end and fulfillment. Through his penetrating view of the universe, he found Christ present in the entire cosmos, from the least particle of matter to the convergent human community. The whole cosmos is incarnational. In *The Divine Milieu* Teilhard claimed, "There is nothing profane here below for those who know how

---

ing with what already exists. See also Ian G. Barbour, "God's Power: A Process View," in Polkinghorne, *The Work of Love*, 16.

[8] This is the doctrine of the primacy of Christ articulated by the Franciscan theologian Duns Scotus (1265–1308). For Scotus's argument on the primacy of Christ, see John Duns Scotus, *Opus Oxoniensis* (Oxon) 3.d.7.a.3, vol. 14 (Paris: Vives, 1894), 348–60; Allan B. Wolter, OFM, *Duns Scotus: Four Questions on Mary* [intro., text, and trans.], 29–30 (Santa Barbara, CA: Old Mission Santa Barbara, 1988).

to see."[9] Christ invests himself organically within all creation, immersing himself in things, in the heart of matter, and thus unifying the world.[10] The universe is physically impregnated to the very core of its matter by the influence of his superhuman nature.[11] Everything is physically "christified," gathered up by the incarnate Word as nourishment that assimilates, transforms, and divinizes.[12] The world is like a crystal lamp illumined from within by the light of Christ. For those who can see, Christ shines in this diaphanous universe, through the cosmos, and in matter.[13] He envisioned the evolutionary process as one moving toward evolution of consciousness and ultimately toward evolution of spirit, from the birth of mind to the birth of the whole Christ.[14] The whole evolutionary process is an intertwining of love and suffering as isolated existence is relinquished for greater union.

We usually think of incarnation as an act separate from creation, but Teilhard reminds us that incarnation and creation are two dimensions of one act of cosmotheandric love. Each star, atom, leaf, plant, and creature is Word-expressed-energy of Love and thus open to more life and being. God creates by letting go

---

[9] Pierre Teilhard de Chardin, *The Divine Milieu: An Essay on the Interior Life*, trans. William Collins (New York: Harper and Row, 1960), 66.

[10] Timothy Jamison, "The Personalized Universe of Teilhard de Chardin," in *There Shall be One Christ*, ed. Michael Meilach (New York: The Franciscan Institute, 1968), 26.

[11] Ursula King, ed., *Pierre Teilhard de Chardin* (Maryknoll, NY: Orbis Books, 2003), 96.

[12] Pierre Teilhard de Chardin, "My Universe," in *Process Theology: Basic Writings*, ed. Ewert Cousins (New York: Newman Press, 1971), 254.

[13] This is the thesis of Teilhard's classic *The Divine Milieu*. See also Teilhard, "My Universe," 249–55.

[14] Pierre Teilhard de Chardin, *The Future of Man*, trans. Norman Denny (New York: Harper and Row, 1964), 309. In the last entry in his journal, made three days before his death on Easter Sunday 1955, Teilhard brought together his principal thesis: *"Noogenesis=Christogenesis (=Paul)"* summed up in Paul's First Letter to the Corinthians (15:28): "that God may be all in all" *(En pasi panta Theos)*.

in love, a paradoxical withdrawal of power that makes new being possible. As divine love empties itself into the other, it empowers the other by withdrawing its own power and allowing the other to flourish as other. One can draw an analogy with a parent's love for a child. The parent's love is so great that all that the parent has is given in love. But the very gift of the parent's love is in the withdrawal of control; the parent withdraws so that the child may grow into his or her own unique creation. The greater the love, the greater the gift of freedom to the beloved.

In a similar way all that God is, is given in love. God is hidden in the appearance of being (that is, the Father is hidden in the Word) and made visible by the energy (Spirit) of love. The self-emptying of divine love into the other is the fullness of love in the other; God "appears" in the other. God is not a superior Being who lords it over us; rather, God stands "under" us, hidden within ordinary reality as the "real," the whole of the whole, the depth of love. Orthodox theologian Vladimir Lossky said: "The love of God for man is so great that it cannot constrain; for there is no love without respect. Divine will always will submit itself to gropings, to detours, even to revolts of human will to bring it to a free consent. . . . God is a beggar of love waiting at the soul's door without ever daring to force it."[15] The self-emptying of God into the other is the fullness of God in the other. This mystery of emptiness and fullness undergirds the humility of God. Divine power is not a force over us but the humility of love beneath us (cf. Phil 2:6–8), the love that makes existence possible. Francis of Assisi grasped the humility of God as the experience of love in ordinary reality. The story is told how Francis abhorred lepers and ran away from them. However, around the time of his conversion, he met a leper and, instead of running away, Francis stopped, kissed the leper's hand, and gave him alms. That encounter changed his life. He later wrote that "what had seemed bitter to me was turned

---

[15] Vladimir Lossky, *Orthodox Theology: An Introduction*, trans. Ian and Ihita Kesarcodi-Watson (Crestwood, NY: St. Vladimir's Press, 1978), 73.

into sweetness of soul and body."[16] From then on he realized that God is hidden in ordinary, fragile reality, sacramentalized by the Eucharist. "God hides himself in a little bread," he said. "Look brothers at the humility of God!"[17]

Creation is not a demonstration of God's boundless power but of God's boundless love, a love so great that creation is drenched in it. In the words of the penitent Angela Foligno, "The whole creation is pregnant with God."[18] We do not see this God because we are not looking for this God. We want a God who will lord it over us and be superior to us, and when we can't find such a God we invent one. But God is wholeness and depth of love, a love that does not absorb others but accepts and affirms them precisely in their otherness; true love gives true freedom to the other. To say God is love is not to find God anywhere other than where love is, in every created being, from quarks to stars to human persons. God is the whole of every whole, love bending low, hiding in the details of nature. The mystery of divine love is hidden in the other, and it is precisely in the other that God shines through (or hides)—in the unbearable wholeness of being. In the world of evolving reality, everything lives between love and nothingness. That is why each being must cling to love, for love is the next creative moment of life, and everything alive is drawn to trust and surrender.

God's Vulnerable Love

The question of God in the face of immense suffering has driven people from religion. So many people ask: Why does God allow bad things to happen to good people? Why does God give free reign to violence, murder, theft, natural disasters, and human

---

[16] Francis of Assisi, "Testament," 3, in *Francis of Assisi: Early Documents*, vol. 1, *The Saint*, ed. Regis J. Armstrong, J. A. Wayne Hellmann, and William J. Short (New York: New City Press, 1999), 124.

[17] Francis of Assisi, "Letter to the Entire Order," 27–29, in Armstrong, Hellmann, and Short, *Francis of Assisi,* 118.

[18] Paul Lachance, trans., *Angela of Foligno: Complete Works* (New York: Paulist Press, 1993), 242.

misery? Christianity has lived with a cognitive dissonance for almost two thousand years. Holding fast to the claim that God is love, it has kept God at a safe distance from this fickle and, at times, violent creation. Keith Ward writes:

> The traditional concept of God in Christianity is that God is eternal, in the sense of being timeless—that is, without temporal relation to anything in time, and without internal relations of a temporal nature. It follows from this that God is strictly immutable. Whatever happens in the created cosmos makes no difference to God, and does not change God in any way. The cosmos is created by a non-temporal act, and God creates every moment of time, from first to last, in one and the same act of intentional causation.[19]

A timeless, immutable, virtually apathetic God who is said to be love is problematic unless, of course, we understand God as one who can express love but never really be *in* love. For the church fathers to say that "God is love" did not betray a vulnerable God but a God whose action of *goodwill* directed itself to other persons. True love was to will and achieve the good of another, not to have emotions. Augustine distinguishes between emotions and moral actions with regard to the perfect love of God: "His pity is not the wretched heart of a fellow-sufferer. . . . The pity of God is the goodness of his help. . . . When God pities, he does not grieve and he liberates."[20] Thomas Aquinas writes that love, like joy, but unlike sadness or anger, can be simply an act of the will and the intellect. Love can be ascribed to God as a purely intellectual capacity.[21] But God is not a Being who loves; God *is* love, and absolute love is utterly faithful. In the words of the prophet Jeremiah, "I have loved you with an everlasting love" (31:3).

---

[19] Keith Ward, "Cosmos and Kenosis," in Polkinghorne, *The Work of Love*, 152.

[20] Augustine, *Contra Adversarium Legis et Prophetarum* 1.40, cited in Paul S. Fiddes, *Creative Suffering of God* (Oxford: Clarendon Press, 1992), 17.

[21] Thomas Aquinas, *Summa Theologia* 1a. 20, 1, cited in Fiddes, *Creative Suffering of God*, 18.

There is no doubt that suffering and violence abound in the crevices of life, but suffering is not a punishment of a vengeful God. God does not abandon us; we abandon God by abandoning ourselves from ourselves, running after little gods. God lives deep within us, as the center of love, but we are often blind to this inner center and drawn by the little gods of power, success, status, and wealth, everything we create for ourselves. Thus we abandon God within for the fleeting gods without. When things go wrong, we run from our little gods and invoke the God of revelation, but we have a difficult time finding this God. The theodicy question is not why God allows bad things to happen to good people but why we abandon God in the face of suffering. If God is love, then our only real hope is in God, because hope is the openness of love to infinite possibilities and new life. Only a God who is *not* love could impose suffering as punishment, unperturbed by the violence and suffering of creation. Such a God could watch from a distance and remain unmoved by the cries for mercy. Dorothy Sölle writes, "When a being who is free from suffering is worshiped as God, then it is possible to train oneself in patience, endurance, imperturbability, and aloofness from suffering.[22] But this is not the God revealed in either the Old or New Testament. The prophet Hosea speaks of God's merciful love toward an errant Israel, revealing the depth of divine love: "I will lure her and lead her to the desert and there speak to her heart" (2:10). Similarly, the prophet Isaiah proclaims: "Since you are precious and honored in my sight, and because I love you, I will give people in exchange for you, nations in exchange for your life" (43:4). The God of Israel shows anger, but it is a deep hurt (so to speak) because of Israel's unfaithfulness. God does not abandon Israel but remains ever faithful in love: "Though the mountains may fall and the hills fade away, my love shall never leave you" (Is 54:10). This God of love appears in Jesus of Nazareth, a God who gets radically involved in the messiness of the world to be God for us. It is in this respect that the ringing words of Dietrich Bonhoeffer, in his famous letter of July 16, 1944, hold true:

---

[22] Dorothee Sölle, *Suffering*, trans. Everett R. Kalin (Philadelphia: Fortress Press, 1975), 43.

God lets himself be pushed out of the world on to the cross. He is weak and powerless in the world, and that is precisely the way, the only way, in which he is with us and helps us. . . . The Bible directs man to God's powerlessness and suffering; only the suffering God can help.[23]

To have faith in a God of unconditional love is to realize how intimately close God is. So close we forget God's presence. In his own day Jesus was immersed in a violent culture, a culture of conflict and anxiety. But he also knew of the deeper truth hidden beneath the surface of human judgment, namely, that this broken, anxious world is oozing with God. He asked us to have faith, to believe that the reign of God is among us and within us. As Patrick Malone writes:

Faith is more than a magical formula to conquer the worry, regret, shame and resentments that cloud our visions and make us jaded and tired. Having faith does not remove every trace of self-absorption and doubt. Those things are part of the human condition. Faith is what brings us into the deepest truth that says we are in the image of an unlimited, unrestricted, unimaginable love. And when we forget that, as Jesus reminded the religious authorities of his day, then religion does become a shield, a crutch, a closed refuge instead of a way to boldly throw ourselves into a harsh world, knowing that is precisely where we discover a generous God.[24]

To love is to risk being rejected by the other. God takes a risk in loving us because the gift of divine love bears with it the possibility of refusal. God's love respects the independence and freedom of the other because love does not seek to control, dominate, or manipulate; rather love seeks to empower the other for the flourishing of life. The age of science fashioned God into a distant deity governing the world from above, a God who is

---

[23] Dietrich Bonhoeffer, *Letters and Papers from Prison*, ed. Eberhard Bethge (New York: Macmillan, 1972), 360.

[24] Patrick Malone, "A God Who Gets Foolishly Close," *America* (May 27, 2000): 22.

deaf to the cries of the poor. But the God of Jesus Christ belongs to the cosmos from the beginning and until the end of time, sharing in the sufferings of every age so as to rise in the glory of ever deepening love. When God and cosmos are severed, then theology becomes a mere abstraction of a nonexisting God.[25]

Crucified Love

Evolution bears witness to the fidelity of divine love because every cosmic death is, in some way, transformed into new life. Hans Urs von Balthasar said that the very act of creation reflects something of a "divine crucifixion," for in creation God reveals his power to be his unconditional love for the world. The act of descending into what is nothing [creation] in order to express himself, according to Von Balthasar, is God's humility, his condescension, his going outside his own riches to become poor.[26] The cross is key not only to sin and human nature, but to God himself. The cross reveals to us the heart of God because it reveals the vulnerability of God's love. Balthasar writes: "It is God's going forth into the danger and the nothingness of the creation that reveals [God's] heart to be at its origin vulnerable; in the humility of this vulnerability lies God's condescension [humility] and thus his fundamental readiness to go to the very end of love on the cross."[27] The mystery of the cross is the mystery of God not possessing but fully communicating the mystery of love in radical openness to and acceptance of the human person. Love lives in persons not ideas. Love is not a concept but a powerful, transforming energy that heals, reconciles, unites, and makes whole. Love draws together—heart to heart, center to center. Love is not what God does; love is what God is. Love is the Godness of God. That is why the cross is significant not as

---

[25] Raimon Panikkar, *The Rhythm of Being: The Gifford Lectures* (Maryknoll, NY: Orbis Books, 2010), 188.

[26] Hans Urs von Balthasar, *The Glory of the Lord: Theological Aesthetics*, trans. Andrew Louth, Francis McDonagh and Brian McNeil, vol. 2, *Studies in Theological Style: Clerical Styles*, ed. Joseph Fessio (San Francisco, CA: Ignatius Press, 1984), 353.

[27] Ibid., 356.

a mystical object of devotion but as the theological center. It is the most revealing statement about God. In *The Crucified God* Moltmann writes:

> When the Crucified Jesus is called the image of the invisible God, the meaning is that *this* is God, and God is *like this*. God is not greater than he is in his humiliation. God is not more glorious than he is in this self-surrender. God is not more powerful than he is in this helplessness. God is not more divine than he is in this humanity. All that can be said about God is said in the cross.[28]

With arms outstretched Christ crucified embraces a sinful world disrupted by human violence, disconnected, and incomplete—a God who is radically in love with the world. The *power* of divine Love is shown in the *powerlessness* of the cross. Cardinal Walter Kasper writes:

> On the cross the incarnation of God reaches its true meaning and purpose. The entire Christ-event must therefore be understood in terms of the cross. On the cross God's self-renouncing love is embodied with ultimate radicalness. The cross is the utmost that is possible to God in his self-surrendering love; it is "that than which a greater cannot be thought"; it is the unsurpassable self-definition of God. This self-renunciation or emptying is therefore not a self-abandonment and not a self de-divinization of God . . . but the revelation of the divine God. . . . God need not strip himself of his omnipotence in order to reveal his love. On the contrary, it requires omnipotence to be able to surrender oneself and give oneself away; and it requires omnipotence to be able to take oneself back in the giving

---

[28] Jürgen Moltmann, *The Crucified God*, trans. R. A. Wilson and John Bowden (New York: HarperCollins, 1991), 205. Similarly, Jon Sobrino writes: "What is manifest on the cross is the internal structure of God himself." See Jon Sobrino, *Christology at the Crossroads* (Maryknoll, NY: Orbis Books, 1978), 226.

and to preserve the independence and freedom of the recipient. Only an almighty love can give itself wholly to the other and be a helpless love.[29]

The cross signifies a God who is radically involved with the world and ultimately concerned for the world. Gregory Baum writes that suffering can have two meanings. On one hand, suffering is due to a lack of something that belongs to our integrity. We suffer because we are personally vulnerable; we can lose our health, our family, our friends, our job, and anything else that is precious to us. This type of suffering may be called suffering *ex carentia* (by deprivation). However, we may also suffer because our friends or family are vulnerable; our heart is torn because they have lost something that belongs to their integrity. We suffer with them because we have extended to them our love and our solidarity; we suffer with them because we have reached beyond ourselves and identified ourselves with them; we suffer because an inner wealth or fullness has allowed us to give ourselves away. Baum calls this suffering *ex abundantia* (out of fullness). Suffering *ex abundantia* is compassion. While God cannot suffer *ex carentia*, because God cannot lose what pertains to God's integrity, God can [and does] suffer *ex abundantia*. Out of the divine plenitude God loves those who suffer, shares their pain, and bears their burdens with them.[30] It is because God is the fountain fullness of love that God can share in the sufferings of the world and through these sufferings draw life into new life. For God's love can neither be overcome by human power nor conquered by force. God's love is the power of love to heal and transform death into life. God is most godlike in the suffering of the cross.

For this reason the cross stands as the center of theology; here we see what God is in the scandalous death of the innocent man

---

[29] Walter Kasper, *The God of Jesus Christ*, trans. Matthew J. O'Connell (New York: Crossroad), 194–95.

[30] Gregory Baum, "Meister Eckhart and Dorothee Soëlle on Suffering and the Experience of God," in *Light Burdens, Heavy Blessings*, ed. Mary Ellen Sheehan, Mary Heather MacKinnon, and Moni McIntyre (Quincy, IL: Franciscan Press, 2000), 235–36.

Jesus. Love shows itself as the power to embrace death and draw it into the wholeness of life; hence, the cross is the *axis mundi*. It is the symbol of love's fidelity at the heart of evolutionary creation. The whole process of evolution, according to Holmes Rolston, is cruciform. "Biological nature is always giving birth, regenerating, always in travail. Something is always dying and something is always living on. . . . This whole evolutionary upslope is a calling in which renewed life comes by blasting the old. Life is gathered up in the midst of its throes, a blessed tragedy lived in grace through a besetting storm."[31] Divine love rises up from the throes of history because love is committed to life; it is the wellspring of new life. Love, poured out for another in the face of death, is the hope of new life. Love means to let go and enter into the storm and to love as passionately, extravagantly, and wastefully as God loves. In light of cruciform nature of creation Rolston writes:

> The abundant life that Jesus exemplifies and offers to his disciples is that of a sacrificial suffering through to something higher. The Spirit of God is the genius that makes alive, that redeems life from its evils. The cruciform creation is, in the end, deiform, godly, just because of this element of struggle, not in spite of it. There is a great divine "yes" hidden behind and within every "no" of crushing nature. God . . . is the compassionate lure in, with, and under all purchasing of life at the cost of sacrifice. Long before humans arrived, the way of nature was already a *via dolorosa*. In that sense, the aura of the cross is cast backward across the whole global story, and it forever outlines the future. . . . The *capacity to suffer through to joy* is a supreme emergent and an essence of Christianity [emphasis added].[32]

It is difficult to explain logically a religion where God is involved in the violence and atrocities of history, the natural disasters, and the deadly diseases that plague humanity. But this God

---

[31] Holmes Rolston, "Kenosis and Nature," in Polkinghorne, *The Work of Love*, 58–59.

[32] Rolston, "Kenosis and Nature," 59–60.

is absurdly close, "so incredibly close that we are forced either to discover God in all the messiness of creation, no matter how confusing or abrasive, or to outright reject him."[33] Too often we want a God who will be strong enough to push our sufferings away. But as Malone writes, "Our only credible action is to bless this world, not by conquering our failures but by allowing God to break through our less-than-stellar lives."[34] This is what love does. It perseveres through the storms, it waits patiently for the beloved, never giving up, always reaching out, making space for something new to happen.

God Within

If God is love then our only freedom and hope are in God. Etty Hillsum, a young Jewish woman, was not particularly religious, but she found freedom within the death walls of a concentration camp by recognizing the human capacity to make an inner place for God to dwell. In a small diary she kept, she left us profound insights on living joyfully in the midst of suffering. Hope, she indicates, is not asking God to do something for us but us doing something for God—welcoming God into our lives. She writes:

> Dear God, these are anxious times. Tonight for the first time I lay in the dark with burning eyes as scene after scene of human suffering passed before me. I shall promise You one thing, God, just one very small thing: I shall never burden my today with cares about tomorrow, although that takes some practice. Each day is sufficient unto itself. I shall try to help You, God, to stop my strength ebbing away, though I cannot vouch for it in advance. But one thing is becoming increasingly clear to me: that *You cannot help us, that we help You to help ourselves.* And that that is all we can manage these days and also all that really matters: that we safeguard that little of You, God, in ourselves. And perhaps in others as well. Alas, there doesn't seem to be much You Yourself can do about our circumstances, about

---

[33] Malone, "A God Who Gets Foolishly Close," 23.
[34] Ibid.

our lives. Neither do I hold You responsible. *You cannot help us, but we must help You and defend Your dwelling place inside us to the last* [emphasis added].[35]

Unless we stop making God an object of power, we cannot really be free—whether we live in peace or violence. God is the cosmotheandric whole of our lives, the utterly faithful One who cannot disown his own self, because his "self" is our very existence (cf. 2 Tim 2:13). The only way to know this God of love is to pray. Thomas Merton writes that "if I find God I will find myself, and if I find myself I will find God," because the essence of who I am lies in God.[36]

We are the instruments and points of God's in-break,[37] the privileged bearers of transcendence.[38] The God of the philosophers has abandoned this world, but the God of Jesus Christ has raised it to new life and continues to be life in the ever newness of cosmic evolution. What we hope for, what we love, depends on how we see our role in evolution. Teilhard describes the human person as "the rising arrow of biological synthesis . . . the last born, freshest, most complicated and subtly varied of the successive layers of life."[39] The human is not a passing phase of life in the cosmos but integral to the whole of life. Being comes together and is deepened in the human person as he or she evolves in and with "God-cosmic" energy. The beauty of the human lies not in the intellect alone but in the body extended into the expanding cosmos that longs for unity and wholeness. We must know ourselves as loved and as being-in-love; in this love is our freedom, our hope, and our zest for life. To make a

---

[35] Annemarie S. Kidder, ed., *Etty Hillsum: Essential Writings* (Maryknoll, NY: Orbis Books, 2009), 59.

[36] Thomas Merton, *New Seeds of Contemplation* (New York: New Directions, 1961), 36.

[37] Ann W. Astell, "Postmodern Christian Spirituality: A *Coincidentia Oppositorum?*" *Christian Spirituality Bulletin* 4 (Summer 1996): 5.

[38] Richard Kearney, *Anatheism* (New York: Columbia University Press, 2010), 91.

[39] Pierre Teilhard de Chardin, *The Human Phenomenon*, trans. Sarah Appleton-Weber (Brighton: Sussex Academic Press, 1999), 156.

place for God within is to enter into the heart, to let go in that inner space where God lives and evolve in greater unity in love. God is born from within when we come to know ourselves in the divine love that lives deep within us. There too we discover that we are not strangers in this evolving universe. We are its future.

Chapter Six

Sacred Secularity

Ever since the Enlightenment, intellectuals of every kind have believed that the principle consequence of modernity has been the decline of religion. Charles Taylor diagnosed the secularism of our age as the interlocking constellation of cosmic, social, and moral orders, purely immanent orders devoid of transcendence and functioning *etsi Deus non daretur*, "as if God would not exist."[1] This phenomenological experience, according to Taylor, constitutes our age as a secular one, whether or not people have religious or theistic beliefs. The word *saeculum* originally meant an indefinite period of time but became a synonym for ungodly. To secularize is to make worldly or to convert religious things into profane ones. Secularity pertains to the world or the values

---

[1] Charles Taylor, *A Secular Age* (Cambridge, MA: Belknap/Harvard University Press, 2007). This phrase is taken from Dietrich Bonhoeffer's letter to Eberhard Bethge (July 16, 1944) in which, describing contemporary Christian life, he wrote, "we have to live in the world *etsi deus non daretur*." He explains this by saying: "God would have us know that we must live as men who manage our lives without him. The God who is with us is the God who forsakes us. The God who lets us live in the world without the working hypothesis of God is the God before whom we stand continually. Before God and with God we live without God. God lets himself be pushed out of the world on to the cross. He is weak and powerless in the world, and that is precisely the way, the only way, in which he is with us and helps us." Dietrich Bonhoeffer, *Letters and Papers from Prison*, ed. Eberhard Bethge (London: SCM Press, 1971), 360.

inherent in earthly activity. It is not necessarily opposed to religion, although secularization has relegated religion to one activity among many.[2] Emile Durkheim described religion as nothing but a metaphor of social order and saw modern secularity as progress, while Nietzsche proclaimed God is dead.

In *Public Religions in the Modern World,* José Casanova states that theories of secularization and modernization have been tightly interwoven.[3] Each of these spheres of activity has its own "internal and lawful autonomy," although each sphere has influenced the other. The rise of secularization encompassed a differentiation of activities including education, medicine, art, and moral guidance in the form of modern therapy. Similarly, religion came to occupy a sphere of its own, no longer claiming oversight over the full range of human activities, but now drawing on its own lights and resources to specialize in meaning, morality, salvation, and consolation. Casanova believes this process of differentiation is the incontestable core of secularization in the West. Although many scholars said that secularization dispenses with religion, including practices and beliefs, this idea has been contradicted by the fact that religion still remains.

Taylor argues that Western modernity, including its secularity, is the fruit of new inventions, newly constructed self-understandings, and related practices, and cannot be explained in terms of perennial features of human life. He traces the path of secularity through the social imaginary, the picture of the world that holds us captive, expressed by the way people imagine their

---

[2] José Casanova defines three different meanings of being secular that shed light on the complexity of the problem: (1) mere secularity or the phenomenological experience of living in a secular world where being religious may be a normal viable option, (2) exclusive secularity or the experience of living without religion as a normal condition, and (3) secularist secularity or the experience of having been liberated from "religion" as a condition for human flourishing. See José Casanova, "Are We Still Secular? Exploring the Post-Secular: Three Meanings of 'the Secular' and Their Possible Transcendence," paper presented at New York University, Institute for Public Knowledge, October 22–24, 2009, 8.

[3] José Casanova, *Public Religions in the Modern World* (Chicago: University of Chicago Press, 1994).

social surroundings in images, stories, and legends.[4] In his view secularization did not kill off religion, since the depths of humanism have survived as spiritual values; however, spirituality, like secularization itself, has become pluralistic and differentiated. Consequently, religion no longer functions as a hegemonic power, at least in the West. The political structures of modern nations, as well as socioeconomic spheres of activity, have come to operate by norms and principles independent of explicit religious dictates. Religion has faded from public space and concentrated itself in personal belief and practice.

The rise of modern philosophy created "God problems," leaving religious seekers unfulfilled. The core of the problem concerns the world. What is God's relationship to the world? Is the *saeculum* opposed to God or the very place where God is revealed? If one turns to the scriptures, one finds little evidence that the world is opposed to God. In the Gospel of John, for example, "the world" has polyvalent meaning.[5] According to Sandra Schneiders "world" refers first to *creation* itself, as we read in the opening creation account of Genesis (1:1–2:4a). God spoke all things into existence and declared them "very good"; thus, the "world" refers to the whole universe emerging in goodness from God's initiative through the Word." The world is also seen as the *theater of human history* "into which every human being is born, including the Word made flesh." The world is our home, the place where we dwell. Third, the world is the place where the *reign of God* unfolds. Jesus prayed to God not to take his disciples out of the world but precisely to keep them safe from evil in the world (see Jn 17:15). The world to which Jesus missions his disciples includes all creation, especially humanity, as it makes its way through history. Finally, the world is a *synonym for evil*, "the domain and the work of the Prince of this World, whom Jesus calls Satan, the Devil, the Father of Lies who is a murderer from the beginning. Jesus engages in a struggle with this personal evil agency which

---

[4] Taylor, *A Secular Age*, 173.

[5] Sandra M. Schneiders, "God So Loved the World . . . Ministerial Religious Life in 2009," a talk on vowed religious life given to the IHM Congregation, June 14, 2009. Schneiders points out that "the Fourth Gospel uses the Greek word for world, 'kosmos,' 78 times, more than the rest of the New Testament put together."

will cost him his life and which, he warns, will cost his disciples theirs if they take up his project." This more nuanced understanding of "world" underscores a complex arena in which the Reign of God and the Kingdom of Satan contend for control, and good and evil intimately coexist in our world. Schneiders interprets this tension as the complexity of forces within which takes place the human struggle in the pursuit of God.[6]

The rise of modern philosophy and science challenged or sometimes dispensed with the "magic" of religious belief. Facing the growing ungodliness of the world, the Catholic Church confirmed the need for separation from the world, especially when challenged by the new social imaginary that emerged at the Enlightenment. Schneiders points out that all the great movements of modernity including the Renaissance, the scientific revolution, the Protestant Reformation, and the Enlightenment were considered opponents to the church's divinely revealed faith and attacks on its claims to divinely sanctioned authority.[7] In response to the progress of modernity, the church reacted by withdrawing into isolation and codifying doctrine into manuals that were to be rigidly followed. The condemnation of modernism at the turn of the twentieth century typifies the church's fear of worldly progress and its challenge to faith.[8]

---

[6] Ibid., 22–24.

[7] Ibid., 15.

[8] Modernism was a general movement in the late nineteenth and twentieth centuries that tried to reconcile historical Christianity with the findings of modern science and philosophy. It arose mainly from the application of modern critical methods to the study of the Bible and the history of dogma and resulted in less emphasis on historic dogma and creeds and in greater stress on the humanistic aspects of religion. Importance was placed upon the immanent rather than the transcendent nature of God. The movement as a whole was profoundly influenced by the pragmatism of William James, the intuitionism of Henri Bergson, and the philosophy of action of Maurice Blondel. Among the leaders of Catholic Modernism were A. F. Loisy in France and George Tyrrell in England. Vital to the Catholic movement were the adoption of the critical approach to the Bible, which was by that time accepted by most Protestant churches, and the rejection of the intellectualism of Scholastic theology, with the corresponding subordination of doctrine to practice. Catholic Modernism was condemned by Pope Pius X in the 1907 encyclical *Pascendi Dominici gregis*.

It was not until Pope John XXIII that alienation of the church from the world was recognized as a looming pastoral disaster. Schneiders states that "not quite a hundred years after Pius IX had slammed the Church's door on modernity, John XXIII threw open the windows of the church on the modern world by calling the second Vatican Council." She writes: "The conciliar turn to the world was a deep conversion, a seismic movement which not only collapsed decrepit structures and cleared the ground for new constructions but challenged the whole Christian world to replace separatist institutionalism with Gospel-based commitment to the flourishing of all creation, especially the human family."[9]

Thomas Merton spoke of the world as "the unquiet city of those who live for themselves and therefore are divided against one another in a struggle that cannot end." One cannot flee the physical world, he states, because flight from the world "is nothing else but the flight from self-concern."[10] The world is a problem, he states, insofar as everybody is a problem to himself, or herself. To renounce the world is not to escape from conflict, anguish, and evil, but from disunity and separation. Flight from the world is not something we do because the world we flee from is as much in the cloister as it is in the marketplace. Rather, flight from the world is an attitude of striving for unity and peace in relation to oneself and others. It is a way of being God-centered wherever one finds oneself. The world as pure object is something that is not there. It is not a reality outside us for which we exist. It is not a firm and absolute objective structure that has to be accepted on its own inexorable terms. The world has, in fact, no terms of its own because it does not exist apart from us. The world reflects who we are and what we think we are in relation to God. It is not the world that is opposed to God. It is we who are opposed to God when we try to control God for our own religious purposes. We are not asked to create an alternate world or to reject this one but to divinize it from within.

---

[9] Schneiders, "God So Loved the World," 16, 20.

[10] Thomas Merton, *New Seeds of Contemplation* (New York: New Directions, 1961), 78–79.

Like Merton, the core of Teilhard's thought is secularization and the key to secularization is evolution.[11] Because our world is in evolution, human activity takes on new meaning and importance; human work is integral to evolution. Teilhard saw human activity as evolution toward the fullness of love. Christianity is thoroughly secular because the universe is organically linked to Christ; Teilhard suggests that the physical universe is the third nature of Christ.[12] N. Max Wildiers states that Teilhard "put the theological problem of secularity in an extremely original and illuminating form and at the same time provided a truly Christian solution that fits in completely with the faith handed down by tradition."[13] Teilhard said we must rid ourselves of the old God of the starry heavens and embrace the God of evolution. Only in this way, he asserted, can the world be seen as a divine milieu.

Christian Secularity

To grasp the dynamism of Christianity and thus the value of Christian life, one must accept evolution as the new Genesis story. Evolution is not background to the human story; it *is* the human story. Until we come to know God in evolution, we shall find the world a problem. Evolution is not simply a biological mechanism of gene swapping or environment pressures. It is the unfolding and development of consciousness in which consciousness plays a significant role in the process of convergence and complexification. Evolution gives rise to religion when consciousness unfolds in a "Thou-embraced-I." In our own time, Teilhard said, religion has shrunk because we have made it a personal matter and have limited it to personal salvation. Religion has become very anthropocentric, as if the only need for an ultimate ground is the human person. We do not realize that religion

---

[11] N. Max Wildiers, "Foreword," in Pierre Teilhard de Chardin, *Christianity and Evolution,* trans. René Hague (New York: Harcourt Brace Jovanovich, 1971), 9.

[12] For a discussion on Teilhard's understanding of the third nature of Christ, see James A. Lyons, *The Cosmic Christ in Origen and Teilhard de Chardin* (London: Oxford University Press, 1982), 183–96; Ilia Delio, *Christ in Evolution* (Maryknoll, NY: Orbis Books, 2008), 76–77.

[13] Wildiers, "Foreword," 12.

belongs to *the whole of humankind* and thus the cosmos. He writes: "The birth of my faith represents no more than an infinitesimal element of a vastly wider and more certain process, common to all men. And thus it is that I find myself obliged by the very logic of my process to emerge from my individualism and confront the general religious experience of humankind, *that so I may involve myself in it.*"[14]

Evolution as a meta-narrative (the story of the "big picture" rather than scientific explanation alone) impelled Teilhard to develop new language that could capture evolution as a dynamic process of love. One of the terms he coined was *amorization,* from the Latin word for love *(amor)*; amorization is the process of unfolding love in evolution. By using this term he did not mean that evolution is an increase in sentiment or emotion. Conversely, amorization is the emergence of personality through union. As elements or persons unite, they differentiate, and their differentiation is the basis of greater union. Amorization is a process of centeredness by which the center of one's personhood becomes more authentic in love through union. Hence, amorization is growth in consciousness and depth of being.

Authentic love begins with freedom of self. This applies to both nonhuman and human life. Nature can do nothing other than be itself, and in being itself it is truly free. A tree does nothing but be a tree, and in this "tree beingness" it expresses its own being-in-Love. It is in the beingness of self that God is revealed. Merton writes:

> A tree gives glory to God by being a tree. For in being what God means it to be it is obeying Him. It "consents" so to speak, to His creative love. It is expressing an idea which is in God and which is not distinct from the essence of God, and therefore a tree imitates God by being a tree. The more a tree is like itself, the more it is like Him. If it tried to be like something else which it was never intended to be, it would be less like God and therefore it would give Him less glory. No two created beings are exactly alike. And their individuality is no imperfection. On the

---

[14] Pierre Teilhard de Chardin, *How I Believe,* trans. René Hague (New York: Harper and Row, 1969), 61, 60.

contrary, the perfection of each created thing is not merely in its conformity to an abstract type but in its own individual identity with itself. This particular tree will give glory to God by spreading out its roots in the earth and raising its branches into the air and the light in a way that no other tree before or after it ever did or will do. Do you imagine that the individual created things in the world are imperfect attempts at reproducing an ideal type which the Creator never quite succeeded in actualizing on earth? If that is so they do not give Him glory but proclaim that he is not a perfect Creator. Therefore each particular being, in its individuality, its concrete nature and entity, with all its own characteristics and its private qualities and its own inviolable identity, gives glory to God by being precisely what He wants it to be here and now, in the circumstances ordained for it by His love and His infinite Art.[15]

Authenticity of self reveals God; in being oneself one expresses God. When divine love becomes incarnate in us, Christ is born anew. God is glorified in the christification of all life, as the poet Gerard Manley Hopkins wrote in his poem "As Kingfishers Catch Fire, Dragonflies Dráw Fláme":

> The just man justices;
> Kéeps gráce: thát keeps all his goings graces;
> Acts in God's eye what in God's eye he is—
> Chríst—for Christ plays in ten thousand places,
> Lovely in limbs, and lovely in eyes not his
> To the Father through the features of men's faces.

While the term *amorization* may disarm us, what Teilhard suggests is that mysticism is at the heart of created life. We are held by an embrace of Love, a "love-field" sustaining us at every moment. This field of love is God, the hidden depth and core of being that makes wholeness of being possible. We must discover this love for the evolution of human life and this means coming home to ourselves and being at home *within* ourselves. This

---

[15] Merton, *New Seeds of Contemplation*, 29–30.

coming home to ourselves is being at home in God and the basis of the mystical life. Ken Wilber says that the mystic comes to a new integrated level of wholeness, a consciousness of being embraced by the whole and thus an ever expanding desire for wholeness. The mystic empties self of selves in order for the authentic self to shine through. Wilber writes:

> The rediscovery of this infinite and eternal Wholeness is man's single greatest need and want. . . . Each person knows or intuits that this is so. . . . But at the same time he is terrified of real transcendence, because transcendence entails the "death" of his isolated and separate self-sense. Because he won't let go of and die to his separate self, he cannot find true and real transcendence, he cannot find that larger fulfillment in integral Wholeness.[16]

The livingness of faith requires the living reality of God, and we can only know this living God through a deep oneness of the heart. Teilhard's vision frees religion from its institutional constraints and opens it up to the heart of life, where love is continuously welling up in the center of everything that exists. The world is not God, yet God is the unlimited depth of love of all that is, a love that attracts, generates, and overflows into new life. God is revealed everywhere, beneath our groping efforts, as a universal milieu, only because God is the ultimate point upon which all realities converge. God "appears" in every element and creature because divine Love is the center, the ground of each being that makes it distinctly "this" and not "that." Evolution is toward greater unity in love and differentiation of core personalities. This union and differentiation is the basis of cosmic personalization by which the cosmic Person, the Christ, emerges as the personal center of a personalizing universe.

To reclaim Christianity as a religion of unity is to understand its core theology in view of evolution. The Trinity strengthens our idea of divine oneness by giving it the structure of unity that is the mark of all real living reality. The Trinity is not a separate divine community of Persons into which creation must

---

[16] Ken Wilber, *Up from Eden: A Transpersonal View of Human Evolution* (Wheaton, IL: Quest Books, 1996), 13, 16.

fit; rather, the whole cosmotheandric process is Trinity. Love (Father) is poured out at the heart of every being through tangential energy (Word) from which radial energy/consciousness/spirit (Spirit) is emerging. Evolution is the rise of spirit/consciousness, which means that religion is not a distinct human phenomenon but integral to the spirit of the earth. As consciousness rises in evolution, "the spirit of the earth discovers a more vital need to worship; *from universal evolution God emerges* in our minds greater and more necessary than ever."[17] God-Omega is the love center of every element, the self-emptying center by which every center exists. God appears in the other, uniting "to form one with something" by being immersed in it, becoming "a particle within it."[18] It is precisely in the other that God comes to be. This cosmotheandric union is creative and dynamic; it means that creation can only have one object—a *universe*—because the whole (God) is constantly seeking greater wholeness. "The whole reveals itself to each of its elements in order to draw it to itself."[19] The Christian response to secularity is not to escape or reject the world, nor is it to live with a double standard of values—spiritual and worldly. Rather, the secular is the realm of Incarnation that means we must see the world in its divine depth, which is shown precisely in the worldliness of human activities and earthly affairs. We have lost sight of Christianity as a religion of personhood rooted in Love. By emphasizing the soul as a form distinct from the body (rather than the constellation of energies in a distinct personality), the human person has become depersonalized, the soul depicted as trapped in matter and destined for a better world. The present form of Christian religion does not promote organic unity but fragments the whole into individual parts, making religion a great exception rather than integral to life and the power to energize life's growth. Christianity, Teilhard writes, "gives the impression of not believing in human progress."[20]

---

[17] Pierre Teilhard de Chardin, *Human Energy,* trans. J. M. Cohen (New York: Harcourt Brace Jovanovich, 1969), 43.

[18] Pierre Teilhard de Chardin, *Activation of Energy,* trans. René Hague (New York: Harcourt Brace Jovanovich, 1970), 263.

[19] Teilhard de Chardin, *How I Believe,* 60.

[20] Ibid., 75.

The Incarnation speaks to us of a world filled with God, but only a heart in love with matter can see this God-filled world. Teilhard's secular mysticism calls for oneness of heart with God: "I merge myself through my heart with the very heart of God." This heart-centered being-in-the world is a penetrating vision that sees the divine depth of worldly things: "God is at the tip of my pen, my spade, my brush, my needle; of my heart and of my thought. By pressing the stroke, the line or the stitch on which I am engaged, I shall lay hold of that last end toward which my innermost will tends."[21] In every action we must adhere to the creative energy of God, to coincide with it and become its living extension. The Urdu poet Mir wrote: "Rose and mirror and sun and moon—what are they? Wherever we looked, there was always Thy face."[22]

A Worldly God

Richard Kearney argues for a return to God *after* God, a new turn to religion that signals an awakening of consciousness of the sacred in secular reality.[23] Nietzsche's death of God was not a true death but an end to the uninvolved, apathetic Unmoved Mover. The idea that God is dead is already contained in the Christian idea of the death of God. God ceases to be an external object in order to mingle in human life, and this life is not simply a return to a non-temporal conclusion. The self-emptying of God into everyday reality is what Incarnation is about. God becomes as "nothing" so as to appear as something, a human person. Jesus himself spoke of God dwelling in the least and lowly: "Whatsoever you do to the least of my brothers and sisters you do for me" (Mt 25:31–46). God, Irenaeus of Lyons wrote, is the human person fully alive. Kearney states: "This is not some anthropological reduction of the infinite to the finite, but a recognition that the infinite is to be found at the core of each

---

[21] Teilhard de Chardin, *Christianity and Evolution*, 75.

[22] Annemarie Schimmel, *Mystical Dimensions of Islam* (Chapel Hill: University of North Carolina Press, 1975), 289.

[23] Kearney, *Anatheism* (New York: Columbia University Press, 2010), 3, 87.

finite now, that the divine word inhabits the flesh of the world, in suffering and action."[24] Christianity is less a religion of formal ritual and worship than a return to human personhood. God is not somewhere in a heavenly sphere or a type of virtual reality; God is truly in our midst, as one of evolutionary us.

Teilhard also argued for a return of God to the world by moving beyond the classic, static metaphysical understanding of God, beginning with the Incarnation as the starting point for knowing God. We are floundering and fragmenting, he indicates, because God is absent from the core of collective human life. By shrinking the Incarnation to a narrow and juridical understanding of sin and salvation, we have lost sight of its organic meaning: divine Love is so profound that God becomes as "nothing" so as to appear as "something." God is not an intellectual idea but love expressed in personal otherness—*this* person of Jesus. God is the one who appears "despised and rejected, a man of sorrows, and acquainted with grief; as one from whom men hide their face" (Is 53:3). God stands like a beggar at the soul's door: "I stand at the door and knock. If anyone hears my voice and opens the door I will come in and eat with him, and he with me" (Rv 3:20).

Teilhard's evolutionary theology places Christianity squarely within cosmic history. He does not see Christianity as normative of all religion but normative of evolution; Christianity fulfills an essential function in evolution. The goal of Christianity is the aim of evolution itself—personal unity in love. Christianity begins with physicality and personal being. God is the name of radical love, and love becomes self-conscious in human persons: "The Father and I are one," Jesus said (Jn 10:30). God is the depth of reality's sacredness. "The world is charged with the grandeur of God" (Gerard Manley Hopkins), but one must be able to see this grandeur. "What do you want?" Jesus asked the blind man. "Lord," he said, "I want to see" (Lk 18:41). That is, I want to be made whole, to be part of the whole, to be able to *see* the whole. Jesus made a paste with his own saliva and dirt and put it on the man's eyes. This is how intertwined God is with earthy us. God is not pure, abstract thought but is present in mud and spit. That is how God works, not like a magician but through the creativity of earth's elements. Who could possibly know

---

[24] Ibid., 137.

this God? Not the cool-headed philosophers but the passionate mystics who pour out tears day and night, beating their breast out of a sense of compunction that divine Love holds us in our authentic being, even when we are in love with false gods. By his actions, Jesus indicated that whoever sees and does not believe that *this* is God and God is like *this*—is blind. Blindness is thinking that we can see what we cannot really grasp: "It is because you say you see that your blindness remains" (Jn 9:41). God is not our idea of God: "My thoughts are not your thoughts, and my ways are not your ways" (Is 55:8). God is the wholeness of love, visibly real to the one who can see; the light that radiates the truth of the world.

Mystic Oneness

Teilhard believed that Christianity has a power to unite in a way that neither "the pantheisms of the East nor those of the West could satisfy." However, he also felt that Christianity was forced and conventional and robbed him of faith in the world.[25] The problem, he realized, is how we understand the Christ. Language carries meaning—and sometimes baggage. For some, the title Christ has become an obstacle to unity because it bears the weight of historical divisions and violence.

However, the power of Jesus' life is in its totality, which includes death and resurrection. Not to include death and resurrection is to miss out on what is thoroughly universal, the power of divine Love to converge; humanity, cosmos, and God are united in a single personal center of love, that is, the risen Christ. It is belief in the resurrection that makes the life of Jesus worth following. The resurrection shows us the *personal* love of God in the *person* of Jesus and the *personalizing* process of evolution. What resurrection says is that human life has cosmic meaning in the heart of Love. We die individually, but we are part of a larger whole. Christ belongs to the whole. Christ symbolizes the personal center of love that bursts forth in Jesus and empowers our own lives to converge in love. Christ represents the capacity of every person to live in love and hence in God. Author and

---

[25] Teilhard de Chardin, *How I Believe*, 76.

speaker Michael Dowd claims that a new type of theist is emerging, one whose creed is based on reality, evidence, and integrity:
"Reality is our God, evidence is our scripture, and integrity is
our religion."[26] But personalization is not individualism. It is
not sheer physicality itself that is God but the ultimate depth
of every particular "this" that is *not* physical, precisely as its
depth/center/transcendence/divinity. Love is the core energy
of cosmic personalism, the depth of being and dynamically
unitive. Religion is not a feeling of inspiration or motivation;
neither is it static love. Rather, religion is the call to wholeness,
to union-in-love. Every world religion shares in this call in its
own unique way. The mystical poets of Islam, in their complete loving surrender to God, speak of the profound unity of
being. The poet Ibn al-Farid wrote: "I knew for sure that we
are really One, and the sobriety of union restored the notion
of separation, And my whole being was a tongue to speak, an
eye to see, an ear to hear, and a hand to seize."[27] One of the
great women mystics of Islam, Rabe'a al-'Adawiya (d. 801),
expressed profound depth of union with God:

> O my God, all the good things you have pre-
>   pared for me
> on this earth, give them to Your enemies.
> And everything you have prepared for me in
>   the other world,
> give it to Your friends, because You are enough
>   for me.
> My God, if I worship you out of fear of Hell,
>   burn me in Hell.
> And if I worship you out of hope of Paradise,
>   keep me out of Paradise.
> But if I worship You solely for Yourself, Do not
>   deprive me of Your eternal beauty.
> O God, all that I do and all that I desire in this
>   world is to remember You,

---

[26] Michael Dowd, "The New Theism: Shedding Beliefs, Celebrating
Knowledge," available on the metanexus.org website.

[27] Schimmel, *Mystical Dimensions of Islam*, 277.

and in the world to come, my only desire is to
    meet You.
This is my desire; now do with me whatever
    You will.[28]

We can find a similar type of mystical poetry among the Jewish
Kabbalist writers. One of the earliest and most important Kabbalists, Nachmanides, writes, "You should remember God and
His love always so that your awareness [is] not separate from
Him when you walk along the way, when you lie down, and
when you wake up, to the point that your words with other
people may be in your mouth and on your tongue, but your
heart is in the Presence of God."[29] Union in love is not specifically Christian nor is it a vague awareness of the divine presence
filling the universe. It is the particular, personal oneness of love
by which everything lives in love. In the late fifteenth century,
the Sufi poet Jami exclaimed:

Neighbor and associate and companion—ev-
    erything is He.
In the beggar's coarse frock and in the king's
    silk—
Everything is He.
In the crowd of separation and in the loneli-
    ness of
Collectedness
By God! Everything is He, and by God! Every-
    thing is He.[30]

---

[28] "A prayer by Rabe'a al-'Adawiya," trans. Tom Michel, SJ (personal
communication). An older translation is available on the thesufi.com
website.

[29] Mark Elber, "Mystical Union with the Divine: Devekut," available
on the netplaces.com website. "The word 'devekut' can refer to a range
of experiences, anywhere from keeping mentally focused on the Eternal
One to total union with the Divine (yikhud). We find the verb form of
the root (dalet, bet, kuf) in Genesis: 'a man shall unite [v'davak] with
his wife and they shall become one flesh' (2:24). Here, clearly the image
is one of union. Ecstatic Kabbalists consistently used the term to refer
to union with God, whereas Theosophical Kabbalists do not always."

[30] Schimmel, Mystical Dimensions of Islam, 283.

Since love is the core energy of evolution and every religion bears a unique expression of love, all world religions are in evolution. The mystical dimension of every world religion is to seek unity with the divine. In an interesting play on numbers, Jewish writer Daniel Matt describes the oneness of God as the oneness of love based on the mystical numerology of the words *one* and *love*:

> The Hebrew word for "one" is *ehad*, and the word for "love" is *ahavah*. In mystical numerology *(gematriyya)*, each Hebrew letter has a numerical value. The *gematriyya* of *ehad* is the sum of its individual letters: 1 *(alef)* + 8 *(het)* + 4 *(dalet)* = 13. The *gematriyya* of *ahavah* is 1 *(alef)* + 5 *(heh)* + 2 *(bet)* + 5 *(heh)* = 13. Oneness and love are equivalent. Together *ehad* and *ahavah* add up to 26. This is the same numerical value assigned to the holiest divine name: *YHVH*, the sum of whose letters (10+5+6+5) also equals 26. God is oneness and love.[31]

Out of this oneness of love is our being in love and our desire for oneness. Love is the whole, and every human person desires to belong to the whole. Religion that empowers the whole empowers evolution for the next level of cosmic life. As long as religions remain in conflict, evolution is thwarted in its forward direction and the earth suffers the pains of division.

Beyond World Religions

Teilhard saw a significant role for Christianity in evolution based on the Incarnation and the involvement of God in history. Although he lived for many years in China he did not see that Buddhism or other Eastern religions could empower evolution toward unity in love in the same way as Christianity. While other religions express dimensions of personal unity, Christianity is a religion of evolution in that it anticipates a new creation that is not individual but communal, the unity of all persons and

---

[31] Daniel C. Matt, *God and the Big Bang: Discovering Harmony Between Science and Spirituality* (Woodstock, VT: Jewish Lights Publishing, 2001), 70.

creation in God. Incarnation is God's involvement in history, but it is also history's involvement with God: the world makes a difference to God.

Christianity, however, cannot conquer the world as the sole religion; the very idea belies the gospel itself. Jesus reached out to the Samaritan woman (Jn 4:4–26), the Gentiles, tax collectors, the blind, the deaf, the lame, and all those outside Torah. Jesus' life overturned the law of exclusivity in order to live in the law of love: "You shall love the Lord your God with all your heart, and with all your soul, and with all your mind. This is the great and first commandment. And a second is like it, you shall love your neighbor as yourself" (Mt 22:36). Divine kenosis means that love, incarnation, and personalization are intertwined. Without self-emptying there is no novelty, without novelty there is no creativity, without creativity, there is no new life: "Unless a grain of wheat falls into the earth and dies, it remains alone; but if it dies, it bears much fruit" (Jn 12:24).

Christianity is a religion of evolution because it is marked by self-emptying love (Phil 2:6) that gathers together and creates anew (Jn 10:30). The life of Jesus Christ anticipates a new creation whereby love of God, love of self, and love of neighbor are gathered into a new unity, a new love, and a new future. In Jesus, evolution "appears" in person; *this* is what evolution is about. Raimon Panikkar writes that Jesus had to disappear for the Christ to emerge or he would have been made king and idol. The going away of the earthly Jesus (kenosis) is the beginning of the risen Christ, the fullness (pleroma) of creation: "Unless I go away, the Paraclete will not come to you; but if I go, I will send him to you" (Jn 16:7). "Otherwise," Panikkar said, "we would rigidify him into concepts, into intellectual containers. We would turn his teaching into a system, imprison him within our own categories and suffocate the Spirit."[32] Teilhard too said that the cosmic Person—the Christ—cannot be realized in history unless incarnation continues in evolution. What took place in the life of Jesus must now take place in humankind, amid the conflicts of history, where the Spirit groans aloud in the pangs of new birth. If Christianity is a religion of evolution toward union in

---

[32] Raimon Panikkar, *Christophany: The Fullness of Man*, trans. Alfred DiLascia (Maryknoll, NY: Orbis Books, 2004), 124.

love—the Christ—then the church (the body of Christ) is to be the phylum of love, the consecration of a new way of being in love. Through kenosis, union, and deeper relatedness, the church is to seek greater wholeness in evolution toward the Christ. Anything or anyone who prevents kenosis and union thwarts evolution and the emergence of Christ. Teilhard writes: "By disclosing a world-peak, evolution makes Christ possible, just as Christ, by giving meaning and direction to the world, makes evolution possible." The synthesis of Christ and the universe is so integral to each other that we can be saved "only by becoming one with the universe."[33]

A New Religious Consciousness?

Reflecting on the future of humanity, Teilhard envisioned an eventual convergence of religions so that the emergence of Christ would ultimately not be limited to a single religion but would be the convergence of psychic, spiritual energy, the unification of the whole.[34] In a 1950 talk to the Congrès Universel des Croyants he stated that "the various creeds still commonly accepted have been primarily concerned to provide every human with an *individual* line of escape and for this reason they fail to allow any room for a global and controlled transformation of the whole of life and thought in their entirety."[35] This stance, Teilhard insisted, can no longer be because the stasis of religion is the stifling of evolution. "No longer is it simply a religion of individual and of heaven, but a religion of mankind and of the earth—that is what we are looking for at this moment, as the oxygen without which we cannot breathe."[36] He spoke of "a general convergence of religions upon a universal personal center of unity who fundamentally satisfies all religions" made possible by the evolution of the computer and the new level of mind through the World Wide Web.[37]

---

[33] Ibid., 81.

[34] Ibid., 77–85.

[35] Teilhard de Chardin, *Activation of Energy*, 240.

[36] Ibid.

[37] Teilhard de Chardin, *How I Believe*, 85; idem, *Christianity and Evolution*, 130.

Casanova notes that in our globalized era "all religions can be reconstituted for the first time as de-territorialized global imagined communities, detached from the civilizational settings in which they have been traditionally embedded." Through the Internet and mass migration, each world religion is being dissociated and reconstituted on the global level through interrelated processes of particularistic differentiation, universalistic claims, and mutual recognition.[38] World religions are becoming more at home in the presence of one another than at home among themselves where they are becoming increasingly divided on issues of divorce, homosexuality, and the participation of women. Teilhard's evolution of religions toward unity-in-love speaks to a new level of complexified religious consciousness that is more relational, communal, and earth centered. It is not a blending of religions into a homogenous whole, a negation of respective doctrines and cultures. Rather, each religion unites according to its "thisness," its core personality. It unites not by losing what it is but by becoming more authentically itself because each unique religious core is the basis of union and hence of unity. Only on this new level of evolutionary convergence can religion be restored to the core of life. In an essay titled "Zest for Living" Teilhard speaks of "unsatisfied theism," not as the cause for new religion but the need to rejuvenate what has been passed on:

> We are surrounded by a certain sort of pessimists who continually tell us that our world is foundering in atheism. But should we not rather say that what it is suffering from is *unsatisfied theism*? . . . If the great spiritual concern of our times is a re-alignment and readjustment of old beliefs towards a new Godhead who has risen up at the anticipated pole of cosmic evolution—then why not simply slough off the old—why not, that is, regroup the whole of the earth's religious power directly and . . . pay no attention to the ancient creeds? . . . Why not have a completely fresh faith, rather than rejuvenation and confluence of "old

---

[38] José Casanova, "Human Religious Evolution and Unfinished Creation," in *The Spirit in Creation and New Creation: Science and Theology in Western and Orthodox Realms*, ed. Michael Welker, 192-202 (Grand Rapids, MI: Eerdmans, 2012), 200.

loves"? First of all, in each of the great religious branches that cover the world at this moment, a certain spiritual attitude and vision which have been produced by centuries of experience are preserved and continued; these are indispensable and irreplaceable for the integrity of a total terrestrial religious consciousness . . . the cosmic forces of complexification, it would seem, proceed not through individuals but through complete branches. What is carried along by the various currents of faith that are still active on the earth, working in their incommunicable core . . . is experiences of contact with a supreme inexpressible which they preserve and pass on.[39]

Without religious convergence, evolution cannot go forward because we cannot harness the energies of love for greater unity and being. Religious convergence is not by way of doctrine but of what we hold together across languages, cultures, and religions: earth, community, peace, and justice. We must enter into communion "with the very source of all interior drive."[40] The convergence of religions must be centered on love, as each religion expresses love and union with the divine in its own particular way. To live from the inner depth of love, as persons in evolution, is to live with purpose and direction not as an "I" but as a "we," a collective whole. To know God as the wholeness of love is to enter into oneness at the heart of all life. That is why prayer and contemplation are essential for the next stage of evolution. Without the eye of the heart or the inner space to welcome the new ways love shows itself in others, we cannot love toward greater unity. God is the ultimacy of love, the heart of life, and the power of the future. Any religion that attempts to grasp or control God kills cosmic hope. To recognize the face of God in the face of the other liberates the other from idolatry, as an object of control or rejection. Rather, the other becomes brother and sister, bound together by the luminous thread of love. The Hindu gesture Namaste means that the God in me recognizes the God in you. We are one because love is one and God is one. According to Sufi poet Ibn al-Fārid, "Both of us are

---

[39] Teilhard de Chardin, *Activation of Energy*, 240–42.
[40] Ibid., 242.

a single worshipper who, in respect to the united state, bows himself to his own essence in every act of bowing."[41]

The greatest danger of religion is to assume any type of sovereign power, because love always lives for the other and with the other. Everything and everyone who lives in love knows this simple truth. That is why the way forward—to evolve—is inward and across boundaries of difference. God is above, below, behind, and beyond the finite because God is the divine milieu in which everything is related. "Love is what we feel when we become aware of our oneness with what we thought was separate from us: a person, a place, a thing, an idea."[42] Religion degenerates into religiosity when God is absolutized by constructing foundations that are purported to be immutable, when fixed structures cannot adapt to changing circumstances. Excessive order, paradoxically, drifts toward chaos, which unexpectedly creates the conditions for the creative emergence of new patterns of order. The livingness of God disrupts and disfigures every stabilizing structure, thereby keeping the playful whole in movement. Just when we think we have a certainty of God, divinity will slip out from under our evolutionary feet and, like the speed of light, elude our grasp to become for us the power of the future.

---

[41] In Schimmel, *Mystical Dimensions of Islam*, 154.
[42] Matt, *God and the Big Bang*, 70.

Chapter Seven

Christian Love

Christianity is a religion of personhood rooted in love; at least this was the core message of Jesus. It lost its core personality early on when it adopted the Greek notion of soul and the supernaturality of the divine. The human person became a synthesis of parts in which the soul held priority over the body, giving the impression that "Christians do not believe in human progress."[1] We set our eyes on another world in hope that we could merit entrance into it. But we humans are not transients, renting a home in the cosmos until we can move to a more permanent one. Human life is not extrinsic to cosmic life, a strange species in an otherwise natural world. We are the latest arrivals in an evolutionary universe; we emerge from the whole and are integral to it. Evolution becomes conscious in us so that our task is not to leave the world but to see it in its divine depth, overcoming the forces of alienation that threaten to depersonalize culture.[2]

Patristic and medieval writers spoke of creation as the first book of revelation. The world, they said, is created as a means of God's self-revelation so that, like a mirror or footprint, it might lead us to love and praise the Creator. However, the book of creation became illegible because humans fell, we might say, upward into a higher consciousness, one that could choose self over

---

[1] Pierre Teilhard de Chardin, *How I Believe*, trans. René Hague (New York: Harper and Row, 1969), 75.

[2] Mary Evelyn Tucker, "The Ecological Spirituality of Teilhard," *Teilhard Studies* 51 (Fall 2005): 13.

others. Thus the light of truth was blurred by sin or alienation of the human from self and others.[3] The significance of Jesus Christ was understood within the static, patristic-medieval cosmos of hierarchy, stability, perfection, and sin. The tradition maintains that Christ came to repay the debt incurred by human sin and reconciled us to God. The Easter exultet still proclaims O *felix culpa*! For if Adam had not sinned Christ would not have come.

Evolution is a new story in which it is more difficult to account for original sin. The geneticist F. J. Ayala has demonstrated that the genetic diversity of the present human population (much of which we inherit from pre-human ancestors) could not possibly have been funneled through a single human couple, so monogenism must be rejected on scientific grounds alone.[4] The problem with original sin, according to Teilhard, is that it requires a static cosmology to be plausible. It arises in a fixed universe of limits. Teilhard did not deny the reality of sin. However, in an evolutionary universe it is not possible to speak of an *origin* of sin because the whole cosmos is still being created. The doctrine was formulated to explain the reality of evil in a fixed world created in original perfection and fallen due to human sin. Daryl Doming states:

> In the late 18th and early 19th centuries it [original sin] was undermined by geology's discovery of deep time, followed by the Darwinian revolution in biology. Simultaneously, the work of biblical scholars confirmed that Genesis had been misread in too literal a fashion. Yet no substitute has been agreed upon for the classic notion of original sin and its mysterious inheritance by all descendants of Adam.[5]

Teilhard could not accept the church's position on original sin because it opposed evolution as the process by which humans develop. Original sin, he said, is simply the "law of imperfection which operates in mankind in virtue of its being *in fieri*"; that is, because evolution is an unfinished process and the human person

---

[3] Bonaventure, *Collationes in Hexaëmeron* 2.20 (V, 340).

[4] F. J. Ayala, "Mitochondrial Eve," *Science* 270 (1995): 1930–36.

[5] Daryl Doming, "Original Sin," *America* (November 12, 2001): 14–21.

is still being created, sin is the inevitable correlate of incompleteness. He sums up his position on original sin in *Christianity and Evolution*:

> Let me say frankly what I think: it is impossible to universalize the first Adam without destroying his individuality. . . . We can no longer derive the whole of evil from one single hominian. I must emphasize again that long before man, death existed on earth. Sin . . . is the general solution to the problem of evil. Since, in the universe we know today, neither one man nor the whole of mankind can be responsible for contaminating the whole, we must remove from his language what represents the expression of the ideas of a first-century Jew [Paul]—instead of trying to preserve precisely those outdated formulations at the expense of the apostle's fundamental faith. . . . Original sin, taken in its widest sense is not a malady specific to the earth nor is it bound up with human generation. It simply symbolizes the inevitable chance of evil which accompanies the existence of all participated being. Wherever being *in fieri* is produced, suffering and wrong immediately appear as its shadow: not only as a result of the tendency towards inaction and selfishness found in creatures but also as an inevitable concomitant of their effort to progress. Original sin is the essential reaction of the finite to the creative act. . . . It is the reverse side of all creation. . . . Strictly speaking, there is no first Adam. The name disguises a universal and unbreakable law of reversion or perversion—the price that has to be paid for progress.[6]

Evolution changes the way we understand Christianity and the phenomenon of religion itself. For many Christians, sin and belief in Jesus Christ go together; if Adam had not sinned, Christ would not have come. This relationship between Adam and Christ, however, is a Pauline development that was enhanced by later writers. Jesus' approach to sin in the Gospels is in the form of healing; power goes out from him that brings to life what is

---

[6] Teilhard de Chardin, *Christianity and Evolution*, trans. René Hague (New York: Harcourt, 1971), 39–41.

disconnected or diseased (see Lk 7:36–50; Mk 1:40–45). The emphasis is on wholeness. Jesus' God-centered life shows a way of relating to others that makes wholes where there are divisions. His love gathers and heals what is scattered and apart. He draws people into community and empowers them to live the law of love. This power continues through the sacraments of baptism and Eucharist. Christians are sent into the world to energize the world and gather all together in love.

Christianity is a religion of "wholemaking," the dynamism of gathering persons into communal wholes; it is a religion of wholeness in relation to other religions of wholeness as well. Each religion has its own core identity that defines it in relation to the larger whole of culture and society. In this respect Christianity is part of a larger cosmic religious phenomenon. It did not arise *de novo* (or descend from heaven) but arose out of an evolution of consciousness (axial consciousness) along with other world religions. Because Christianity emerged within a larger whole, it belongs to the larger whole. If we continue to see Christianity separate and exclusive from the larger whole, we risk losing its illuminative value. By isolating itself from cosmic evolution, Christianity forfeits its transformative power:

> Our Christology is still expressed in exactly the same terms as those which three centuries ago could satisfy those whose outlook on the cosmos it is now physically impossible for us to accept. . . . What we now have to do without delay is to modify the position occupied by the central core of Christianity—and this precisely in order that it may not lose its illuminative value.[7]

Religions, in general, express a human consciousness of ultimacy, otherness, and transcendence. How these are expressed define religions in particular ways. Christianity has a particular "thisness" based on God's self-involvement in history; because of *this* particularity it must find its relationship to the larger whole in a way that is symbiotic and synergistic. Teilhard said: "I find myself obliged by the very logic of my progress to emerge from my individualism and confront the general religious experience

---

[7] Ibid., 77.

of mankind, *that so I may involve myself in it.*"[8] We can only understand Christianity within a larger whole, however, if we accept
evolution as the starting point for the Christian phenomenon: "If
we Christians wish to *retain* in Christ the very qualities on which
his power and our worship are based, we have no better way—
no other way, even—of doing so than fully to accept the most
modern concepts of evolution."[9] Here, of course, is the watershed
between the church and modern culture, for the church remains
ambivalent with regard to evolution. The church recognizes evolution as a possible scientific explanation of biological life but does
not accept it as *the* explanation of all life. Hence, evolution is not
considered in its philosophical implications and is not integral to
the development of theology or doctrine. At a recent celebration
of Charles Darwin's *On the Origin of Species*, Cardinal William
Levada, prefect of the Congregation of the Doctrine of the Faith,
introduced the event by saying it provided "a favorable occasion
for a new and qualified exchange about the theory of biological
evolution *free from any reduction to an ideological system claiming to become the key of interpretation of the whole of reality*"
(emphasis added).[10] The church maintains that evolution is a
theory not a fact (*pace,* modern science). Without evolution as
the starting point for revelation, however, Christianity becomes
increasingly irrelevant to the world of which it is a part. One
can sense Teilhard's frustration when he writes: "The truth about
today's gospel is that it has ceased, or practically ceased, to have
any attraction because it has become *unintelligible*."[11] The question Christians must ask: What is the significance of Christ in an
evolving world, at the heart of a humankind that is seeking its
future? To understand what this means in the twenty-first century
is to discover Jesus Christ in a new way.[12]

---

[8] Teilhard de Chardin, *How I Believe*, 60.

[9] Ibid., 79.

[10] Cardinal William Levada, "Address," in *Biological Evolution: Facts
and Theories: A Critical Appraisal 150 Years After "The Origin of Species,"* ed. G. Auletta, M. Leclerc, R. A. Martinez (Rome: Gregorian and
Biblical Press, 2011), 7.

[11] Teilhard de Chardin, *Christianity and Evolution*, 91.

[12] I have begun explorations for a new Christology in two previous
books: *Christ in Evolution* and *The Emergent Christ*. My purpose here

The Cosmic Person

The doctrine of incarnation requires faith in God's self-involvement in history. We can consider God becoming flesh both historically and cosmologically. These ways are not exclusive, but the West has focused on the historical while the East has emphasized the cosmological. The historical way looks at the human history of God in the person of Jesus of Nazareth, that is, the context and community in which Jesus was born and lived out his public ministry. The cosmological way seeks to understand the person of Jesus Christ within the larger context of reality; the historical is understood within the larger framework of the cosmological. Among some patristic and medieval writers such as Origen, Irenaeus of Lyons, Hugh of St. Victor, and Bonaventure, the cosmological held priority over the historical. When a dispute arose in the Middle Ages about the relationship between being and goodness, the authors of the *Summa Fratris Alexandri* argued that relegating goodness to being in the Godhead would give rise to a "cosmo-morphic" error.[13] It is no surprise that Franciscan theologian Duns Scotus saw love and not sin as the reason for the Incarnation. Scotus looked at the larger picture of reality, not the narrow picture of human sin. He saw an intimate connection between creation and Incarnation, grounded in the infinite love of God. Love is the reason for everything that exists, and God is love. God wanted to self-express outwardly in a creature who would be a masterpiece and love God perfectly in return. This is Scotus's doctrine of the primacy of Christ. Christ is the first in God's intention to love. Creation is not an independent act of divine love that was, incidentally, followed up by divine self-revelation in the covenant. Rather, the divine desire to become incarnate was part of the divine plan from all eternity: "He is the image of the invisible God, the firstborn over all creation. For by him all things were created: things in heaven and on earth, visible and invisible. . . . He is before all things,

---

is to understand the evolution of Christ in light of cosmic personalism and the fundamental energy of love.

[13] Kevin Keane, "Why Creation? Bonaventure and Thomas Aquinas on God as Creative Good," *Downside Review* 93 (1975): 116.

and in him all things hold together" (Col 1:15, 17). Christ is the masterpiece of love, the *summum opus Dei*. Because creation is centered on incarnation, every leaf, cloud, fruit, animal, and person is an outward expression of the Word of God in love. When Jesus comes as the incarnation of God, there is a "perfect fit" because everything has been made to resemble Christ. Sun, moon, trees, animals, and stars all have life in Christ, the personal Word of Love, through whom all things are made (cf. Jn 1:1).[14] As the motif or pattern of creation, Christ is the perfect divine-human-cosmic communion who exemplifies the meaning and purpose of all creation, namely, the praise and glory of God in a communion of love.

Christogenesis

The emphasis on love and not sin as the reason for Christ was obscured by the need to define the Incarnation more precisely. The church fathers defended the Incarnation at the Council of Chalcedon in 451 as a true union of divinity and humanity, defining *person* and *nature* and the union of natures without division, separation, or confusion. Jesus Christ is one person subsisting in two natures: divine and human. The definition presupposes an understanding of *person* and *nature* based on Greek philosophy. Since the fifth century Christian orthodoxy has maintained that divine and human natures are fully unified in Jesus Christ (according to the First Council of Ephesus in 431) but that the two natures also remain distinct (according to the Council of Chalcedon in 451); a oneness of person subsisting in two natures. The two natures, distinct but unified, participate in an exchange of properties; the properties of the divine Word can be ascribed to the man Christ, and the properties of the man Jesus Christ can be predicated of the Word *(communicatio idiomatum)*. However, there remains disagreement in the exact dynamic of this incarnational union. Those leaning toward an Antiochene Christology stressed the distinction of natures and therefore a more tightly

---

[14] Mary Beth Ingham, *Scotus for Dunces: An Introduction to the Subtle Doctor* (New York: Franciscan Institute Publications, 2003), 264–66.

regulated communication of properties; those adherents of Alexandrian Christology underscored the unity of Jesus Christ and therefore a more complete communication of properties.

But what exactly *is* "divine nature" and "human nature" based on modern physics and biology? What is human personhood in an evolving cosmos? These are difficult questions and are not easily answered without engaging modern physics and biology, including quantum physics, chaos theory, systems biology, genetics, and neuroscience. F. LeRon Shults took up this task in his book *Science and Christology*, but there is still much work needed to develop a contemporary systematic understanding of Jesus Christ that is consonant with reality as science now understands it.[15] The modern understanding of personhood today cannot ignore consciousness or the complex interaction of mind-brain-body and the evolution of these.

Although the evolutionary nature of personhood is complex, we can say that divine love comes to explicit consciousness in a way that belongs entirely and originally to the person, Jesus of Nazareth. Divine love explodes in the person of Jesus in an explicit way so that he is recognized as the Christ, *the* cosmic Person, the paradigm of relationality. The whole process of evolution that leads to the birth of Jesus is punctuated by cataclysmic events, violent explosions, and catastrophic extinctions followed by periods of relative stability. This emergence is not some dramatic leap into existence. On the contrary, God's appearance is hidden in the depth of Big Bang evolution. Jesus appears not simply as the perfect union of divine human and cosmic natures but on the edge of emergent chaos. The poet Denise Levertov captures the Incarnation as the unexpected interruption of mystery:

> It's when we face for a moment
> The worst our kind can do, and shudder to
>   know
> The taint in our own selves, that awe
> Cracks the mind's shell and enters the heart:
> Not to a flower, not to a dolphin,

---

[15] F. Leron Shults, *Science and Christology* (Grand Rapids, MI: Eerdmans, 2008).

To no innocent form
But to this creature vainly sure
It and no other is god-like, God
(out of compassion for our ugly
Failure to evolve) entrusts,
As guest, as brother,
The Word.[16]

After the death of Jesus his disciples experienced his resurrection as the Christ, Omega, the integrated whole. The early church had a sense of Jesus on the edge of chaos and emphasized a new power in the human person because of the risen Christ. Jaroslav Pelikan showed that as Christianity developed from the early church onward the images of Jesus Christ changed as culture changed.[17] In light of where we are today, we can say that Jesus began as anointed prophet and is now evolution's future.

In our own time consciousness again plays a significant role in understanding the Christ. A new universe is emerging through evolution and hence a new consciousness is emerging, one that is integral rather than mythic or mental-rational.[18] Integral consciousness is the consciousness of the whole integrated reality of God-cosmos-anthropos. To know this cosmotheandric God we must return to the senses and to the flesh as our most intimate element that enfolds us in the systole and diastole of being. The flesh is not matter but an element of Being, the *entre deux* between the whole of being and each individual fragment. "God is not simply a principle of which we are the consequence, a will whose instruments we are. There is sort of an impotence of God without us and Christ attests that God would not be fully God

[16] Denise Levertov, "On the Mystery of the Incarnation," *A Door in the Hive* (New York: New Directions, 1989), 50.

[17] Yale theologian Jaroslav Pelikan expounded on a series of shifting Christ images from the patristic to the Middle Ages in his book *Jesus Through the Ages: His Place in the History of Culture* (New Haven, CT: Yale University Press, 1999).

[18] German thinker Jean Gebser developed the idea of integral consciousness and was influential on the American philosopher Ken Wilber. See Carter Phipps, *Evolutionaries: Unlocking the Spiritual and Cultural Potential of Science's Greatest Idea* (New York: Harper, 2012), 198–209.

without becoming fully human."[19] Knowledge of God, therefore, begins with the felt experience, a withinness that is at once real but ineffable, felt but ungraspable. Saint Augustine asked, "What do I love when I love You?"

> Not bodily beauty, and not temporal glory, not the clear shining light, lovely as it is to our eyes, not the sweet melodies of many-moded songs, not the soft smell of flowers and ointments and perfumes, not manna and honey, not limbs made for the body's embrace, not these do I love when I love my God.
>
> Yet I do love a certain light, a certain voice, a certain odor, a certain food, a certain embrace when I love my God: a light, a food, an embrace for the man within me, where his light, which no place can contain, floods into my soul; where he utters words that time does not speed away; where he sends forth an aroma that no wind can scatter; where he provides food that no eating can lessen; where he so clings that satiety does not sunder us. This is what I love when I love my God.[20]

Teilhard extended this felt withinness to his scientific observation of evolution. He described a cosmological force of attraction by which elements unite, complexify, and personalize as they differentiate. Beginning with the human person as the self-reflective "I" of evolution, Teilhard suggested that *someone* and not something is coming to birth at the heart of evolution. He used the term *Christogenesis* to indicate that evolution is, from the point of Christian faith, the birth of the cosmic Person. In this respect Christianity does not begin with the historical person of Jesus but with Big Bang evolution. The primordial soup of the early Big Bang was a sea of particles and energy that quickly formed into fundamental molecules and forces. The ubiquity of evolutionary convergence in view of the exuberant diversity of elements on both biological and cosmological levels impelled Teilhard to identify convergence as a principal factor of evolution. He saw

---

[19] Merleau-Ponty, *Signs,* cited in Richard Kearney, *Anatheism* (New York: Columbia University Press, 2010), 91.

[20] Augustine, *The Confessions of St. Augustine,* trans. John K. Ryan (New York: Doubleday, 1960), 233–34.

a mutual complementarity between nature's dynamic movement toward greater unity and the revelation of God as Trinity. God is dynamically interior to creation, gradually bringing all things to their full being as Trinity-in-unity by a single creative act spanning all time. God does act outside creation but "from within, at the core of each element, by animating the sphere of being from within. Where God is operating, it is always possible for us to see only the work of nature because God is the formal cause, the intrinsic principle of being, although God is not identical with being itself."[21] Or, as Teilhard writes, "the whole reveals itself to each of its elements in order to draw it to itself."[22] The Trinity shows the essential condition of God's capacity to be the personal summit of a universe that is in process of personalization; love generated as evolutionary Word expressed in Spirit-energy reaches its summation in Jesus Christ, in whom we see the direction of evolution. Christogenesis means that evolution is not mere chance or random processes; it involves directed change, organized becoming, patterned process, and cumulative order.[23]

Teilhard recognized that there is a unifying influence in the whole evolutionary process, a centrating factor that continues to hold the entire process together and move it forward toward greater complexity and unity. The ultimate mover of the entire

---

[21] Ilia Delio, *The Emergent Christ: Exploring the Meaning of Catholic in an Evolutionary Universe* (Maryknoll, NY: Orbis Books, 2011), 37.

[22] Teilhard de Chardin, *How I Believe*, 60.

[23] In *Nonzero: The Logic of Human Destiny*, Robert Wright states that despite the scientific materialist, there is ample evidence for direction in nature. He writes: "People who see a direction in human history, or in biological evolution, or both, have often been dismissed as mystics or flakes. In some ways, it's hard to argue that they deserve better treatment. . . . Through natural selection, there arise new 'technologies' that permit richer forms of non-zero-sum interaction among biological entities: among genes, or cells, or animals, or whatever . . . both organic and human history involve the playing of ever-more-numerous, ever-larger, and ever-more-elaborate non-zero-sum games. . . . History, even if its basic direction is set, can proceed at massive, wrenching human cost. Or it can proceed more smoothly—with costs, to be sure, but with more tolerable costs. It is the destiny of our species—and this time I mean the inescapable destiny, not just the high likelihood—to choose" (New York: Pantheon Books, 2000), introduction.

cosmogenesis, he indicates, is something that is simultaneously *within* the sequence of beings as tendency, desire, and purpose, and *in front* of the advancing wave of development, beckoning it, as its ideal culmination. Teilhard identified this Mover with God. The evolutionary pressure is the presence of God at every stage, helping, driving, drawing. We always assumed that God could be located "above," he writes, but now we realize that he can also be situated "ahead" and "within" as well. This cosmotheandric process of evolution reflects the power of divine love as the unitive center of being, converging separate elements into greater union. Incarnation is not a separate event from creation but the act of creative personalization through unitive love. Love is the energy that empowers union; union generates new creation, and each new creation is more whole and united in love—more personal. Creation, incarnation, and redemption are not separate, independent acts, Teilhard asserts, but a single act of divine love that gives birth to more personal being in evolution. Divine love enfolding evolution is creative, personalizing and redemptive, as being unifies and complexifies. Evolution, therefore, is a cosmic birthing process toward personal unity by which the whole is gathered together in love. In *How I Believe* Teilhard writes:

> If we Christians wish to *retain* in Christ the very qualities on which his power and our worship are based, we have no better way—no other way, even—of doing so than fully to accept the most modern concepts of evolution. Under the combined pressure of science and philosophy, we are being forced, experientially and intellectually, to accept the world as a coordinated system of activity which is gradually rising up toward freedom and consciousness. The only satisfactory way of interpreting this process is to regard it as irreversible and convergent. Thus, ahead of us, a *universal cosmic center* is taking on definition, in which everything reaches its term, in which everything is explained, is felt and is ordered. It is, then, in this *physical pole* of universal evolution that we must, in my view, locate and recognize the plenitude of Christ. . . . By disclosing a world-peak, evolution makes Christ possible, just as Christ

by giving meaning and direction to the world, makes evolution possible.[24]

Through his penetrating view of the universe Teilhard found Christ present in the entire cosmos, from the least particle of matter to the convergent human community. "The Incarnation," he declared, "is a making new . . . of all the universe's forces and powers." Personal divine love is invested organically with all of creation, in the heart of matter, unifying the world.[25] By taking on human form Christ has given the world its definitive form—personalization. God could not create unless God was incarnate, and to be incarnate is to share in the sufferings and evil inherent in the struggles of evolution. By saying that cosmogenesis is Christogenesis, Teilhard showed that the world is longing to become more personalized. Our universe is a personalizing universe, marked by divine omnipresence shining through both the glory and pain of the world.

The Novelty of Jesus

Christification is personlization of the universe by which love unifies and rises in consciousness. In this sense all religions participate in the evolution of the cosmic Person—christogenesis—through their own particular forms of worship, prayer, ritual, and belief. While cosmic personalization demands that religions converge toward a common personal center, Teilhard also saw a particular role for Christianity in evolution. Zachary Hayes claims that the life, death, and resurrection of Jesus Christ means that evolution, from a Christian perspective, has purpose and aim. It is not a mere plurality of unrelated things but a true unity in divine love incarnate. He writes: "God creates toward an end.

---

[24]Teilhard de Chardin, *How I Believe*, 79–80.

[25]Pierre Teilhard de Chardin, *The Human Phenomenon*, trans. Sarah Appleton-Weber (Brighton: Sussex Academic Press, 1999), 211; Timothy Jamison, "The Personalized Universe of Teilhard de Chardin," in *There Shall Be One Christ*, ed. Michael Meilach (New York: The Franciscan Institute, 1968), 26.

That end as embodied in Christ points to a Christified world."[26]
What may appear from the sciences as a mechanical process is,
on another level, a limitless mystery of productive love. God's
creative love freely calls from within the world a created love
that can freely respond to God's creative call. That created love
is embodied in Christ in whom all of creation finds its goal.

If incarnation is what this universe is about, a cosmotheandric
evolution of love, then evolution is an unfolding theophany, an
unveiling of divinity in creation. Evolution is Trinity enfolding
space-time. Love overflows into space-time Word, energized by
the Spirit of new creation. God is not so much behind creation as
its cause, but in front of creation as its future. God is the name
of love's excess, which gives rise to being and transcends being.
God, therefore, is always the "more" of what any finite being
can express. God emerges from within as ever newness in love
and is the future of every new love.

The particular Christian contribution to evolution and cosmic
personalization is the law of love—not the idea or concept of
love—but the reality of union and integral wholeness. Christian
life is transformative life because it takes God as its starting point
acting in history. In the person of Jesus of Nazareth a new God
consciousness of love becomes radically expressed in a way that
departs from other religions. This new religious consciousness
evokes a new way of action. Jesus is a new Big Bang in evolution,
an explosion of love that ignites a new way of thinking about
God, creation, and future: "I have come to cast fire on the earth
and how I wish it were ablaze already" (Lk 12:49).

The Gospels open with the word *metanoia*, "repent," indicating a summons to a complete change of life for both the
individual and society. This change is a not a single event but
a permanent newness of life. Christianity emerges out of older
concepts of order; it is more dynamic than the classical hierarchic
pyramid with God at the top, humans in the middle, and plant
and animal life below. The new Christian order is not about fix-
ity of place in the hierarchy but inclusiveness within the whole
concept of order itself, a *holarchy*. Jesus' intimate experience
of God and his self-identity with the Father ("The Father and

---

[26] Zachary Hayes, *A Window to the Divine: A Study of Christian
Creation Theology* (Quincy, IL: Franciscan Press, 1997), 90–91.

I are one") empower him to act in the name of love by healing and reconciling all that is unloved in human persons. He
gathers what is scattered, healing the sick, eating with sinners,
speaking with women, dining with tax collectors and Gentiles,
dealing with each person as one called into greater wholeness.
The story of Jesus' encounter with the Samaritan woman (Jn
4:4–26) shows the new religious consciousness that erupts in
this man from Galilee:

> Now Jesus learned that the Pharisees had heard that he was
> gaining and baptizing more disciples than John although
> in fact it was not Jesus who baptized, but his disciples. So
> he left Judea and went back once more to Galilee. Now
> he had to go through Samaria. So he came to a town in
> Samaria called Sychar, near the plot of ground Jacob had
> given to his son Joseph. Jacob's well was there, and Jesus,
> tired as he was from the journey, sat down by the well.
> It was about noon. When a Samaritan woman came to
> draw water, Jesus said to her, "Will you give me a drink?"
> (His disciples had gone into the town to buy food.) The
> Samaritan woman said to him, "You are a Jew and I am a
> Samaritan woman. How can you ask me for a drink?" (For
> Jews do not associate with Samaritans.) Jesus answered her,
> "If you knew the gift of God and who it is that asks you
> for a drink, you would have asked him and he would have
> given you living water." "Sir," the woman said, "you have
> nothing to draw with and the well is deep. Where can you
> get this living water? Are you greater than our father Jacob,
> who gave us the well and drank from it himself, as did also
> his sons and his livestock?" Jesus answered, "Everyone
> who drinks this water will be thirsty again, but whoever
> drinks the water I give them will never thirst. Indeed, the
> water I give them will become in them a spring of water
> welling up to eternal life." The woman said to him, "Sir,
> give me this water so that I won't get thirsty and have to
> keep coming here to draw water." He told her, "Go, call
> your husband and come back." "I have no husband," she
> replied. Jesus said to her, "You are right when you say you
> have no husband. The fact is, you have had five husbands,
> and the man you now have is not your husband. What

you have just said is quite true." "Sir," the woman said, "I can see that you are a prophet. Our ancestors worshiped on this mountain, but you Jews claim that the place where we must worship is in Jerusalem." "Woman," Jesus replied, "believe me, a time is coming when you will worship the Father neither on this mountain nor in Jerusalem. You Samaritans worship what you do not know; we worship what we do know, for salvation is from the Jews. Yet a time is coming and has now come when the true worshipers will worship the Father in the Spirit and in truth, for they are the kind of worshipers the Father seeks. God is spirit, and his worshipers must worship in the Spirit and in truth." The woman said, "I know that Messiah" (called Christ) "is coming. When he comes, he will explain everything to us." Then Jesus declared, "I, the one speaking to you—I am he."

In his encounter with the woman at the well, Jesus broke three Jewish customs: first, he spoke to a woman; second, she was a Samaritan woman, a group the Jews traditionally despised; and third, he asked her to get him a drink of water, which would have made him ceremonially unclean from using her cup or jar. This shocked the woman at the well. But Jesus lived in unrestrained love, inwardly free from laws and customs that hindered wholeness and community. Empowered by the Spirit he did the unthinkable—he spoke with a Samaritan woman.

Jesus emphasized the priority of human values over conventionally "religious" ones. He preached against religious alienation and challenged abstract religious laws. When some disciples complained that he was gathering food on the Sabbath he said: "The Sabbath was made for man, not man for the Sabbath" (Mark 2:27). Jesus consistently opted for the human person against the claims of legalistic religion. When he had to choose between the good of a suffering human person, such as healing the blind man with mud ("Go, wash in the pool of Siloam") and the claims of formal and established legalism ("This man is not from God because he does not keep the Sabbath"), he chose the human person (Jn 9:1–41). Throughout the New Testament we see the explicit contrast between mere interior religiosity that is fixed to laws and abstract ideas, and the love that makes whole, uniting humans to humans and humans to God. The self-righteous Pharisees were continuously testing Jesus: "Are we blind too?" they asked. Jesus said, "If you were blind, you would not be guilty of sin; but now that you claim you can see, your guilt remains" (Jn 9:41). Jesus ushered in not a new religion but a new humanism. God is love, not infinite power. Thomas Merton points out that God gives himself to us without reservation, in love, becoming one of us. Love is the creative secret of God, the hidden mystery, manifest and active in all aspects of life but especially in the human person. He writes: "Christianity does not teach man to attain an inner ideal of divine tranquility and stoic quiet by abstracting himself from material things. It teaches him to give himself to his brother and to his world in a service of love in which God will manifest his creative power through men on earth."[27]

Jesus was a "wholemaker," bringing together those who were divided, separated, or left out of the whole. He initiated a new way of "catholicity," a gathering together of persons in love.[28] At the end of his life he prayed: "That they will all be one, just as you and I are one—as you are in me, Father, and I am in you. And may they be in us so that the world will believe you sent me" (Jn 17:21). He gathered together what was divided and confronted systems that diminished, marginalized, or excluded human persons. He challenged others not by argument or attack but out of a deep center of love. Jesus said, "Do not resist an evil person. If someone strikes you on the right cheek, turn to him the other also" (Mt 5:39). Faith in Christ should move us to be loving and free, to create new wholes, and in doing so, to create a new future for the human person, for society, and for the whole earthly community.

Dying to Love

If evolution is about kenosis and pleroma, self-emptying and full-ness, then the greatest evolutionary act of Jesus was his death on

---

[27] Thomas Merton, *Love and Living*, ed. Naomi Burton Stone and Brother Patrick Hart (New York: Harcourt, 1979), 147–50.

[28] For a greater explanation of Jesus and catholicity, see Delio, *The Emergent Christ*, 59–71.

the cross, a conscious decision to remain faithful in love despite the forces of hatred and opposition. His attentiveness to the inner voice of love (Lk 22:42, "Not my will but yours be done") over the voices of fear and death (Mt 26:39, "Let this cup pass from me") exemplified Jesus' commitment to love in the face of suffering; to love unto death for the sake of life. Jesus' act of ultimate love was ultimately free: "No one takes it [my life] from me, but I lay it down of my own accord" (Jn 10:8). His life recapitulates the process of evolution itself; suffering and death mark the passage from isolated existence into personal unity.

The life of Jesus shows us that to live within the confines of the expected, which seems to provide stability, security, and certainty, is to be dead even when alive; to be exposed to the unexpected is to be open to the creativity of life and death. The cosmic Person (the Christ) can only emerge when humans are willing to let go of isolated existences for the sake of greater union. The power of love that evolves the cosmos toward personalization is love unto death for the sake of life. God's freedom in love is uncoercive and utterly faithful. If we seek a divine monarch, an omnipotent power who will save us from death, we are outside the Christian God revealed in the cross. Walter Kasper writes:

> God's self-emptying, his weakness and his suffering are not the expression of a lack, as they are in finite beings; nor are they the expression of a fated necessity. . . . He suffers out of love and by reason of love, which is the overflow of his being. . . . Because God is the omnipotence of love, he can as it were indulge in the weakness of love; he can enter into suffering and death without perishing within. . . . God on the cross shows himself as the one who is free in love and as freedom in love.[29]

On the cross God is powerless, lowly, and abandoned; only in the Resurrection do we believe that *this* God is the innermost center of the universe, the power of love that lives beneath our feet as

---

[29] Walter Kasper, *God of Jesus Christ*, trans. Matthew J. O'Connell (New York: Crossroad), 195.

the absolute power of the future. Karl Rahner writes: "When the vessel of his body was shattered in death, Christ was poured out over the cosmos: he became actually, in his very humanity, what he had always been in his dignity, the innermost center of creation."[30] A Christian theology of the cross awakens the human capacity to love in the face of opposition. Kearney states, "Christian caritas as a refusal of exclusivist power is a summons to endless kenosis."[31] To be free in love, however, we must know ourselves as being loved, and this means accepting ourselves as lovable. Jesus was free in love because he lived in truth and authenticity of being. We discover our true selves in love when we realize we are not alone and therefore have no need to defend our isolated egos. The lovability of our lives is our particular inscape, our "thisness," not simply our genome or phenotypes, but the unique constituency of relationships that makes each "I" a living "Thou" with a distinct personality. To realize our human capacity to love is the beginning of divinization because in the beauty of our "I" is the living Thou waiting to be called upon as God. As Etty Hillsum realized: "You God cannot be God unless we create a dwelling place for you in our hearts."[32] Love lives in the freedom to be for another. Merton writes:

> The forms and individual characters of living and growing things, of inanimate beings, of animals and flowers and all nature, constitute their holiness in the sight of God. . . . The pale flowers of the dogwood outside this window are saints. The little yellow flowers that nobody notices on the edge of that road are saints looking up into the face of God. This leaf has its own texture and its own pattern of veins and its own holy shape, and the bass and trout hiding in the deep pools of the river are canonized by their beauty and their strength.[33]

---

[30] Karl Rahner, *On the Theology of Death* (New York: Herder and Herder, 1961), 66.

[31] Kearney, *Anatheism*, 55.

[32] Annemarie S. Kidder, ed., *Writings of Etty Hillsum* (Maryknoll, NY: Orbis Books, 2009), 59.

[33] Thomas Merton, *New Seeds of Contemplation* (New York: New Directions, 1961), 30.

If we find ourselves in a violent world today, it is not only because we have lost sight of the human person but because we have lost sense of love. We equate love with self-gratification, not with the core beauty of our individual being. Without real love at the center of our lives, we are not free; hence, we cannot be for another. We must instead separate ourselves from the other in order to exert some type of autonomy over and against the other. The remarkable medieval woman Clare of Assisi (d. 1253) spoke of the cross as a mirror. We are to gaze into this mirror of the cross each day, she said, and to study our face within it. Our tendency is to see violence outside ourselves not within ourselves; the other is violent, not me—but violence is a mirror of who we really are. In the mirror of the cross we are to reflect on our inner worlds and see if they are one with our outer worlds or in conflict with them. Clare asks that we gaze on the cross and consider our own violence: where we fail in love and where find freedom in love. To know ourselves is to be one in love with God and thus to bear God in our lives.

Miroslav Volf describes a "phenomenology of embrace" that opens a path to authentic love. An embrace, Volf writes, begins with opening the arms. "Open arms are a gesture of the body reaching for the other. They are a sign of discontent with my own self-enclosed identity and a code of desire for the other. I do not want to be myself only; I want the other to be part of who I am and I want to be part of the other." A self that is "full of itself" can neither receive the other nor make genuine movement toward the other. Open arms signify that I have "created space in myself for the other to come in and that I have made a movement out of myself so as to enter the space created by the other." Volf indicates, however, that one does not stop at the embrace for the embrace is not to make two bodies one; it is not meant to dissolve one body into the other. If the embrace is not to cancel itself, therefore, the arms must open again; this preserves the genuine identity of each subject of the embrace.[34] Nor should we try to understand the other if we are to preserve the alterity or genuine identity of the other in the embrace. If

---

[34] Miroslav Volf, *Exclusion and Embrace: A Theological Exploration of Identity, Otherness, and Reconciliation* (Nashville, TN: Abingdon Press, 1996), 141–44.

we try to understand the other on our own terms, we make the other into a projection of ourselves or try to absorb the other into ourselves. A genuine embrace entails the ability-not-to-understand but to accept the other as a question right in the midst of the embrace, and to let go, allowing the question of the other to remain mystery.[35]

This embrace of God is not without pain. Every effort to love—every embrace—has the possibility of refusal and resistance: "To be what one must in loving God, one must admit that one can be the opposite; one must admit that one can revolt. The resistance of freedom alone gives sense to the union."[36] There is no expansion without contraction; there is no birth without pain; there is no evolution without suffering and death. We cannot expect our embrace of another to be accepted; neither can we expect God to work "miracles" in the face of opposition. Sin is a disordering of loving-communion with others and with God, a will to power over and against the other. Authentic being empowers the embrace of love, and with each new act of love there is a new future.

God is love, and love is the core of evolution; so too, love is God, and God is the core of evolution. Through billions of years with billions of violent events—cosmic cataclysms, massive explosions, biological extinctions, war, cannibalism, tornados, earthquakes, death—divine love has persevered without perishing because divine love can never be extinguished. Love pushes through what appears to be dead and breathes into it new life. Love forever seeks more union, more being, more consciousness. That is why humanity has no real future and cannot evolve without returning to love at the core of being. The law of progress and the law of love must be joined together for the future of earthly life. God will not save us, indeed, cannot save us, if we are without love; without love we are without God, and therefore we are already dead. We must, therefore, return to ourselves—*this* self with its genomic configuration, its evolutionary

---

[35] For an explanation of embrace and not-understanding, see ibid., 145–56.

[36] Vladimir Lossky, *Orthodox Theology: An Introduction*, trans. Ian and Ihita Kesarcodi-Watson (Crestwood, NY: St. Vladimir's Press, 1978), 72.

history, and its power to love—because only *this* self can love. This return to self is the core of the gospel and Christianity's role in evolution, underscoring the law of love by which every person can be made whole in love. From the depth of inner love, Christ, the cosmic Person, will be born.

Chapter Eight

Love, Learning, and the Desire for Power

Christian love was never, from the outset, a type of emotionalism or individual piety. Rather, it demanded thoughtfulness, a vision of the heart that could see the truth of reality. The fathers of the church developed a holy alliance of learning and loving through knowledge of the scriptures, philosophy, astronomy, physics, grammar, and rhetoric. Meditation and contemplation were integral to the philosophical quest for truth. Contemplation was serious business because it was the gateway to the real. The purpose of education in the ancient world *(paideia)* was to show individuals how to define themselves authentically and spontaneously in relation to the world—not to impose a prefabricated definition of the world, still less an arbitrary definition of the individual alone. Learning was a matter of interior freedom, which meant the capacity to find oneself on the deepest possible level and from there to act. What early scholars showed was that the world is more real in proportion to the people in it; to be consciously alive as a human person was to render the world more fully and consciously alive.

It is not surprising that the earliest learning centers were monasteries, out of which the university arose. Thomas Merton draws a comparison between the monastery and university in this way:

> A university, like a monastery is at once a microcosm and a paradise. Both monastery and university came into being in a civilization open to the sacred, that is to say, in a civilization which paid a great deal of attention to what

137

it considered to be its own primordial roots in a mythical and archetypal holy ground, a spiritual creation. Thus the *Logos* or *Ratio* of both monastery and university is pretty much the same. Both are "schools," and they teach not so much by imparting information as by bringing the clerk (in the university) or the monk (in the monastery) to direct contact with "the beginning," the archetypal paradise world. This was often stated symbolically by treating the various disciplines of university and monastic life, respectively, as the "four rivers of paradise." At the same time, university and monastery tended sometimes to be in very heated conflict, for though they both aimed at "participation" in and "experience" of the hidden and sacred values implanted in the "ground" and the "beginning," they arrived there by different means: the university by *scientia*, intellectual knowledge, and the monastery by *sapientia*, or mystical contemplation.[1]

In a fascinating study titled *The Sacred Cosmos* Peter Ellard unpacks the dynamism of the intellectual life of the School of Chartres in the twelfth century. Scholars promoted study of the natural cosmos in tandem with grammar and scripture, so that knowledge of the cosmos would lead to knowledge of God. "Liberal arts are used as a way for humanity to understand the cosmos, both on the local and universal level, and it is through the knowledge obtained in the process that one is led to knowledge of God."[2] The basis of study was rooted in the word *cosmos* itself. Greek philosophers such as Pythagoras, Plato, and the Ionians coined the term to describe the universe as ordered, structured, interrelated, and interconnected rather than chaotic. All that is, they believed, exists as a harmonious whole. Because it is ordered and rational, the cosmos could be investigated, studied, and known.[3] William of Thierry held

---

[1] Thomas Merton, *Love and Living*, ed. Naomi Burton Stone and Brother Patrick Hart (New York: Harcourt, 1979), 7.

[2] Peter Ellard, *The Sacred Cosmos: Theological, Philosophical, and Scientific Conversations in the Twelfth-Century School of Chartres* (Scranton, PA: University of Scranton Press, 2007), 16.

[3] Ibid., xxiv–xxvn1.

that divine love is the basis of all that exists. God, he said, does not merely love but *is* love and is present in the cosmos as the ontological core of its being. This love is not something added but is fundamental to the cosmos. The cosmos would not exist and could not exist without it.[4] Ellard highlights the deep, integral relationship between the human person (microcosm) and the cosmos (macrocosm), and the role of learning (study) in the cosmic whole. He writes:

> Rather than seeing the sense world as lacking value or goodness and as being distant from God, William and Thierry presented it in most positive terms as a way to God. They recognized its sacred character not in and of itself simply because it does not and cannot exist in and of itself. Its existence is tied to—and cannot be understood apart from—God. The cosmos, for William and Thierry, is a sacred image of God and it contains the Spirit of God in its very being. Humanity's primary task is to experience the world, to contemplate and understand it, and thereby to proceed to knowledge of God and, ultimately, to union and consummation with God.[5]

In the following century Scholastic theologians such as Thomas Aquinas and Bonaventure continued the pursuit of knowledge as contemplation and prayerful integration of living in the cosmos. Bonaventure, in particular, saw the study of theology as the path to personal holiness. Knowledge, he indicated, was not the end of study but the means to love. Wisdom is knowledge deepened by love, and the highest wisdom, contemplative wisdom, entails a love that transcends all understanding and knowledge:

> But if you wish to know how these things come about, ask grace not instruction, desire not understanding, the groaning of prayer not diligent reading, the Spouse not the teaching, God not man, darkness not clarity, not light

---

[4] Ibid., 161.
[5] Ibid., 204.

but the fire that totally inflames and carries us into God by ecstatic unctions and burning affections. This fire is God, and his furnace is in Jerusalem; and Christ enkindles it in the heat of his burning passion.[6]

What Bonaventure pointed out, like his contemporaries, is that true knowledge is found in neither book learning nor information; it is the life of the spirit. Only a combination of the spiritual life and learning can lead to a penetrating vision of the truth of reality. He described the contemplative theologian as a *perscrutator*, a treasure hunter or a seeker of pearls, one who fathoms the unsuspected depths of the divine mystery, searching out its inmost hiding places and revealing its most beautiful jewels.[7] The searcher of divine depths must be on the journey to God. There is no purely speculative conceptual determination of God; God is not the consequence of pure thought. To make God into a purely speculative act creates confusion. Rather, theology is to discover the depths of God so as to orient one toward an encounter through union in love. Love becomes a conceptual determination (of God) at the junction of theory and practice; that is, love discloses God. Emmanuel Falque states: "Any strictly theo-logical truth, one that has its roots in God, will no longer be content with its unique objective determination. Such a truth will take on a performative sense, one that is transforming for the subject that states it, or it will not exist. . . . Knowledge through love is the only thing that puts in motion whoever comes to know them."[8]

Bonaventure warned against intellectual pursuits divorced from soul building and God seeking as dead ends: "Christ goes away when the mind attempts to behold this wisdom through intellectual eyes; since it is not the intellect that can go in there,

---

[6] Bonaventure, *Itinerarium mentis in Deum* 7.6 (5:313), trans. Ewert Cousins, *Bonaventure: The Soul's Journey into God, The Tree of Life, The Major Life of Saint Francis* (New York: Paulist Press, 1978), 115.

[7] Emmanuel Falque, "The Phenomenological Act of *Perscrutatio* in the Proemium of St. Bonaventure's Commentary on the Sentences," trans. Elisa Mangina, *Medieval Philosophy and Theology* 10 (2001): 11.

[8] Ibid., 18.

but the heart."[9] The type of knowledge that leads to wisdom
and to the depth of reality is self-involving. Learning is not the
acquisition of knowledge (by which we shut ourselves off from
the world) but the self-emptying needed to encounter the mystery
of God. Merton writes: "Learning to be oneself means learning to
die in order to live. It means discovering in the ground of one's
being a 'self' which is ultimate and indestructible which not only
survives the destruction of all other more superficial selves but
finds its identity affirmed and clarified by their destruction."[10]
Knowledge is transformative and performative, for the one who
sees the truth of things becomes a revealer of the truth in a life
well lived. What Bonaventure described is what most medievalists maintained, that true knowledge forms an inner wholeness.
Knowledge renders one more part of the cosmic whole when it
is deepened by love. It is never an end in itself but always a step
toward ever deeper, richer love and transforming union.[11]

The goal of the university was to liberate the spark within,
the inmost center *(scintilla animae)*, a freedom beyond freedom,
a self beyond all ego, a being beyond the created realm, a consciousness that transcends all divisions, all separations. Knowledge, therefore, was in the service of love. "To activate this spark
is *not* to be like Plotinus, alone with the Alone," Merton writes.
Rather, "the 'spark' which is my true self is the flash of the Absolute recognizing itself in me."[12] The human person on the journey
to wholeness of self and self-in-world reflected back to the cosmos that which one had learned. The place where knowledge of
the whole could be pursued was called a university because the
breadth of knowledge between the arts and sciences deepened the
relationship between microcosm (human person) and macrocosm
(world); knowledge of self, knowledge of cosmos, and knowledge
of God were bound together in a harmonious whole—turning as
one—and the luminous thread that held all together was love.

---

[9] Bonaventure, *Hex.* 2.32 (5:342), trans. José De Vinck, *Collations on
Six Days* (Paterson, NJ: St. Anthony Guild Press, 1970), 39.

[10] Merton, *Love and Living*, 5.

[11] Zachary Hayes, "Bonaventure of Bagnoregio: A Paradigm for
Franciscan Theologians?" in *The Franciscan Intellectual Tradition*, ed.
Elise Saggau (New York: The Franciscan Institute, 2002), 56.

[12] Merton, *Love and Living*, 10.

What Must I Know?

The breakdown between knowing and loving began with the rise of heliocentrism and the advent of modern science. Whereas in the Middle Ages the power to unify the many came from the one God who created heaven and earth, in the Enlightenment the power to unify the many was sought in the individual. The changing scientific world view threw the harmonious whole of theology, philosophy, and cosmology into doubt and disbelief. This transition of knowledge from object to subject imposed a burden on the human person to make sense of the world by rational thought alone. Descartes's self-thinking subject initiated a downward trend of disconnectedness. Thinking became detached from anything outside of self so that the self-initiated thought collapsed into a dead end under its own weight.

What was the purpose of knowledge in a world divorced from God? The university became a system of objective knowledge, methodical and mechanistic. Knowledge was no longer in the service of love but in the service of power. Love was reduced to sentiment or inward piety, untethered from the world of meaning and purpose. Objective knowledge rose as humans became decentered in the cosmos. God became divorced from the cosmos, and emphasis was placed on logical reasoning and the intelligibility of the natural order. William Ockham helped invent modernity by denying the reality of universals outside of the human mind and human language and by emphasizing the divine will. God's will cannot be limited by structures of human rationality, he claimed, for absolute volitional freedom and omnipotence means that God can do whatever God desires. Our only certainty can come from direct sensory observation or from self-evident logical propositions, not from rational speculations about invisible realities and universal essences. Ockham's "razor" held that conceptual entities should not be multiplied unnecessarily.[13] What cannot be observed cannot be known. God creates the universe, according to Ockham, but the patterns we

---

[13] See Richard E. Rubenstein, *Aristotle's Children: How Christians, Muslims, and Jews Rediscovered Ancient Wisdom and Illuminated the Middle Ages* (New York: Harcourt, 2003), 252–53.

discover are the products of our mental processes, not evidence of divine intentions. Human knowledge therefore is limited to the contingent and empirical. God's reality and human rational knowledge are infinitely distant from each other. By separating religion from science, one could approach nature with a new optimism:

> Creation presents itself as a gift to us. The gift, however, bears no connection to the giver—except in the tautological sense that a gift must be given. Therefore, nature as creation can be unpacked. And since we are cut off from God except in the act of faith, we might as well unpack that gift and make ourselves at home here.[14]

The range of knowledge that made up the university no longer related to a harmonious whole but to a mechanized universe. As disciplines developed into specialties and sub-specialties, the university became a "multiversity." Instead of educating to know the universe as a web of interconnected life, education became the study of highly specialized fields. Not only did students concentrate in a discipline, but they did so to the exclusion of others. The whole idea of developing human identity integral to the cosmos was subsumed in the drive for mastery and success. Elaine Ecklund notes, "Movements to secularize the academy had relegated religious perspectives to the sidelines, or shut them out altogether."[15] The separation of science from humanistic fields such as religion, history, and English created a model of university life that did not allow any positive role for religious people, institutions, or ideas on campus. One had to leave religion at the door or wholly privatize it. As a result, students did not learn how to connect science with areas of meaning and value. By separating religion from university education, Eckland suggests, the university lost its soul.

Surprisingly, it was the German philosopher Immanuel Kant who sought to revive the whole interlocking constellation of being-through-knowledge following the rise of science. For

---

[14] Cited in ibid., 254.

[15] Elaine Howard Ecklund, "Religion, Science, and the Academy," *Harmonist* (September 20, 2010).

Kant, ontology was transformed into epistemology. Whereas the medievalists (following the ancients) sought understanding by observing and reflecting on the cosmos, Kant combined intuition, understanding, and sense experience in the human person as cosmic traveler. His brilliant philosophical system showed that all knowledge is synthetic and thus presupposes unification at every level. The world is like a work of art that the subject must engage, thus placing a significant emphasis on the role of consciousness in the act of knowing. Kant recognized wholeness in nature long before modern biologists discovered open systems. His holistic account of nature as organized being with formative power plays out in his epistemology. Inner teleology and outer teleology must be related if knowledge is to have value; self-consciousness and self-conscious subjectivity presuppose otherness or encounter. Mark Taylor writes: "What Kant discovered is the principle of constitutive relationality, in which identity is differential rather than oppositional."[16] Hence the human person cannot presume a role in creation; rather, one must intelligently engage the path to greater wholeness by asking: What must I know? What must I do? What must I hope for?

It was perhaps the Reformation more than German philosophy that influenced modern education. The reversal of transcendence in immanence at the heart of the Protestant tradition lodged itself in radical subjectivity of "unhappy consciousness."[17] The combination of Reformation theology and education fit nicely with a mechanistic world. The Reformers' focus on sinful humanity placed a much greater emphasis on grace and the power of God to save. Since the real is always elsewhere, God remains remotely in transcendence and humans are trapped in a world of despair, darkness, and death. Knowledge is the means to exit the trap of worldly despair by creating the conditions for a new paradise. The rise of specializations in law, science, mathematics, and literature aimed to create the new Adam and a new Garden of Eden. Money, wealth, power, and success were not only signs of being blessed by God, but keys to life and happiness.

---

[16] Mark Taylor, *After God* (Chicago: University of Chicago Press, 2007), 110.
[17] Ibid., 154.

The university became a new Eden, the place where the world could be recreated and humankind restored to its central place in the cosmos. The anthropocentrism of the university, with the human person at the center of all knowledge (and hence center of the universe), stripped the world of its divine character and left the world of nature to fend for itself.

Since the rise of the modern university, knowledge has advanced without soul, becoming power without aim. The modern university has become an obstacle to the universe, that is, integral wholeness, insofar as it does not educate us humans to bear the universe in our beings or a consciousness that the universe bears us in its being. Merton writes: "It mass produces uneducated graduates who are unfit for anything except to take part in an elaborate and complete artificial charade which they call 'life.'"[18] Instead of education for the flourishing of life's wholeness, we educate to disconnect and die. Our universities have become fragmented silos of specialties where no two people speak the same language on any given day. Students are encouraged to succeed in their studies, not to contemplate truth, as if success is the goal of study. If contemporary education is failing the cosmos, it is because we have lost the integral relationship between living and loving. Unless we change the way we think, we will not change the way we act. Our mechanized world of mechanized systems with mechanized humans can no longer continue. We are fragmenting fast. The beginning of a sustainable future must begin with the integral knowledge of God, self, and cosmos.

The Role of Thought in Evolution

The starting point for educational reform is awakening to the fact that we no longer live in a mechanistic universe. Ours is an evolutionary universe. Mechanisms can operate efficiently, but as closed systems they cannot evolve. Despite the fact that evolution has been known for over a hundred years, we continue to educate according to a mechanized course of study. One chooses a major and then breaks it down into parts, consuming large amounts of information all along the way. Do we ever ask: What

---

[18] Merton, *Love and Living*, 11.

forms the whole, the universe of study? How is human identity formed in relation to the cosmos through study? The integral relationship between living and loving has become irrelevant to the mastery of a discipline in modern education. We no longer educate to love.

British anthropologist Gregory Bateson, in *Steps to an Ecology of Mind*, criticizes our Western form of knowledge because it is too linear and does not account for the interplay of consciousness and experience. He described the individual, society, and ecosystem as part of one large cybernetic system that he called Mind.[19] We know things within the larger realm of consciousness not as objects outside ourselves but interrelated to ourselves, in what cyberneticists call "feedback loops."[20] Only when thought and emotion are combined are we able to obtain real knowledge, that is, a knowledge that belongs as much to the body as to the mind. Theodore Roszak writes: "Information does not create ideas; ideas create information. Ideas are integrating patterns that derive not from information but from experience."[21]

We cannot envision a new world without changing the way we think. In a world saturated with bits of information, we need to reclaim loving at the heart of thinking. As the medievalists remind us, thinking is integral to loving *(amor ipse notitia est)*. Teilhard de Chardin emphasized that thinking undergirds evolution because without real thought, the process of amorization cannot go forward. To think is to unify, to make wholes where there are scattered fragments, "not merely to record it, but to confer on it a form of unity it would have had if it had not been thought."[22] Thinking is a spiritual act. It is that long, deep,

---

[19] Gregory Bateson, *Steps to an Ecology of Mind: Collected Essays in Anthropology, Psychiatry, Evolution, and Epistemology* (Chicago: University of Chicago Press, 2000).

[20] For an extensive discussion on cybernetics, see Fritjof Capra, *The Web of Life: A New Scientific Understanding of Living Systems* (New York: Doubleday, 1996), 51–71.

[21] Theodore Roszak, *The Cult of Information* (Berkeley and Los Angeles, CA: University of California Press, 1994), 87–88.

[22] Pierre Teilhard de Chardin, *The Human Phenomenon*, trans. Sarah Appleton-Weber (Brighton: Sussex Academic Press, 1999), 176.

hard look at reality where the knowing process becomes more than the vision itself. Thinking requires use of the intellect as well as judgment, consciousness, and connectivity to the object of thought. It is not mere information but the synthesizing of information into ideas and insight. Thinking is the work of the spirit, not only the human spirit but God's Spirit. Each time the mind comprehends something it unites the world in a new way.[23] It participates in the generation of the divine Word flowing from the fountain of love, creating a new unity through the Spirit. Teilhard writes: "To discover and know is to actually extend the universe ahead and to complete it."[24] We pursue knowledge not to gain information or control life but to organize life for a greater unity and deepening of love.

Teilhard discusses two types of knowledge: one is an abstract and timeless knowledge of "the world of ideas and principles," which he instinctively distrusted. The second is a "real" knowledge that is in constant development—the conscious actuation of the universe about us. The first type of knowledge leads to geometry and theology, while the second leads to science and mysticism; a type of mysticism not based on possession of a complete truth from heaven but part of the ongoing process of earth.[25] He warns against any abstract knowledge that is divorced from physical reality, since abstract knowledge is a faded reality compared to boundless presence. Abstract knowledge is conceptual understanding that undergirds a will to power, since only the individual can hold concepts. Such knowledge cannot further evolution nor can it deepen love because it is isolated in the knower. It forms individual ideas but leaves the physical relational world adrift. Even among physicists, Teilhard notes, the advent of quantum physics and the non-deterministic nature of reality has led to the imposition of the investigator's mind on shifting patterns of phenomena.[26] This has been unhelpful to furthering evolution. A brief comparison of mechanistic and

---

[23] Ibid.
[24] Ibid., 35.
[25] Ibid., 40.
[26] Ibid., 5.

holistic systems shows that the difference between linear and holistic thinking results in a difference of values:

Thinking		Values	
Mechanistic	*Holistic*	*Mechanistic*	*Holistic*
rational	intuitive	expansion	conservation
analysis	synthesis	competition	cooperation
reductionist	integrative	quantity	quality
linear	nonlinear	domination	partnership

Source: Capra, *The Web of Life*, 10.

True knowledge must engage physical reality because this reality is the basis of who we are. Discovery of the world is ultimately self-discovery and discovery of God. The human's evolving consciousness must be seen as integral to the physical world, and the physical world must be seen as integral to the human's desire to know. Teilhard rejected Scholastic theology because it divorced knowledge from experience. Abstract knowledge is sterile and lifeless. This type of abstract knowledge has made theology impotent to effect real transformation of life in evolution. Rather, knowledge must deepen and make whole that which is real and that in turn will lead to greater unity. This type of organic knowledge requires faith in the power of matter to reveal God. Faith and thought belong together. Faith begins with trust in the ultimate goodness (or love) at the heart of being. It is trust in the reality of being alive. It is not so much an inner spiritual experience detached from the real but a wholehearted surrender to the ineffable, ultimate depth of being itself, to God. Although we usually think about faith as separate from reason and supernatural by grace, Teilhard says that faith and reason are built into the fabric of evolution. The one who believes "forms an intellectual synthesis." Religion, education, and evolution go together. Each person is to know so as to bring into existence something new; to gather "the dust of experience into a unity." Each person is to build his or her soul by bringing the widely scattered elements of experience into a unified whole.[27]

---

[27] King, *Teilhard's Mysticism of Knowing*, 37.

The Catholic Intellectual Tradition

The Catholic intellectual tradition is based on the maxim that faith seeks understanding *(fides quaerens intellectum)*; blind faith is ripe for deception. Teilhard suggests that the Catholic intellectual tradition can play a vital role in the forward movement of evolution, if it embraces evolution as the narrative of unfolding reality. His evolutionary epistemology illuminates a new way of knowing that is free from fixed concepts or defined essences. He opts for an active engagement of the mind in the evolution of consciousness. In *Where Is Knowing Going?* Jesuit theologian John Haughey returns to the root of the word *catholic* to discover a dynamic principle of "wholemaking" that is consonant with Teilhard's thought. The word *catholic* connotes a divine presence of wholemaking or leavening the stuff of life to create a greater whole.

> Right out of the block the term catholicity means openness and in contrast to what is incomplete, partial, sectarian, factional, tribal and selective. The term catholicity promises a worldview that is universal in classical Greek; kata (a preposition) and holos (a noun) when coupled become *kath-holou* an adverb meaning "wholly" and *katholikos*, a substantive that is best rendered "catholicity" in English. The word connotes movement towards universality or wholeness.[28]

Building on the insights of Bernard Lonergan, Haughey sees the work of epistemology as thinking that makes greater wholes. For Lonergan, the best route to knowledge is to develop a strong grasp of one's own subjectivity and of the operations of one's own consciousness rather than seeking more and more information about stuff "out there."[29] The knowing process is an orientation to the real and the potentialities of being but one must be

---

[28] John Haughey, SJ, *Where Is Knowing Going: The Horizons of the Knowing Subject* (Washington, DC: Georgetown University Press, 2010), 40.

[29] Ibid., 42.

conscious of one's openness to being. For too long we have let concepts developed by others do our thinking for us. Our educational system is like cardboard boxes in a room that someone fills with mental stuff. In Lonergan's view, thinking begins with a subject's grasp of oneself as open to the real. Notions give birth to concepts when we encounter reality with unrestricted wonder, and attend to the real as an act of engagement. The knowing process is not the grasp and regurgitation of facts; it is engagement with reality as we encounter reality, living into the questions of our deepest desires. God is the name of genuine unrestricted love bubbling up at the heart of life, attracting more insight, wonder, and creativity. Haughey speaks of catholicity as a virtue of ceaseless wonder that, by nature of its own inner spiritual dynamism, cannot be controlled or manipulated. As a dynamic engagement of the mind, catholicity is bound up with personal authenticity, having a grasp of one's own self and self-consciousness. Lonergan suggests that personal authenticity is built on fruitful dialogue, for it is in genuine understanding of self that knowledge expands into being itself. This approach allows us to see the knowing process in a way that extricates us from the tethers of concepts. By conceptual preoccupation "we let concepts spawned by other minds do our thinking for us."[30] Knowledge that forms from the dynamism of the mind's thought processes is not information gathering or storing concepts in a mental warehouse; rather, knowledge is the energy of desire. Information can tell us about things, but knowledge is an exploration of the mind that seeks to form wholes out of thought fragments gained from experience, judgment, and reflection. We seek to know to fall more deeply in love.

Haughey's notion of catholic as wholemaking is consonant with Teilhard's epistemology of intellectual synthesizing unity. Both scholars (like Lonergan) see an openness of the mind to more being and hence a deepening of truth. Teilhard identifies coherence and fecundity as the two criteria of truth. Revealed knowledge must fit into a greater whole of which it is a part and lend itself to more life. Truth, therefore, cannot be static or rigidly defined; rather, it is part of life and is a forward-moving process. It is the diaphanous appearance of God to the one who

---

[30] Ibid., 42–43.

can see into the depth of being and who can harness being into the fire of life. While Teilhard's principles of coherence and fecundity are helpful to discern what is true and good, Haughey's principle of wholemaking illuminates unity and beauty. Beauty is the harmony of contrasts, and thinking enhances beauty. As the mind gathers the fragments of knowledge into a more unified synthesis, it promotes beauty in the world. The active engagement of the mind orients itself toward the wholeness of life. The "whole" is actualized by the observer, who transforms the perceived data into wholes; each perceiver is a "particular actualizing of the whole."[31] When the task of study is understood in this dynamic context, it does not aim to refine what has already been defined. Rather, it aims to make wholes out of what is received from the past and perceived in the present. An epistemology consonant with evolution demands a "turn to the whole," directing us away from radical subjectivity of unhappy consciousness and from particularities that isolate, opening us up to the dynamic engagement of reality. Instead of neatly packaged concepts, the mind is drawn to make sense of experience (or data), even though it may not yet be explicit. Knowledge progresses as we discover more about the world we live in. When the mind can engage reality as a question rather than imposing prefabricated answers on it, then one can participate creatively in evolution.

Education as Wholemaking

While the Catholic intellectual tradition has the capacity to transform human persons into evolutionary wholemakers, it has succumbed to the mechanistic system of the secular university. Although theology woke up in the twentieth century to the larger philosophical and cultural shifts of postmodernity, feminism, the option for the poor, and religious pluralism, it did not wake up to modern science. Theology and philosophy still are not integrated throughout the whole gamut of study but have settled into academic silos in the same way that the sciences have sequestered

---

[31] Pierre Teilhard de Chardin, *Christianity and Evolution*, trans. René Hague (New York: Harcourt, 1971), 100; King, *Teilhard's Mysticism of Knowing*, 5.

themselves in silos of specializations. Religion and science are estranged (and usually housed on opposite ends of the campus). As a result, there are few theologians or theologically interested philosophers at universities where the most significant scientific work is done. Students continue to be trained in theology departments independent of any broader integration with the sciences in the university. Paul Crowley writes:

> While the Church in fact has a distinguished history of serving as a patron to the natural sciences (despite the debacle surrounding Galileo), theology in general has become a discipline so tightly bound by narrowly dogmatic and ecclesiastical concerns that it risks becoming irrelevant to a larger culture . . . that is increasingly framed by the paradigms and epistemes of the natural sciences. The challenge . . . is not only one engaging science per se, but engaging a culture where religion as a serious voice is too readily dismissed, due in part to the hegemony of secular worldviews where a certain "scientism" prevails, even as an absolute form of knowledge. On the other hand, theology itself cannot expect to be taken seriously by the sciences if it forgets that its chief concern is the inexhaustible mystery we call God, and instead presents its own set of absolutes to the sciences. . . . If theology cannot engage the sciences, then it has no voice at the table concerning the significant issues facing humanity today. If theology cannot engage a culture that has been framed by the paradigms of science, then theology itself risks self-marginalization. Christian faith itself is at risk of seeming irrelevant, and God increasingly distant from the horizon of human understanding.[32]

We need to rediscover the link between knowledge and love, a penetrating vision of wisdom by which one knows in a way more deeply than the mind alone can grasp. Knowledge is to deepen our participation in the whole, not to control it. When we are

---

[32] Paul Crowley, SJ, "Jesuit Theology, Scientific Culture and the Challenge of Climate Change," in *Shaping the Future: Networking Jesuit Higher Education in a Globalizing World*, ed. Frank Brennan, SJ (Washington, DC: Association of Jesuit Colleges and Universities, 2010), 24.

unconscious of our connectedness to the world of things, we cannot be intelligently related to them. We know objects as data not as mirrors of reflection. The self that is divorced from the world of conscious experience is a self that tries to control the world of experience. One knows intellectually but not intelligently; that is, one knows from the operations of the brain but not from the body of the whole person, the senses, and the emotions. Our modern system of knowledge is an efficient, mechanized system of information gathering that can now be done by a computer as well as by a human person. Knowledge is taken in as a product for individual gain. One consumes information, takes it in, chews it up, and spits it out without necessarily being changed by it. Consumptive knowledge leads to individual power without regard for the inherent good of the other. Such knowledge cannot make the human person whole; neither can it connect the human person to the larger whole of family, community, and universe. When knowledge isolates and individualizes, it fragments love into a thousand little pieces.

Wisdom is knowledge deepened by love. It is found in the experience of the sacred and the inner heart. It brings to light the depths of things in a way that both reveals and veils the divine mystery. The wise person thinks with the heart. If the world is edging toward a posthuman one, it is because we are educating to disconnect ourselves from human personhood and desire, including our longing for wholeness, wellness, and community. Evolution depends on wisdom and our capacity to love. And education plays a vital role in how we love.

Chapter Nine

Technology and Noogenesis

The decentering of the human person in the cosmos and the mechanization of our educational system have left a gaping hole in the heart of the cosmos. Evolution has become a blind process while love presses onward toward more being and consciousness. If love cannot find a place to dwell in the disconnected human person, where should it direct its energy? Toward anything that will connect us to more being and consciousness, hence the meteoric rise of computer technology. Whereas the Black Death gave new impetus to the rise of science in the Middle Ages, the prevalence of war and violence in the twentieth century gave new impetus to the rise of computer technology. Just as an apocalyptic mentality emerged after the Black Death and the decimation of Western Europe, so too, a new apocalyptic spirit arose in the twentieth century marked by two world wars and the rise of nuclear power. Alan Turing, a British intelligence office and cryptanalyst, developed the computer to decipher German codes. Turing believed that a machine could be made to mimic human intelligence. In 1950 he developed a test in which a computer was set up to fool judges into believing that it was human. The test was performed by conducting a text-based conversation on a subject. If the computer's responses were indistinguishable from those of a human, it had passed the Turing test and could be said to be "thinking." John McCarthy coined the term *artificial intelligence* in 1956, defining it as "the science and engineering of making intelligent machines."[1] Although the computer was invented for the purpose of intelligence, the potential of its power was quickly seized upon in a century of violent wars and rampant death. Nick Bostrom writes: "In the postwar era, many optimistic futurists who had become suspicious of collectively orchestrated social change found a new home for their hopes in scientific and technological progress."[2] The success of the computer to process complex information at speeds beyond human mental power made its development attractive. Within a short span of fifty years, computer-based technology has become the principal organizer of modern life.

Transhumanism

Up to the twentieth century the philosophical challenge was to think nature—and ourselves in the presence of nature. Today, the philosophical challenge is to think technology . . . and ourselves in the presence of technology.[3] Technology has come to define who and what we are; it has become the mirror of our deepest desires. Noreen Herzfeld writes:

> In today's world, technology is central to our understanding of ourselves and the environment around us. . . . Technology plays an undeniably greater role in our lives than it has at any previous time in human history. That greater role is also seen in the power to create something new. . . . To create the new is to go outside of nature . . . the German existentialist Martin Heidegger observes that the ancient craftsman certainly made something new when he constructed a chair. A doctor might bring new health to a patient. However, neither imposed a new form on nature; rather, each worked with what is already implicit

---

[1] Leora Morgenstern and Sheila A. McIlraith, "John McCarthy's Legacy," *Journal of Artificial Intelligence* 175 (January 2011): 1–24.

[2] Nick Bostrom, "A History of Transhumanist Thought," *Journal of Evolution and Technology* 14, no. 1 (April 2005): 4.

[3] Carl Mitcham, "The Philosophical Challenge of Technology," *American Catholic Philosophical Association Proceedings* 40 (1996): 45.

in the wood or the body. . . . The new products of modern technology do not simply "disclose" or shape nature but transform and replace nature. In this way, modern technology gives us heretofore undreamed of power.[4]

The term *transhumanism* refers to technologies that can improve mental and physical aspects of the human condition such as suffering, disease, aging, and death; it is "the belief that humans must wrest their biological destiny from evolution's blind process of random variation . . . favoring the use of science and technology to overcome biological limitations."[5] The term was first used by Julian Huxley, brother of Aldous Huxley and friend of Pierre Teilhard de Chardin. In *Religion without Revelation*, Huxley wrote:

> The human species can, if it wishes, transcend itself—not just sporadically, an individual one way, an individual there in another way—but in its entirety, as humanity. We need a name for this new belief. Perhaps transhumanism will serve: man remaining man, but transcending himself, by realizing new possibilities of and *for his human nature*.[6]

While Huxley saw transhumanism as a positive step for the whole of humankind, transhumanists today focus on individual enhancement. Transhumanists build on the idea that the mind is a powerful information processor whose information can be repackaged in a different medium. Mind is essentially what we are, and the body houses the mind. In the not-too-distant future, transhumanists claim, it may be possible to repackage the mind in a new medium.

In a 2006 *New York Times* article "Merely Human? That's So Yesterday" Ashlee Vance explored the futuristic vision of Ray

---

[4] Noreen Herzfeld, *Technology and Religion: Remaining Human in a Co-created World* (West Conshohocken, PA: Templeton Press, 2009), 9.

[5] Archimedes Carag Articulo, "Towards an Ethics of Technology: Re-Exploring Teilhard de Chardin's Theory of Technology and Evolution, available on the scribd.com website.

[6] Julian Huxley, *Religion Without Revelation* (1927; reprint Westport, CT: Greenwood Press, 1979), 195.

Kurzweil (who coined the term *Singularity*), "a time, possibly just a couple decades from now, when a superior intelligence will dominate and life will take on an altered form that we can't predict or comprehend in our current, limited state. At that point, human beings and machines will so effortlessly and elegantly merge that poor health, the ravages of old age and even death itself will all be things of the past." Kurzweil continues: "We will transcend all of the limitations of our biology. . . . This is what it means to be human—to extend who we are."[7] The Singularity will not be engaged by all, however. Rather, "the Haves, who have financial means and intelligence to embrace the new technology, will live on for hundreds of years while the Have-Nots, who are hampered by their antiquated, corporeal forms and beliefs will eventually die out."[8]

Article 1 of the World Transhumanist Association's declaration, according to its website, states: "Humanity stands to be profoundly affected by science and technology in the future. We envision the possibility of broadening human potential by overcoming aging, cognitive shortcomings, involuntary suffering, and our confinement to planet Earth." Although Kurzweil's dawning age of Techno sapiens seems out of science fiction, it looms over us as the dawning real. Techno sapiens is arising not only through artificial intelligence but also through genetics and neuroscience. In the area of synthetic biology, organisms can now be synthesized in the laboratory from DNA blueprints and chemical parts. Whereas the cost of synthesizing DNA in 1999 was about a hundred thousand dollars, in 2009 a DNA synthesizer could be purchased on eBay for less than a thousand dollars.[9] Some synthetic biologists anticipate that in the near future we will be able to design our own offspring. For the first time in evolution, technology affords our species control of its own destiny, or as the editors of *Nature* wrote in 2007, "God has competition."[10] Kevin Kelly, a leader in transhumanism, says that

---

[7] Ashlee Vance, "Merely Human? That's So Yesterday," available on the nytimes.com website.

[8] In ibid.

[9] Michael Specter, "A Life of Its Own," *The New Yorker* (September 28, 2009), 61.

[10] In ibid., 61.

the future of evolution is about "the marriage of the born and the made."[11] But no one seems to be attending to this marriage, and the pace of technology is increasing exponentially, outstripping our ability to absorb it or reflect on our use of it. Michael Specter writes: "When the IBM 360 computer was released in 1964, the top model came with eight megabytes of main memory, and cost more than two million dollars. Today, cell phones with a thousand times the memory of that computer can be bought for about a hundred dollars."[12] The myth of technology is appealing, and the power of technology is seductive. We now have the power not only to evolve ourselves through technology but also to direct the course of evolution. In biological evolution nature influences or mutually interacts with the species, but in technological evolution the species controls nature. Biological evolution and technological evolution have become co-terminus, and a new posthuman species is emerging in evolution. W. Brian Arthur writes that "conceptually, biology is becoming technology. And physically, technology is becoming biology."[13] In the past, evolution proceeded by way of natural selection; today, evolution advances by creativity and invention. This has been going on for the last hundred years, Kurzweil states. Only now are we becoming conscious of what is happening to us and by us. We must now see what this new age of technology holds for us.

InfoPhilia

Artificial intelligence is spawning a philosophical shift today, from reality constructed of matter and energy to reality constructed on information.[14] We not only project onto our technologies our dreams and desires, but our technologies have become extensions of our very selves. Books such as *Being Digital* indicate

---

[11] Kevin Kelly, *Out of Control: The New Biology of Machines, Social Systems, and the Economic World* (New York: Basic Books, 1994), 6.

[12] Specter, "A Life of Its Own," 64.

[13] W. Brian Arthur, *The Nature of Technology: What It Is and How It Evolves* (New York: Free Press, 2009), 208.

[14] Stephen R. Garner, "Praying with Machines: Religious Dreaming in Cyberspace," *Stimulus* 12, no. 3 (2004): 20.

that information has come to define reality. With artificial intelligence, Stephen Garner writes, "the essence of a person can be separated from their body and represented in digital form—an immortal digital soul waiting to be freed—an idea that some see as medieval dualism reincarnated."[15] The term *cybergnosticism* has been coined to describe the "belief that the physical world is impure or inefficient, and that existence in the form of pure information is better and should be pursued."[16] Michael Heim sees strong links between artificial intelligence and Platonic, Gnostic, and Hermetic traditions that emphasize the goodness of spiritual reality and corruption of material reality, an idea consonant with cyber life and posthumanism:

> Cyberspace is Platonism as a working product. The cybernaut seated before us, strapped into sensory-input devices, appears to be, and is indeed, lost to this world. Suspended in computer space, the cybernaut leaves the prison of the body and emerges in a world of digital sensation.[17]

The power of technology is seductive. Americans alone spend billions of dollars each year to enhance their bodies and promote wellness through technology. One has only to consider the endless string of television commercials that promise better bones, better heart, and a better body—a newer, younger, more agile, and healthier you. The prospect of carrying around one's own gene card is now on the horizon. Like carrying a credit card, the gene card will carry all of a person's DNA information and provide constant health monitoring. In the future it may also serve as an identity card. Kurzweil extends the utopian health ideal to immortality by downloading the brain into neurochips. As we move beyond mortality through computational technology, our identity will be based on our evolving mind file. We will be software not hardware. By replacing living

---

[15] Ibid., 20; see also D. O. Berger, "Cybergnosticism: Or, Who Needs a Body Anyway?" *Concordia Journal* 25 (1999): 340–45.

[16] Garner, "Praying with Machines," 20.

[17] Michael Heim, *The Metaphysics of Virtual Reality* (New York: Oxford University Press, 1993), 89.

bodies with virtual bodies capable of transferral and duplication, we will become disembodied superminds.[18] Hence, we will be able to achieve some type of immortality or extended life. Robert Geraci states, "Our new selves will be infinitely replicable, allowing them to escape the finality of death."[19] This futuristic "post-biological" computer-based immortality is one also envisioned by Hans Moravec, who claims that the advent of intelligent machines (Machina sapiens) will provide humanity with personal immortality by mind transplant. We will be able to "wake up matter" by infusing it with intelligence and information.[20]

Many transhumanists look to a postbiological future where super informational beings will flourish. Through mechanical means we will be able to overcome the limitations of the body, including suffering and death, and attain artificial eschatological paradise. Bart Kosko, a professor of electrical engineering at the University of Southern California, writes: "Biology is not destiny. It was never more than tendency. It was just nature's first quick and dirty way to compute with meat. Chips are destiny."[21] Carter Phipps enlightens us on the cyber-punk slang "meat is messy," meaning that the biological human body is bloody, sticky, and breaks down. The digitized body will be free and unconstrained by the physical and temporal limitations of the flesh.[22] Katherine Hayles, in *How We Became*

---

[18] Kurzweil defines the Singularity as the point at which machines become sufficiently intelligent to start teaching themselves. When the Singularity happens, he states, the world will irrevocably shift from the biological to the mechanical. See Ray Kurzweil, *The Age of Spiritual Machines: When Computers Exceed Human Intelligence* (New York: Viking, 1999), 3–5.

[19] Robert Geraci, "Spiritual Robots: Religion and Our Scientific View of the Natural World," *Theology and Science* 4, no. 3 (2006): 235.

[20] See, for example, Hans Moravec, *Robot: Mere Machine to Transcendent Mind* (New York: Oxford University Press, 1999).

[21] Bart Kosko, *The Fuzzy Future: From Society and Science to Heaven in a Chip* (New York: Harmony Books, 1999), 256.

[22] In Carter Phipps, *Evolutionaries: Unlocking the Spiritual and Cultural Potential of Science's Greatest Idea* (New York: Harper, 2012), 128.

Posthuman, writes, "In the posthuman, there are no essential differences, or absolute demarcations, between bodily existence and computer simulation, cybernetic mechanism and biological organism, robot technology and human goals." She concludes with an admonition: "Humans can either go gently into that good night, joining the dinosaurs as a species that once ruled the earth but is now obsolete, or hang on for a while longer by becoming machines themselves. In either case . . . the age of the human is drawing to a close."[23] Similarly, Robert Jastrow claims, "Human evolution is nearly a finished chapter in the history of life," although the evolution of intelligence will not end because a new species will arise, "a new kind of intelligent life more likely to be made of silicon."[24] While artificial intelligence transhumanists aim toward a new virtual body, they also anticipate a new virtual creation where the earthly garden will wither away and be replaced by a much greater world, a paradise never to be lost.[25]

In *Alone Together* Sherry Turkle says that what was considered normative among older generations, such as personal friendship, dating, conversation, and phone calls, is becoming obsolete among the youth, who can no longer distinguish between real and simulated reality. She notes that 9/11 marked a transition point in that the phone became not simply a helpful instrument but a part of one's personhood; to lose one's cell phone now is to lose a part of one's life. According to Turkle, the average teenager texts about six thousand messages a month. In an interview she said: "Teenagers prefer to text than talk because talking for them involves too much information, too much tension, too much awkwardness. They like the idea of a communication medium in which there doesn't need to be awkwardness. You leave before you're rejected." People are frightened by the world we've made, she states. The economy isn't going right; global warming continues. "We celebrate our technologies because . . .

[23] Katherine Hayles, *How We Became Posthuman: Virtual Bodies in Cybernetics, Literature, and Informatics* (Chicago: University of Chicago Press, 1999), 3, 283.

[24] Robert Jastrow, "Toward an Intelligence Beyond Man's," *Time* 111 (February 20, 1978): 59.

[25] Moravec, *Robot,* 143ff.

people imagine that science and technology will be able to get it right."[26] Technology provides a ray of hope that we can be saved from destruction.

Technology and Ecology: Competing Myths?

The relationship among iPhones, Google, and institutional religion may not seem obvious, but the loss of human identity has stimulated the scientific imagination to fill in the deep hole left by the absence of religion from our everyday lives. The hope for more life and deeper consciousness, once the stuff of religion, has been transferred to a technological utopia. The "I–Thou" relationship has mutated into an "I–phone" relationship. The emergence of a technologically driven, health-crazed culture has been on the rise since the dawn of the modern age. The need to find a new body and new personal identity is becoming more urgent in a culture of consumerism in which the primary commodity is the human person. The financial collapse of the banking industry in 2008, the incredible Ponzi schemes that stripped millions of peoples of their life savings, the failure of the Eurozone to achieve financial stability, and the continuation of global warming all seem to reflect the fact that we no longer know where we are going or what we are doing here. Body and soul have come apart, and there is very little that holds us together.

The rise of postmodernity and the deconstruction of systems can be traced to the rise of modern science, the Protestant Reformation, and the decentralization of the human person. Mark Taylor writes:

> The emergence of the new notion of subjectivity in Protestantism led to the privatization, decentralization, and deregulation of religion, which ran directly counter to the centralization and universalization of authority that the church hierarchy had imposed during the High Middle

---

[26] Interview, Sherry Turkle, September 22, 2009, on her forthcoming book *Alone Together: Why We Expect More from Our Technologies and Less from Each Other* (New York: Basic Books, 2011). The interview is available on the pbs.org website.

Ages. These developments, in turn, contributed to the information and communications revolution that began with print and continues in today's network culture. As religion was privatized and every believer became a priest, the centralized hierarchical authority of the church broke down and authority was distributed among individual believers. Rules and regulations no longer were imposed from above but now emerged from the bottom up through individuals who were separate but equal. These changes were brought about by and promoted literacy and education.[27]

The invention of the printing press played a significant role in the spread of the Reformation. Taylor states: "The coemergence of printing and the Reformation transformed the way in which information was produced, distributed, and consumed in the early modern period."[28] Printed words were "out there" on a flat surface, in a radical sense dead, "subject to dynamic resurrection."[29] The subjective control of word-event became the subjective control of nature itself. The Reformers' need to save the subject was aided by the printed word, which, as the word of God, could directly affect a person's life. This was important because modern science arose as a dominant cultural force, pushing humans into an aimless cosmic peregrination. The Reformation offered the human person divine protection and grace in a restless world. However, the Reformation overvalued the individual to the exclusion of the larger whole, shaping personal salvation into radical subjectivity. Some scholars see that the consequences of the Reformation are now evident in economic collapse, greed, and, we might add, anti-ecological consciousness.[30] Historian Lynn White claims that the emphasis of Christianity on human salvation and dominion over nature made it possible to exploit

---

[27] Mark Taylor, *After God* (Chicago: University of Chicago Press, 2007), 73–74.

[28] Ibid., 74.

[29] See Walter Ong, *Orality and Literacy: The Technologizing of the Word* (London: Methuen, 1982), 32–33.

[30] See, for example, Brad Gregory, *The Unintended Reformation: How a Religious Revolution Secularized Society* (Cambridge: Belknap/Harvard University Press, 2012).

nature in a mood of indifference to the feelings of natural objects. In the post-Reformation period, all but humans have been excluded from grace.[31]

It is not surprising that the Protestant Reformation focused on the human subject as the object of salvation, not only in response to a corrupt church but to a church out of touch with modern science. By the time we entered the twentieth century the cry "God is dead" could be heard throughout Western culture, as nihilism and alienation emerged in the forms of communism, Marxism, and existentialism. We created technologies to resurrect ourselves from what seemed like endless destruction—war, poverty, industrialization, and increasing anonymity. Instead of saving ourselves, however, we have become more controlling of ourselves and one another out of fear and distrust. The will to mastery has become more urgent as technology threatens to slip from human control.

The lure of artificial intelligence is its promise of a better life through artificial means. Just as Platonists spoke of true reality in a world beyond, so too proponents of artificial intelligence promote a better life apart from this biological one. The primacy of mind over body, however, stands at odds with the whole ecological movement of interrelatedness. Artificial intelligence enforces an unhealthy dualism that draws attention away from the earth. Ecology tells us we are part of the web of life, while information technology promises to liberate humans from the burden of finite, earthly reality. The human person, wedded to the artificial screen, is caught between care for the earth and flight from the world. Although we are socially linked through various Internet sites and have immediate access to information, we are simultaneously connected and disconnected. We sit alone as we privately engage in our social Internet worlds. The technology that joins us together keeps us apart, creating in real time a virtual community that ultimately abandons nature.

Noreen Herzfeld discusses the prevalence of violent video games among teenage boys where one can play in the "god mode" and control life and death. She indicates that playing violent video games may be rewiring the human brain or at least

---

[31] Lynn White, "The Historical Roots of Our Ecologic Crisis," *Science* 155 (March 10, 1967): 1205.

enhancing those brain centers associated with violence and aggressive behavior.[32] Children today are suffering from nature deprivation because their playground is the artificial screen. Some scholars suggest that Eric Harris and Dylan Klebold were driven to violently massacre their classmates at Columbine High School because of the influence of the video games *Doom* and *Wolfenstein 3D*. One psychiatrist said that their lives were most gratifying while playing in a virtual world. Addiction to violence through constant exposure to violent imagery may be desensitizing youth to violence and perhaps depersonalizing them as well. Herzfeld notes that the prevalence of cyberviolence can only exacerbate ecological destruction, as these lead increasingly to the disconnect between the human person and the natural world.

Internet technology offers a controlled world free of suffering and death. Yet, as R. Louv points out, nature means natural wildness, biodiversity, and abundance. "It serves as a blank slate upon which a child draws and reinterprets the culture's fantasies . . . a creation that is somehow richer than the scientifically accessible world, because it interacts more intimately with a person."[33] A thoroughly domesticated nature can no longer fulfill this role. When the artificiality of a random number algorithm such as a computer game replaces the surprises of natural richness, we lose something of human life. When we replace the earth with an artificial screen we cut ourselves off to its secret workings. We become so vulnerable in the face of the void that we have to keep filling up our lives with more stuff, including information. Technology pushes us along at such rapid speeds that the human brain cannot absorb the information sufficiently to process. Hence, we are increasingly overwhelmed and fragmented. José Arguelles believes that the speed of the machine has now surpassed the speed of thought. The result is "great psychic turbulence, opening fractures and

---

[32] Herzfeld, *Technology and Religion*, 74. Herzfeld writes: "Immersion in cyberspace sets up a cybernetic loop between the human and the machine, a loop that allows each to be changed by the others. The player becomes the game, and the game plays the player."

[33] Richard Louv, *Last Child in the Woods: Saving Our Children from Nature—Deficit Disorder* (Chapel Hill, NC: Algonquin, 2005), 7.

fault lines in the collective unconscious."[34] For protection, the human nervous system "numbs out" to protect itself from this destructive energy.

Most of nature's changes are slow and mysterious. Have we ever seen, for example, a rosebud unfurl? Only by spending time in nature can we act on behalf of nature. By shutting ourselves up in artificial environments we lose the sense of what it means to be created, contingent, and finite. Alfred Kracher writes: "Nature can frighten . . . and this fright serves a purpose, to awaken in us our dependency on God, the earth and other people." He goes on to say that "a planet ruled by predictability where all contingency is eliminated is also a planet dominated by unchecked evil."[35] If we can control our relationships, our loves, and our dislikes, we not only control evil unwittingly, but we can become evil unknowingly. Harmony requires wildness—the unpredictability of nature, the contingency that makes the world what it is—a sense of astonishment, wonder, and awe.

Computer technology depends on individual control, preempting relationships of dependency on one another and the earth. If we do not like our virtual friends, we can delete them. Artificial intelligence can lend itself to community without commitment and mutuality without responsibility. It can lead to narcissism, self-indulgence, and isolation if it is not used reflectively to further wholeness and unity. Technologies of the self, whether a cyber self or new genetic self, "are self-asserting rather than self-transforming, enhancing the ego rather than surrendering it to a greater reality and purpose." R. Cole-Turner points to the pelagian lure of technology, which "offers the illusion of a managed grace whereby the self can fix itself up without changing." We believe we have created the means to control the self, Cole-Turner states, "when in truth we have increased only the

---

[34] José Arguelles, *Manifesto for the Noosphere: The Next Stage in the Evolution of Human Consciousness* (Berkeley, CA: Evolver Editions, 2011), 35.

[35] Alfred Kracher, "Nature and Technology as Competing Myths," in *Creation's Diversity: Voices from Theology and Science*, ed. William B. Drees, Hubert Meisinger, and Taede A. Smedes (London: T&T Clark, 2008), 83–84.

power of the self to control, leaving the self unchanged yet self-changing. . . . Technology is not out of control because it is a real power, but because we cannot control what is supposed to control it: namely, ourselves."[36] By artificially controlling our lives we are cutting ourselves off from the richness of life.

Entering the Noosphere

Teilhard de Chardin was acutely aware of internal forces that could thwart the direction of evolution toward the Omega point. In his own day he was concerned about the use of resources, limited food supplies, and whether or not an expanding population would be able to live amiably and in peace under conditions he no longer described as "convergence" but as "external compression."[37] He described humanity as facing an insurmountable "wall," and the human reaction as being either the *extroversion* of "escape" or the *introverted pessimism* of Sartre's "existentialism," that is, other-worldliness or despair.[38] Human evolution faces forces of opposition that threaten to devolve and fragment it. The danger Teilhard worried about most is that humanity, in losing its faith in God, would also lose what he called its "zest for living."[39] He questioned whether or not "a scientific justification of faith in progress was now being confronted by an accumulation of scientific evidence pointing to the reverse—the species doomed to extinction."[40] The only solu-

---

[36] Ronald Cole-Turner, "Biotechnology and the Religion-Science Discussion," in *The Oxford Handbook of Religion and Science*, eds. Philip Clayton and Zachary Zimpson (New York: Oxford University Press, 2006), 941–42.

[37] Pierre Teilhard de Chardin, *The Future of Man,* trans. Norman Denny (New York: Harper and Row, 1964), 235.

[38] In Richard W. Kropf, "Teilhard and the Limits to Growth: The Evolutionary Dynamic toward 'UltraHumanity,'" 8, paper presented at the annual meeting of the Catholic Theological Society of America, Halifax, Nova Scotia, June 2010.

[39] See Pierre Teilhard de Chardin, *Activation of Energy,* trans. René Hague (New York: Harcourt Brace Jovanovich, 1970), 229–43.

[40] See Teilhard de Chardin, *The Future of Man,* 298–303.

tion, he indicated, is not an improvement of living conditions, as desirable as that might be; rather, the inner pressures of history are the catalyst for evolution toward more being. The choice is between compression or some new breakthrough into a new state of human, that is, to evolve.

Teilhard was fascinated by the new technology emerging around him. He visited the cyclotron at Berkeley, California, and described the immense energy in the universe that science could now study. He was also fascinated by the emerging computer technology and foresaw that computers could lead us to a new stage of consciousness. He saw that technology has initiated the next step of evolution, the noosphere, but we must take hold of this new level of consciousness and evolve.[41] The word *noosphere* means a sphere of the mind, from the Greek *nous* or mind. It is a provocative idea that has influenced many cultural leaders, such as Al Gore and Mario Cuomo. Teilhard writes:

> The idea is that the Earth [is] not only becoming covered by myriads of grains of thought, but becoming enclosed in a single thinking envelope so as to form a single vast grain of thought on the sidereal scale, the plurality of individual reflections grouping themselves together and reinforcing one another in the act of a single unanimous reflection.[42]

The noosphere is a psychosocial process, a planetary "neo-envelope" *essentially linked with the biosphere* in which it has its root, yet is distinct from it. It is the natural culmination of biological evolution and not a termination of it. Just as earth

---

[41] Ibid., 204. "In the 1920s Teilhard coined the word *noosphere* in collaboration with his friend Edouard Le Roy. Derived from the Greek word *nous* or mind in the sense of integrating vision, the noosphere describes the layer of mind, thought and spirit within the layer of life covering the earth." See Ursula King, "One Planet, One Spirit: Searching for an Ecologically Balanced Spirituality," in *Pierre Teilhard de Chardin on People and Planet*, ed. Cecelia Deane-Drummond (London: Equinox, 2008), 82.

[42] Pierre Teilhard de Chardin, *The Phenomenon of Man*, trans. Bernard Wall (New York: Harper and Row, 1959), 251–52.

once covered itself with a film of interdependent living organisms that we call the biosphere, so humankind's combined achievements are forming a global network of collective mind, a new intersubjectivity.[43] The noosphere is a new stage for the renewal of life and not a radical break with biological life. If there is no connection between noogenesis and biogenesis, according to Teilhard, then the process of evolution has halted and man is an absurd and "erratic object in a disjointed world."[44] If evolution is the emergence of consciousness, then the development of the World Wide Web has ushered in a new type of consciousness unparalleled in human history. The noosphere is a level of shared consciousness that transcends boundaries of religion, culture, and ethnicity. It is a sphere of collective consciousness, a new interior consciousness that is showing itself in the way culture is organizing itself around social networks. The age of nations has passed, according to Teilhard, and unless we wish to perish, we must shake off our old prejudices and build the earth. The power of the computer to link humanity together on a new level of consciousness suggests a forward movement of spiritual energy. The noosphere is an organic whole and points to a new type of superconvergence and unification.[45]

With the rise of technology Teilhard saw a forward movement of spiritual energy, a maximization of consciousness and a complexification of relationships. Computer technology extends the outreach of human activity, but it depends on a broader use of human activity and how humans will control psychic, spiritual energy needs and powers.[46] He did not see evolution as a disruption in the organic whole but instead a greater unification of the whole in and through the human person who is the growing tip

---

[43] Michael H. Murray, *The Thought of Teilhard de Chardin* (New York: Seabury Press, 1966), 20–21.

[44] In Robert J. O'Connell, *Teilhard's Vision of the Past: The Making of a Method* (New York: Fordham University Press, 1982), 145.

[45] W. Henry Kenny, SJ, *A Path Through Teilhard's Phenomenon* (Dayton, OH: Pflaum Press, 1970), 110.

[46] Joseph A. Grau, *Morality and the Human Future in the Thought of Teilhard de Chardin: A Critical Study* (Lanham, MD: Associated University Press, 1976), 274.

of evolution. Julian Huxley, in introducing *The Phenomenon of Man*, states that Teilhard's thought implies that "we should consider inter-thinking humanity as a new type of organism whose destiny it is to realize new possibilities for evolving life on this planet."[47] Evolution is progress toward more being and technology is the new means:

> It is not *well being* but a hunger for *more-being* which, of psychological necessity, can alone preserve the thinking earth from the *taedium vitae*. . . . It is upon its point (or superstructure) of spiritual concentration, and not upon its basis (or infra-structure) of material arrangement, that the equilibrium of Mankind biologically depends.[48]

Teilhard distinguishes "more being" from "well being" by saying that materialism can bring about well being but spirituality and an increase in psychic energy or consciousness brings about more being.[49] He imagines psychic energy in a continually more reflective state, giving rise to ultrahumanity.[50] The noosphere is the evolutionary convergence of mind through technology; humankind does not dissipate itself but continually concentrates upon itself.[51] Hence, the noosphere is a super-convergence of psychic energy, a higher form of complexity in which the human person does not become obsolete but rather acquires more being through interconnectivity with others. In this respect the noosphere is not the realm of the impersonal but the realm of the *deeply personal* through *convergence* or the bringing together of diverse elements, organisms, and even the currents of human thought—a medium of collective consciousness that enhances more being. Teilhard writes: "It is a mistake to look for the extension of our being or of the noosphere in

---

[47] Julian Huxley, "Introduction," in Teilhard de Chardin, *The Phenomenon of Man*, 20.

[48] Teilhard de Chardin, *The Future of Man*, 317.

[49] Grau, *Morality and the Human Future in the Thought of Teilhard de Chardin*, 275.

[50] Kenny, *A Path Through Teilhard's Phenomenon*, 105.

[51] Teilhard de Chardin, *The Future of Man*, 316.

the impersonal. The future universal cannot be anything else but the *hyperpersonal.*"[52]

Ultrahumanity

Teilhard's vision of evolution is not based on personal enhancement (like the transhumanists) but on community and creativity. He sees the convergence of human and machine intelligence as completing the material and cerebral sphere of collective thought. His hopeful vision of transhumanism is a richer and more complex domain through the connectedness of minds joined together, a collective or global mind for the forward movement of cosmic evolution. He imagines psychic energy in a continually more reflective state, giving rise to "ultrahumanity," by which he means the need for humanity to enter into a new phase of its own evolution.[53] The value of science, according to Teilhard, can only be for the deepening of spirituality, since knowledge increases mind and mind deepens spirit. He writes: "However far science pushes its discovery of the essential fire and however capable it becomes someday of remodeling and perfecting the human element, it will always find itself in the end facing the same problem—how to give to each and every element its final value by grouping them in the unity of an organized whole."[54] Teilhard recognized the insufficiency of science to effect the transition to superconsciousness; that is, science cannot fulfill the cosmic need to evolve. "It is not a tête-à-tête or a corps-à-corps we need; it is a heart to heart." Integral to the noosphere is the role of love and "the rise of . . . a cosmic spiritual center . . . the rise of God."[55] By seeing technology within cosmotheandric evolution, Teilhard suggested that the noosphere is a new level of God in evolution and thus a new

---

[52] Pierre Teilhard de Chardin, *The Human Phenomenon*, trans. Sarah Appleton-Weber (Brighton: Sussex Academic Press, 1999), 185.

[53] Kenny, *A Path Through Teilhard's Phenomenon*, 105.

[54] Teilhard de Chardin, *The Phenomenon of Man*, 250.

[55] Teilhard de Chardin, *The Future of Man*, 75, 120; see also Kenny, *A Path Through Teilhard's Phenomenon*, 138.

level of consciousness and spirituality. At its depth, reality is a process constituted by a drive for transcendence; the human drive for self-transcendence is an expression of nature's restlessness. Science and technology also express this restlessness. We encounter God, share in God, through this restless desire to explore, create, and transcend. Theologian Philip Hefner states, "If self-generation, autopoiesis—the making of ourselves—is written into the very substance of nature . . . we must consider that it is a clue to the nature of reality and, therefore, to the nature of God."[56] When we participate in the drive for new possibilities, we participate also in God. Kurzweil too speaks of evolution as a "spiritual process," becoming more "God-like" through more knowledge and creativity. But Kurzweil's God is not incarnational; rather, God is an ideal. For Teilhard, the noosphere is not a level of individual enhancement but a collective amorization that unifies and converges life in evolution.

> To love is to discover and complete one's self in someone other than oneself, an act impossible of general realization on Earth so long as each can see in the neighbor no more than a closed fragment following its own course through the world. It is precisely this state of isolation that will end if we begin to discover in each other not merely the elements of one and the same thing, but of a single Spirit in search of Itself.[57]

If God is arising within evolution as Omega or unity in love, then technology can further this evolution by leading us on to the next level of consciousness. Whereas artificial intelligence transhumanists view consciousness as an epiphenomenon in the evolutionary process, Teilhard describes evolution as the process of unfolding consciousness. It is not the brain as a giant information processor that draws us together; it is love that unites in a way that new being can emerge that is more unified, more one

---

[56] Philip Hefner, *Technology and Human Becoming* (Minneapolis, MN: Fortress Press, 2003), 81–84.

[57] Teilhard de Chardin, *The Future of Man*, 95.

in the rich diversity of personalities. In other words, artificial intelligence can help evolve the emerging body of Christ.[58]

Evolution, Religion, and Technology

Teilhard's integrative vision of religion and technology in evolution is a corrective to the radical dependence on technology in our own age. Although he was a scientist and valued the contribution of science and technology to the progress of humanity, he was not mesmerized by science as the panacea for life's ills. His clear vision of evolution as a process of Christogenesis allowed him to appreciate technology and the role it could play in furthering this process. He intuitively knew in the mid-twentieth century that if the church did not adopt evolution as the new Genesis story, human life and culture would dissipate. His intuition has become reality. Because neither Christianity nor world religions have adopted evolution as the human story, institutional religions have become untethered from daily life and the dynamic spirit of human evolution. War, injustice, poverty, and violence continue to plague the earth, while anticipation of other-worldly life dominates religious rhetoric. We have no real sense of belonging to a christogenic web of life.

Building on the old Genesis story of paradise and bodies free from suffering and death, transhumanists see technology as the fulfillment of what religion promises. Human beings have the capacity to invent new bodies and thus fulfill their deep religious desires for salvation and immortality. In short, the power of religion has been transferred to technology, especially artificial intelligence and genetics; the exponential rate of technology's development makes new bodies within our reach. But the unreflected cyber life may not be worth living. Social networks, for example, can give the appearance of belonging, but with the

---

[58] Teilhard describes it in two essays written in 1950, the first of which (dated January 6) describes his belief, "On the Probable Coming of an 'Ultra-Humanity'" (*The Future of Man*, 270–80), and the second (dated January 18), with the title in the form of a question, "How May We Conceive and Hope that Human Unanimisation Will Be Realized on Earth?" (*The Future of Man*, 281–88).

touch of a button the person you thought you loved and who loved you can delete you. We can marry a robot or have "robo-friends," but who will challenge us to grow in love? The cyber world can become a new flight of the alone to the alone if we fail to use technology to deepen the heart of love.

Teilhard saw that technology could further religion as the core of evolution. To reiterate his insight: "Religion, born of the earth's need for the disclosing of a God, is related to and co-extensive with, not the individual human but the whole of humankind."[59] As we advance from individual conscious-ness to collective consciousness, we see that reality is a single organic evolutionary flowing. The noosphere is not simply a new level of global mind; rather, the new level of global mind is the emergence of Christ. As we come together in a new level of consciousness, we have the capacity to unite in a new way. Through a collectivization of consciousness, Teilhard sees the possibility of a new global unity in love. Christianity has the capacity to lead evolution toward more being and consciousness and thus to the fullness of Christ. However, the new emerging level of global consciousness, the noosphere, means that each individual path to divinity must be left behind; religions must converge with other religions. Christianity, in this respect, is less a formal religion than a divinization of humanity and cosmos. Tribalism opposes evolution when the bounds of separateness resist the urge to unify. For evolution to advance to the next level of shared humanity and deepened consciousness, religions must unify on the level of love and consciousness of an ultimate ground. The seeds of this evolution are already planted in the forms of interreligious dialogue, ecumenism, and interreligious aims such as the interreligious eco-justice network. World reli-gions are becoming more at home in the presence of one another than at home because of dialogue and Internet communication. The lines of religious differences are becoming blurred or erased through the immediate and undifferentiated Internet and social networking; hence, a new shared consciousness is emerging based on the values we hold as a species.

---

[59] Teilhard de Chardin, *How I Believe*, trans. René Hague (New York: Harper and Row, 1969), 61.

Technology is not outside the realm of religion but integral to its purpose and development. We cannot know how to use or develop technology, however, if we do not know where we are going or why we are going at all. Evolution is not a blind, mechanical process but a dynamic unfolding of consciousness and complexity. Life develops as a creative process of vitality and subjectivity. The next stage of evolution depends on the spiritual power of religions. World religions must awaken to their role in evolution and seek to unite for the sake of the earth and for the ongoing evolution of planetization. Evolution proceeds toward the Omega point not by information or individual enhancement but by the human arrow and the deepening of love. Teilhard did not see evolution as a disruption in the organic whole but as a greater unification of the whole in and through the human person: "We should consider inter-thinking humanity as a new type of organism whose destiny it is to realize new possibilities for evolving life on this planet."[60] Through the inner law of convergence-complexity, God is being born from within; "from universal evolution God emerges in our minds greater and more necessary than ever."[61] As we advance from individual consciousness to collective consciousness we perceive a new age in which we can no longer divide up life, space, and time into self-isolated fragments. Rather, reality is a single, organic, evolutionary flowing. In this respect, the noosphere is not simply a new level of global mind; it is the emergence of Christ.[62] Technology plays a role in evolutionary convergence, especially through collective consciousness, but the endpoint is not technology or Techno sapiens; it is Omega, being-in-love. As biogenesis yields to noogenesis, love will emerge more unified through collective consciousness. We must strive not to enhance ourselves or transcend our biological limits. Instead, we must deepen our capacity to love.

---

[60] Teilhard de Chardin, *The Future of Man*, 20.

[61] Teilhard de Chardin, *Human Energy*, trans. J. M. Cohen (New York: Harcourt Brace Jovanovich, 1969), 43.

[62] Kenny, *A Path Through Teilhard's Phenomenon*, 123–24.

Chapter Ten

Contemplative Evolution

Computers were developed to help us think faster and more efficiently, but now they are beginning to think for us as well. We are addicted to the power of the mind and are lured into buying silicon chips that will provide faster speed and more efficient information. We are what we think and the better we can think (we think), the better off we will be. Although the processing power of the human brain can still outpace the fastest computer, the development of faster chips is closing the gap. What is less accounted for is the human brain's energy limits of computational power. When the human brain is bombarded by huge amounts of information, it simply cannot generate enough energy to process and hence fatigues. A fatigued brain makes for a perfect "couch potato," and the vicious loop from computer to television to cell phone back to computer only serves to reinforce the mind-body dualism and a fatigued brain.

But what if Descartes was wrong about the human brain as the only real thinking machine and we have built modern technological culture on the faulty premise of mind-brain dualism? In 1994 neurologist Antonio Damasio published a landmark work titled *Descartes' Error: Emotion, Reason, and the Human Brain* in which he showed that emotions are part of the brain. A defect in the emotional brain shows up as a defect in thinking. Damasio found that patients with brain damage in the frontal lobes, due to disease or injury, performed normally on intelligence tests but could not prioritize tasks, manage time, or feel the tragic events of life by showing emotion. In a more recent book

Damasio looked to the Dutch Jew Baruch Spinoza, a contemporary of Descartes, who challenged his *cogito* theory and lost.[1] In Spinoza's book *The Ethics*, published after his death in 1677, he argues that body and mind are not two separate entities but one continuous substance. He claims that the mind exists purely for the body's sake, to ensure its survival.

Neuroscientists are now beginning to see that history may have sided with the wrong man. Consciousness is not a matter of the brain alone but a complex and indivisible mind-brain-body system. By tracing information systems in lower species, Damasio points out that in evolutionary history organisms must have begun with a concern only for their internal problems and prospects, then gradually moved to a concern for proximal problems, and then advanced to more distal problems. What he realized is that "nature appears to have built the apparatus of rationality [mind] not just on top of the apparatus of biological regulation, but also *from it* and *with it*."[2] Even quantum physics suggests that the mindfulness of nature seems to begin with the Big Bang. As the brain complexified in evolutionary history, the ability to process more complex interactions developed. What we call the "self" or the "I" is not an isolated module in the brain but neural representations that depend on the senses and sensory cortices, emotions spread throughout the body, and somatic experience. The division between reason and passion, or cognition and emotion is, from a neurological point of view, a fallacy. The mind is engaged in telling the story of the body's events and uses that story to optimize the life of the organism. Emotions are central to cognition and thus survival.[3]

The discovery of the thinking body or the mind-brain-body complex relates to what we know about nature on the whole; every aspect of nature is part of an unbearable wholeness of being. Organisms are resilient patterns of energy flow, and to understand living systems, we must come to see them not

---

[1] Antonio R. Damasio, *Looking for Spinoza: Joy, Sorrow, and the Feeling Brain* (Boston: Houghton Mifflin Harcourt, 2003).

[2] Antonio R. Damasio, *Descartes' Error: Emotion, Reason, and the Human Brain* (New York: Avon Books, 1994), 128.

[3] Emily Eakin, "Spinoza vs. Descartes," *New York Times* (April 19, 2003).

mechanistically, as machines, but as stable, complex, dynamic organizations.[4] We are wholes within wholes all the way back to the Big Bang. This wholeness of Big Bang being, theologically, speaks to us of the unbridled wholeness of love that we name God. Love at the heart of being empowers life toward more being and more life; God is the energy of wholeness and the irresistible lure to greater wholeness. God is the integral whole that attracts every whole toward greater wholeness. This divine wholeness in love—Trinity—pours itself into otherness to become oneness. God's love empties into being; God is the being of being, the breath of breath, transcending every breath (leaving us breathless at times), by the sheer excess of love. God's love is always the more of what any finite being can express; hence, God is always the horizon of what we are coming to be. God emerges from within by means of union in love as ever newness in love and the future of every new love.

Conscious Love

Wholeness is salvific. Wholeness is healthy and life giving, which is probably why wholeness is not something one can purchase or possess. Rather, wholeness is the experience of oneness at the heart of being; the "I" knowingly embraced by a "thou," an ineffable bond of love and peace. The emergence of love in evolution is not merely a physical law of attraction for the propagation of the species; it is the longing for oneness, for belonging to another. Every human person desires to love and to be loved, to belong to another, because we come from another. We are born social and relational.[5] We yearn to belong, to be part of a larger whole that includes not only friends and family but neighbors, community, trees, flowers, sun, earth, stars. We are born of nature and are part of nature; that is, we are born

---

[4] Freeman Dyson, "Our Biotech Future," *New York Times Book Review* (July 19, 2007).

[5] For an interesting discussion on sociality from the point of the physical sciences, see Howard K. Bloom, *The Global Brain: The Evolution of Mass Mind from the Big Bang to the Twenty-first Century* (New York: Wiley, 2001).

into a web of life and are part of a web of life. We cannot know what this means, however, without seeing ourselves within the story of the Big Bang universe. Human life must be traced back to the time when life was deeply one, a Singularity, whereby the intensity of mass-energy exploded into consciousness. Deep in our DNA we belong to the stars, the trees, and the galaxies. "Biologists tell us that we are entwined with all life-forms on our planet; our fortunes rise and fall with them. Physicists have discovered that the very atoms of our bodies are woven out of a common superluminal fabric."[6] As this incredible cosmos unfolded, love deepened through the unification of elements into more complex-conscious entities. Love and consciousness intertwined in the Big Bang universe and emerged in the human person as yearning and desire for another—marriage, friendship, community—the interweaving evolution of "I" and "thou." Deep within we long for unity because, at the most fundamental level, we are already one. We belong to one another because we have the same source of love; the love that flows through the trees is the same love that flows through my being; the love that etches the trace of transcendence on my neighbor's face is the same love that details my own face. We are deeply connected in this flow of love, beginning on the level of nature where we are the closest of kin because the earth is our mother.

Yet, my conscious human life separates me from other forms of life and distinguishes me as a human being. As a human, I have a higher level of self-consciousness and this higher con-sciousness is both the source of my anxiety and my hope that I can evolve into greater unity. The very thing I desire, unity, I fear because unity demands the loss of my separate self. The world of nature reminds me of my cosmic heritage, what I am created for, and tells me that separate, autonomous being con-tradicts evolution toward greater unity. Individualism opposes evolution. Homo sapiens are the last arrival in the evolutionary story, the most complex and intelligent species and, yet, the most unnatural species alive. We separate ourselves from the whole and refuse to be part of the whole; we kill and maim our own species, as well as other species. We lock ourselves up

---

[6] Nick Herbert, *Quantum Reality: Beyond the New Physics* (New York: Anchor Press, 1985), 250.

in artificial environments with artificial lighting and sit behind artificial computer screens, sometimes creating artificial lives online because our own lives are so boring and empty. We boast of our intelligence as human creatures but we have lost the human center that feels for another, that weeps for the poor and oppressed, that has a righteous anger in the face of injustice, that forgives our enemies and shows mercy to the wounded. Being created for wholeness in love we are the most loveless of creatures filled with fear, jealousy, anger, hurt, resistance, and rivalry. A center empty of love is ripe for extinction because there is nothing to live for.

In the life of Jesus a power of love emerged that challenged rote cultic practices and religious tribalism, a power to direct evolution toward greater oneness.[7] Jesus showed us a "conscious love," one that sees, feels, and unites with others for the sake of life. Conscious love gives birth to unity because it is love for and with another; it is the type of love that sees the world with new eyes and a new heart; it is love that is not afraid of oneness because it knows the One-God at the heart of life. The evolution of Jesus' life is the movement from lawful religion to spirit-filled life. Jesus initiates a new Big Bang; his life symbolizes a new Singularity, an explosion of cosmic love that ushers in a new presence of God. This new spirit of love is deeply religious without being formally religious, deeply secular without being profane. The way of Jesus is, in the words of Dietrich Bonhoeffer, "not to be religious in a particular way, to make something of oneself on the basis of some method or other," but to be truly human.[8] "It is not the religious act that makes the Christian," Bonhoeffer wrote, "but participation in the sufferings of God in the secular life."[9] This participation is a way of love that unifies,

---

[7] I am not saying that Jesus had a consciousness of evolution; rather, the power of love that broke through in his life allows us to reflect on his life in the context of the universe as we now understand it.

[8] Dietrich Bonhoeffer, *Letters and Papers from Prison*, ed. Eberhard Berthge (London: SCM Press, 1971), 361.

[9] Ibid. Bonhoeffer's insight does not negate the place of worship; rather, it amplifies the need for worship. As Irenaeus wrote, "The glory of God is the human person fully alive." See also Teilhard's insights in *How I Believe*, 60–61, esp. n. 1.

makes whole, and lifts up into more being and life that which is dark, fragmented, and incomplete.

Teilhard grasped the meaning of the gospel life in evolution in his provocative essay "The Evolution of Chastity," where he writes: "The day will come when, after harnassing the ether, the winds, the tides, gravitation, we shall harness for God the energies of love. And, on that day, for the second time in the history of the world, man will have discovered fire."[10] Fire is a powerful symbol of transformation. It conjures up images of intense heat and blinding light as well as death and destruction. Where there is fire, there is transformative energy. Science can tell us what physical fire is, but religion tells us what spiritual fire does; it forges what exists into its Godlike identity. The path to this transformation is wisdom. Science is knowledge that opens windows to the inner depths of the cosmos, but religion involves a type of knowledge that includes the heart, the core of cosmic personalization. Wisdom is knowledge deepened by love and leads to greater wholeness because it is knows and sees with the inner eye of the heart. If love is absent from the core of knowledge—whether on the level of science, university education, or Christian faith—the end result is division, confusion, and separation. Love goes further than knowledge alone, because love is the essence of all that exists.

Love and Worship

Christian life is a consciousness of evolution in love and a new way of being in love. It is the outflow of an inner love that begins with self-knowledge. Who or what is the "thou" of my "I"? Whom do I belong to, and who belongs to me? When we fail truly to know ourselves, we fail to know the cosmos and our role in the cosmos. Knowledge loses its function in the overall direction of life. That is why we must return to the universe, to the stars and the galaxies, to the solitude of the desert and mountain. The way forward is the way inward—to recover the

---

[10] Teilhard de Chardin, "The Evolution of Chastity," in *Toward the Future*, trans. René Hague (New York: Harcourt, 1975), 86–87.

mystical dimension of life beginning in the human heart as that heart extends into the cosmos. We need to find the Omega center within us, that depth of love that makes each of us unique and distinct, that God-centered love which holds us together moment to moment and constantly creates us anew.

To return home to ourselves is to commit ourselves to new life. Jesus began his public ministry with a plea for conversion, to change the way we think about things, to unlearn the habits that keep us separate and isolated, to settle down in our own skin. Jesus said, "If you make my word your home you will learn the truth, and the truth will set you free" (Jn 8:31–32). We are not free because we are not at home in ourselves; there is a restless drive to become something other, to do something else, to be anywhere else but where we are in the present moment. We are Descartes's children; our bodies are in one place, but our minds are in another. Learning to navigate our dualistic lives has rendered love a consumer product. Merton says that "we unconsciously think of ourselves as objects for sale on the market." We want to be wanted because do not want ourselves; thus we come to consider ourselves and others not as persons but as products that can be exchanged commercially. "We do not give ourselves in love, we make a deal that will enhance our own product, and no deal is final. Love becomes a mechanism of instinctive needs."[11] All persons have a call to love if they are alive, but Christians have a commitment to love: "A new command I give you: Love one another. As I have loved you, so you must love one another" (Jn 13:34). Anything that opposes the law of love opposes the work of God.

If the forward movement of evolution depends in a particular way on Christian love, then we must find new ways to love, learning to think and act in ways that make greater wholes, to orient ourselves toward the future of integrated wholeness, *to reinvent ourselves in love.* How do we get out of our dualisms and into the holism of love? We need a revolution of evolution, Heather Eaton states: "Evolution bends the mind, expands the

---

[11] Merton, *Love and Living*, ed. Naomi Burton Stone and Brother Patrick Hart (New York: Harcourt, 1979), 29.

horizon, and reverses the reference points. Earth is not our context, it is our source."[12]

We all want to belong to someone; we are love creatures. We yearn for wholeness, happiness, and peace in love. But the more we look outside ourselves, the less we are settled within ourselves. The very yearning of the human heart is thwarted by modern culture's preoccupation with material things. Love cannot be bought or purchased; it is not a commodity to exchange. Love is the law of evolution written on the human heart. We are created to love and to evolve in love. Unless we wake up to this reality we will continue to devolve and block evolution's thrust toward more consciousness and being. Love lives in the depths of evolving life, but to know this love we must withdraw from the busy world, enter quietly within ourselves, cherish solitude, and return to nature as our kin. Conscious love requires the space of simplicity where love can dwell by letting go of what we try to possess. It needs the peace of solitude, coming home to ourselves where we find the love that creates and sustains us in our innermost being. We must surrender within where God is seeking to be born.

The saints are icons of evolving love. When Francis of Assisi heard the words, "Go, rebuild my church which has fallen into ruin," he first took the words literally to mean repairing the broken-down church where he was praying. So he gathered stones and began to rebuild the walls of the church. In time, however, he realized that the church is not built with stones but with human hearts centered in divine Love. So he threw himself into the project of love, making the love of God the sole purpose of his life. This was not a starry-eyed love sequestered in the privacy of a cloister. Francis encountered divine Love in the disfigured hand of a leper. Overcoming his revulsion of lepers, he found a God who delights to be among the simple and rejected. The world is pregnant with God, he discovered, but it is only a heart in love who can see God. The love revolution that Francis

---

[12] Heather Eaton, "An Ecological Imaginary: Evolution and Religion in an Ecological Era," in *Ecological Awareness: Exploring Religion, Ethics, and Aesthetics,* ed. Sigurd Bergman and Heather Eaton, Studies in Religion and the Environment series, vol. 3 (Berlin: LIT Verlag, 2011), 12.

initiated upset many people, but it changed the world around him. Seeing the beauty of Love's many expressions, he made his whole body a tongue by which he preached the gospel.

Love is not a marketing tool; it is a form of worship, a transcendent spiritual power. It is the deepest creative power in human nature. It is bearing life as gift. It responds to the full richness, the variety, the fecundity of life itself. It "knows" the inner mystery of life and enjoys life as an inestimable fortune in a way that materialism or consumerism could never fathom. Christianity was never intended to be a religion of the book, an intellectual exercise, or a cultural artifact. In Jesus a new temple of worship was disclosed, the temple of the human person in whom God dwells: "I will destroy this temple that is made with hands, and in three days I will build another, not made with hands" (Mk 14:58). What broke open in his life was a new dynamism of love, a catholicity of uniting fragmented humanity beyond mere religion. Catholicity is what we do and how we act; it is the way our love gives birth to God. The cult of religious worship was shattered in the revealed truth of Jesus' life, that all life is holy and anyone who negates life or depletes the energy of love is not of God. Christianity, therefore, is the drama of evolving love and the art of creating (and being created) in love: "The Word was made flesh and lived among us" (Jn 1:14). By *art* I mean the way life is lived creates a harmony of contrasts; it gathers together and engages others in the beauty of life itself. This art of Christian life emerges from our patterns of relatedness.

When Francis of Assisi, a rather comely man, was laid out for burial, one of the friars exclaimed how beautiful he appeared. His beauty was not physical but a radiant goodness, a "metaphysical" light permeating his ravaged body. By the time he died, he had suffered from depression, in addition to the physical suffering of glaucoma, gastrointestinal disorder, and leprosy.[13] He had become something of an outcast in the very community he had founded. Yet throughout his life he made it his aim to love the poor, the weak, and the unlovable. He persisted in love until the end of his life. His beauty arose from a deep inner center of love. Similarly, many people have commented on the beauty

---

[13] Joanne Schatzlein and Daniel Sulmasy, "The Diagnosis of St. Francis: Evidence for Leprosy," *Franciscan Studies* 47 (1987): 181–217."

of Mother Teresa of Calcutta, not because of her physical appearance but because of her artful love of the poor. She spoke of loving the poor as doing "something beautiful for God." She too suffered in darkness and experienced many years of doubt and depression, yet she persevered in love.[14] The insistence on always having what you want, on always being satisfied, on always being fulfilled, makes love impossible. "To love," Merton says, "you have to climb out of the cradle where everything is 'getting' and grow up to the maturity of giving, without concern for getting anything special in return."[15] Love becomes the luminous presence of God when we relinquish the need to control our lives and the lives of others. It creates personality in us not by adding anything special but by chiseling away the stuff we smother our lives with, as if we could become something other than ourselves. It knows, understands, and meets the demands of life insofar as it responds with warmth, abandon, and surrender. Merton writes that "the meaning of our life is a secret revealed to us *by the one we love*."[16] If this love is unreal, the secret will not be found. In fact, we never really find ourselves until we allow ourselves to fall in love with another. Our attitude toward life is also our attitude toward love. Our love, or our lack of it, our willingness to risk it or our determination to avoid it, will in the end be an expression of ourselves: of who we think we are, of what we want to be, of what we think we are here for.[17] Love affects more than our thinking and our behavior toward those we love. It transforms our entire life. Love gives rise to beauty by gathering together what is separate within us; it harmonizes our energies, creating a new oneness of heart through which our inner light flows and illumines the darkness around us. Genuine love is a personal revolution in wholemaking. Love takes our ideas, our desires, and our actions and welds them together in one experience and one living reality. The former superior general of the Jesuit Order, Pedro Arrupe, illumined the heart of love:

---

[14] For an account of Mother Teresa's spiritual darkness, see Mother Teresa and Brian Kolodiejchuk, *Come Be My Light* (New York: Image, 2009).

[15] Merton, *Love and Living*, 34.

[16] Ibid., 35.

[17] Ibid., 27–28.

> Nothing is more practical than finding God,
>> than
> falling in Love in a quite absolute, final way.
> What you are in love with, what seizes your
>> imagination,
> will affect everything.
> It will decide what will get you out of bed in
>> the morning,
> what you do with your evenings,
> how you spend your weekends,
> what you read, whom you know,
> what breaks your heart, and
> what amazes you with joy and gratitude.
> Fall in Love, stay in love,
> and it will decide everything.[18]

Love is life, and the fullness of love is the fullness of life. When we learn to love, to love unto tears, then change and growth, new relationships and new explorations, become not a threat but an opportunity to expand our love. In love, life breaks through the limits of being onto new, undreamed-of horizons, forging a new future in love. That is why Jesus' law of love is the law of Christian discipleship, for the one who loves will make greater wholes than Jesus (Jn 14:12).

Christian life is an evolution in love, living the beatitudes of poverty, peace, charity, and humility in ways that challenge what is separate, creating new unities; the deep connective tissue of oneness will not let us rest with separateness. We are to orient our lives toward love and to resist systems that stifle love. But this path is not easy. Love challenges us not to sink into the status quo, but the challenge is great; it can tear apart our hearts as we long for more wholeness but fear the cost of oneness. We struggle to evolve through the pains of resistance because we are imprisoned by our fears. As long as we remain in the old temple with old laws and old rituals, we are old wine that has lost its flavor. New wine must be put into new wineskins (Mk 2:22). What is the new wine in an evolving universe? It is the

---

[18] Pedro Arrupe, SJ, "Fall in Love," available on the ignatianspirituality .com website.

new spirit of catholicity, of wholemaking, that emerged in the life of Jesus—the dynamism of liberating love.

Transformation

Despite the church's efforts to promote the good news among us, the ladder-climbing culture of modernity has made us unfree in our own skin, distrustful of others, and unloving creatures. The movie *American Beauty* aptly disclosed the empty lives of a plastic-card-carrying species, the sacrifice of real relationship for money and success. It opens with the main character, Lester Burnham, reflecting on the emptiness of his life: "I'm forty-two years old. In less than a year, I'll be dead. . . . And in a way, I'm dead already."[19] The story of Lester's meaningless life then unfolds to a tragic end. The last scene of the movie is his daughter's boyfriend playing a video of a small, plastic bag blowing in the wind. The wind carries it in a circle, sometimes whipping it about violently, or, without warning, sending it soaring skyward then letting it float gracefully down to the ground. The narrator's melancholic voice reflects on the freedom of the bag to be swept away by an uncontrollable force of air. Yet this same plastic bag when placed over the human mouth can suffocate the very breath of human life. And this is the gist of the movie, the snuffing out of human life by plastic lives of consumerism, careerism, and isolation. The story is the failure of love and freedom in the life of a man who seems, on the surface, to be successful.

Personhood is the freedom to be oneself and to love what one is without possessing one's being; to know oneself in another. When Archbishop Oscar Romero realized his friend Father Rutilio Grande had been brutally murdered fighting for the rights of the poor, he could no longer justify his privileged, ecclesial life. He descended in solidarity with the poor and became the "voice of the voiceless," giving his life "as a ransom for many." His last sermon before his assassination tells us of the deep inner love that moved him to act:

---

[19] *American Beauty*, script available on the dailyscript.com website.

You have just heard in Christ's gospel that one must not love oneself so much as to avoid getting involved in the risks of life that history demands of us, and that those who try to fend off the danger will lose their lives, while those who out of love for Christ give themselves to the service of others will live, like the grain of wheat that dies, but only apparently. If it did not die, it would remain alone. The harvest comes about only because it dies, allowing itself to be sacrificed in the earth and destroyed. Only by undoing itself does it produce the harvest. . . . This holy mass, now, this Eucharist, is just such an act of faith. . . . May this body immolated and this blood sacrificed for humans nourish us also, so that we may give our body and our blood to suffering and to pain—like Christ, not for self, but to bring about justice and peace for our people.[20]

When do we find ourselves not as separate entities but as one whole body of life? When is the human person, regardless of race, economic status, or religion, integral to who I am? Romero's life shows that conversion, the commitment to life, can only come about through letting go of the need to control and accepting the risk of encounter. Johann Metz writes: "Failing to risk the poverty of encounter, we indulge in a new form of self-assertion and pay the price for it: loneliness. Because we did not risk the poverty of openness (Matthew 10:39), our lives are not graced with the warm fullness of human existence. We are left with only a shadow of our real self."[21] The letting go of power and privilege is a kenosis of love, a pattern of cruciform love that gathers the lost, forgotten, and disposable, making greater wholes out of divided humanity and forging a new future. For Romero, this path of wholemaking cost him his life. Justice is not an achievement but an evolution in love. The poverty of the cross is love that gathers disparate human beings into a new

[20] Archbishop Oscar Romero, *Voice of the Voiceless: The Four Pastoral Letters and Other Statements* (Maryknoll, NY: Orbis Books, 1996), 193.

[21] Johannes Metz, *Poverty of Spirit* (New York: Newman Press, 1960), 45.

body that is more whole, more one, and more loving. God's love can neither be overcome by human power nor conquered by human force. God is the power of love to heal and transform what is dead into new life.

Modernity has created a false God of war and destruction. The biggest no to theism, Kearney writes, was not Nietzsche's death of God but the actual disappearance of God from the world in the concentration camps of Europe.[22] Fundamentalism has continued this "straw God" to justify political action. George Bush, for example, used explicitly evangelical language to demonize the "axis of evil," confessing that "God" guided his decision to bomb Afghanistan. He claimed he was on a mission from God when he launched the invasions of Afghanistan and Iraq, saying "God told me to end the tyranny in Iraq."[23] Since 9/11 there has been a heightened awareness of evil, and some religious believers show a militant spirit in the name of God as we engage in the battle between good and evil. Lieutenant General William G. Boykin publicly stated about a 1993 battle in Somalia that America's Christian God is superior to the God of the Muslim enemy: "I knew that my God was bigger than his. . . . My God was a real God, and his was an idol."[24] When one God is "bigger" than another God, then we are no longer talking about God. The name itself has been emptied of content.

The logic of the Christian God is the logic of self-involvement, a kenosis of self. Love gives to the other not "some thing" but someone, the irreplaceable self of differentiating love. The lover allows the other to affect him or her; one becomes vulnerable in love. The suffering of love is not a passive "being affected" but an active allowing others to affect one. Because God is love, God can suffer, and by this suffering love, reveal his divinity. Cardinal Walter Kasper states: "Because God is the omnipotence of love, he can as it were indulge in the weakness of love; he can enter into suffering and death without perishing

---

[22] Richard Kearney, *Anatheism* (New York: Columbia University Press, 2010), 58.

[23] Ewen MacAskill, "George Bush: 'God Told Me to End the Tyranny in Iraq,'" *The Guardian* (October 7, 2005).

[24] Quoted in Vijay Prashad, "In God We Trust," *Frontline* 21, no. 6 (March 13–26, 2004).

therein. . . . Thus God on the cross shows himself as the one who is free in love and as freedom in love."[25] Love finds itself in the other so that life is generated between self and other as a single being in love. This is wholemaking in action and the sacrament of Eucharist.

Miroslav Volf explains:

> The grounding of unity and universality in the scandalous particularity of the suffering body of God's Messiah is what makes Paul's thought so profoundly different from the kinds of beliefs in the all-importance of the undifferentiated universal spirit that would make one "ashamed of being in the body." Far from being one against the many, the significance of Christ crucified is the self-giving of the one for the many. The crucified Messiah creates unity, therefore, by giving his own self.[26]

Because Christ unites different bodies into one body through his suffering on the cross, it is the cross with its gift of self-giving love that is the basis of community. The cross is not merely Christ's passion, but it is also God's passion. This embrace by the crucified Christ is the meaning of Eucharist. "The Eucharist," Volf writes, "is the ritual time in which we celebrate this divine making-space-for-us-and-inviting-us-in." However, it is not simply being embraced by God but an empowering of love by which we are to embrace others, including our enemies: "Having been embraced by God, we must make space for others in ourselves and invite them in—even our enemies."[27] In receiving the Eucharist each person receives the whole Christ—head and members—so that the entire body is present in each member.[28] In this way each person is internal to the very being of each other.

---

[25] Walter Kasper, *God of Jesus Christ,* trans. Matthew J. O'Connell (New York: Crossroad), 195.

[26] Miroslav Volf, *Exclusion and Embrace: A Theological Exploration of Identity, Otherness, and Reconciliation* (Nashville, TN: Abingdon Press, 1996), 47.

[27] Ibid., 129.

[28] John Zizioulas, *Being as Communion: Studies in Personhood and the Church* (Crestwood, NY: St. Vladimir's Seminary Press, 1985), 58.

Our relationship to Christ is our relationship to one another. If we say yes to the embrace of the crucified Christ, then we must be willing to offer that embrace to our neighbor, our brother or sister, whoever he or she might be. Eucharist means finding oneself internally related to every other in the field of love; it is the source of a truly catholic—wholemaking—personality and the emergence of a new humanity bound in love. Albert Haase writes that "everyday, in some way, we are challenged to become the bread that is broken for the hungry of the world."[29] The Eucharist is a social self-definition of relationships that transform strangers into family. It is a sacrament of evolution that should empower new patterns of relatedness in the evolving cosmos. Through baptism we are immersed into cosmic evolution as Christogenic evolvers. In the Eucharist we engage in the *beginning* of a new future. Those who participate in the Eucharist are asked to "re-member"—to be membered to—the death and resurrection of Jesus, not as a past event but as the power of the future. A eucharistic community is a new energy field by which relationships generate new patterns of love, mercy, compassion, and forgiveness. Each eucharistic celebration marks the beginning of a new future. As sacraments of evolution, baptism and Eucharist are public commitments to emergent creativity, to new expressions of Christian love that generate more love, more being, and more consciousness. But we need to ritualize these sacraments of integral wholeness in a way that reflects our new inner consciousness, one that is more ecological and communal. Liturgy can empower noogenesis if it can celebrate Christian life in ways that express global consciousness and cosmic Christogenesis. If liturgy, life, and culture can meet on the level of consciousness, we will evolve to a new level of love.

Cosmic Personalization

In his death and resurrection Jesus shows what is intended for the whole cosmos, a new way of being human with new healthy

---

[29] Albert Haase, *Swimming in the Sun: Discovering the Lord's Prayer with Francis of Assisi and Thomas Merton* (Cincinnati: St. Anthony Messenger Press, 1993), 143–44.

relationships for the whole cosmos—new life, new bodies for a new cosmos. What happens in Jesus is anticipation of the future of humanity and of the cosmos, not annihilation of creation but its radical transformation through the power of God's life-giving Spirit. Bonaventure wrote:

> All things are said to be transformed in the transfigura-tion of Christ in as far as something of each creature was transfigured in Christ. For as a human being, Christ has something in common with all creatures. With the stone he shares existence; with plants he shares life; with animals he shares sensation; and with angels he shares intelligence. Thus all things are transformed in Christ since in his hu-man nature he embraces something of every creature in himself when he is transfigured.[30]

In Jesus God arrives as the future; we see in the life of Jesus the creative power of love and the promise of new life. The world is an evolving community in which self-identity is found less in oneself than in one's ongoing relations to others. The ideal of human interpersonal relations is not individual self-fulfillment in distinction from another but mutual transformation through self-gift to the other and reception of the other as gift.

The primacy of love in evolution and the direction of evolu-tion toward more being in love led Teilhard to suggest that, on the level of Homo sapiens, individualism cannot sustain itself in evolution. We must renounce the idea that each individual person contains the ultimate value of his or her existence and realize that our purpose consists in serving the continuation of the evolution process in the universe. Christianity is the power of gathering into community what is yet unrelated or unloved. It is a religion of evolution and a religion of the earth where each person or living thing is part of a larger whole. Nature reminds us that an organism

> is a functional *and* a structural unity in which the parts exist for *and by means of* one another in the expression of

---

[30] Bonaventure, "Sermon IX," trans. Zachary Hayes, in "Christ, Word of God and Exemplar of Humanity," *The Cord* 46, no. 1 (1996): 14.

a particular nature. This means that the parts of an organism—leaves, roots, flowers, limbs, eyes, heart, brain—are not made independently and assembled, as in a machine, but arise as a result of interactions with the developing organism. . . . Thus organisms are not molecular machines. They are functional and structural unities resulting from a self-organizing, self-generating dynamic.[31]

Teilhard grasped the organic nature of life when he wrote: "The entry into the superhuman will not open ahead to some privileged few, or to a single people . . . only to the thrust of All Together in the direction where all can rejoin and complete one another in a spiritual renewal of earth."[32]

Christianity *is* the religion of cosmic personalization because it is a religion of love that is centered not on the individual but on the collective whole—the community. Christ is the cosmic person—the communal whole—coming to birth in evolution. Teilhard posited a dynamic view of God and the world in the process of becoming *something more* than what it is because the universe is grounded in the personal *center of Christ*. The incarnation of Jesus speaks to us of a world that is now being personalized in and through the human person, who is no longer the center but the *arrow* of the evolutionary process. The destiny of humanity and the aim of the cosmos are intertwined in the mystery of Christ. If creation is to move forward toward its completion and transformation in God, what took place in the life of Jesus must take place in our lives as well. God evolves the universe and brings it to its completion through the cooperation of human beings. Thus, it matters what we do and how we live in relation to God, for only through our actions can we encounter God.

Teilhard spoke of the human person as a co-creator. By this he meant we are not passing through a stormy world like a ship on a turbulent sea; rather our choices and decisions shape the

---

[31] Brian Goodwin, *How the Leopard Changed Its Spots: The Evolution of Complexity* (New York: Simon and Schuster, 1994), 197.

[32] Pierre Teilhard de Chardin, *The Human Phenomenon,* trans. Sarah Appleton-Weber (Brighton: Sussex Academic Press, 1999), 173.

future direction of evolution. We are created to evolve into a new future; the choices we make in love and for love co-create our future. When we see ourselves as part of a larger whole, we act of behalf of the whole of which we are part. "I no longer see myself as 'protecting the rainforest' but rather that 'I am part of the rainforest protecting myself. I am that part of the rainforest emerged into thinking."[33] Ken Wilber refers to the emergence of this new level of consciousness as the experience of the "econoetic self"; we do not recognize ourselves as merely strands in the web but we try to perceive reality from the perspective of the web as a whole: "You are doing something no mere strand ever does—you are escaping your 'strandedness' transcending it, and becoming one with the entire display; to be aware of the whole system shows precisely that you are not merely a strand."[34] Finding ourselves in deep communion with the whole earth community is integral to Christogenic life and a new basic for ethics. A thing is right when it tends to preserve the integrity, stability, and beauty of the whole biotic community. It is wrong when it tends to do otherwise.[35] We need a new way of acting and being in the world that broadens diversity, deepens interiority, and strengthens the bonds of relationality.

The Christian is one who is connected through the heart to the whole of life, attuned to the deeper intelligence of nature, and called forth irresistibly by the Spirit to express creatively his or her gifts in the evolution of self and the world. Jesus is brought into being through community and participates in the co-creation of it. Hence what is truly christological, revealing of divine incarnation and salvific power, must reside in connectedness and not in single individuals. We are called to live on the cusp of this evolutionary breakthrough, and this requires

---

[33] John Seed, Joanne Macy, Pat Fleming, and Arne Naess, *Thinking Like a Mountain: Towards a Council of All Beings* (Philadelphia: New Catalyst Books, 2007), 36.

[34] Ken Wilber, *A Brief History of Everything* (Boston: Shambhala, 1996), 205.

[35] Mark Hathaway and Leonardo Boff, *The Tao of Liberation: Exploring the Ecology of Transformation* (Maryknoll, NY: Orbis Books, 2009), 295–97.

our conscious participation as co-creative agents of love—to be Christ anew; that is, to penetrate the truth of the Christ mystery within ourselves, in other persons, and in nonhuman creatures as well. To live the mystery of Christ is to live in the freedom of the Spirit (2 Cor 3:17). Living in freedom requires that we recognize the connectedness that is a basic reality of our existence. We are wholes within wholes; all we do affects all the other wholes of which we are a part. We are always becoming part of a greater whole, trusting that the Creator is continuing to create in and through us. Living in freedom means being content to be incomplete and unfinished, not judging ourselves or others, for everything is incomplete (cf. Mt 7:12). Christian life is to live attentively to the intricate connectedness of all that exists and to engage evolutively in love.

Hope and Future Life

Love does strange things. It does not function logically or systematically; it is often spontaneous, creative, and provocative. To say that love is the heart of the universe is to realize there is spontaneity and creativity in our midst. The more we try to control the Spirit of love, the more it escapes our limited human grasp. Christian life in the twenty-first century must accept the past as gift, welcome the God of the future, and let love guide this Christic adventure of emergent creativity. God seeks to become God at the heart of evolution, a birthing within that can take place when we abandon messianic expectations, accept incompleteness as part of the creative process, recover the capacity of wonder and awe, and live in the primacy of love. When love is stifled, controlled, manipulated, or supplanted by law, when authority presses down from above, threatening to extinguish the burning desire to evolve, when love is overpowered by fear, then evolution is thwarted, defeated in its urge to go forward.

Evolution works on different principles than a mechanistic structure. Life functions as a process not as a machine; it is unfinished and in the process of being completed by participation. Thus we need to create new structures to fit the moment; when the needs change, so too do the structures. It is time to "de-engineer" our thinking, which means examining how mechanistic we have become—even in our treatment of one another. The principle of evolving life is the *future*, that is, the openness of life to more life and the infinite possibilities of life for life. A world opened to the future makes the present rich in possibilities to create something new.

Christianity is a religion of evolution, a consciousness of divine love–empowered reality. In the past Christianity meant a flight from the world. In an evolutionary universe, however, it is a flight from separateness. Even Albert Einstein, who did not believe in a personal God, saw the intricate relatedness that exists:

> A human being is part of the whole, called by us "Universe"; a part limited in time and space. One experiences oneself . . . as something separated from the rest—a kind of optical delusion of one's consciousness. . . . Our task must be to free ourselves from this prison by widening our circle of compassion to embrace all living creatures and the whole of nature in its beauty.[36]

We are no longer in Plato's cave, but we have yet to get out of Newton's cave, seeing ourselves as separate little atoms, needing to preserve our autonomy. God cannot help us; we must help God be God by making room in our lives for divine Love to thrive. Christian life is not about laws and authority and power; these are the very things Jesus overturned. It is about love; law is to empower the spirit of love so that love may abound (cf. 2 Cor 3:6). The more divine love can shine through the core of our lives, the freer we are to overcome the impasses we find ourselves in, the feeling of abandonment or of being crushed by powerful forces beyond our control. God is a beggar of love seeking to be love at the heart of this evolutionary creation; yet God cannot enter into our world without us. Our challenge today is to stay the course of love in a world that resists love, fears love, and rejects the cost of love. God continues to push through evolutionary life to emerge in a new, more illuminative way as God, but the forces of resistance are great. The challenge, therefore, is not to argue or defend evolution but to drench ourselves in

---

[36] Albert Einstein, "Address to the World Jewish Congress," New York, February 12, 1950.

it, to go inward and meet, in silence and solitude, a power no human power can vanquish. This is divine love, always dynamic and ever new, love that empowers us to go beyond ourselves by imagining and creating a world worthy of love.

We must suffer through to something higher, something more unified, more conscious, more being in love. Hope must be born over and over again, for where there is love, there is hope. Christian life is birthing love into greater unity; it is our contribution to a universe in evolution. We point the way to something more than ourselves, something up ahead that we are now participating in, where heaven and earth will be renewed (Rv 21). Teilhard saw that evolution is larger than the scope of the human person alone. Beyond the level of collective consciousness, he posited a mega-synthesis, a convergence of interplanetary or even intergalactal consciousness.[37] We must widen our vision to a christification of the galaxies, a new unity of all cosmic life. To do so we must fix our eyes on the future, on forging new relationships of love that include the earth, all peoples, other religions, all planets, and all galaxies. We need to reimagine ourselves in love, realizing that on the evolutionary time line, Christianity was born this morning and is just waking up to the newness of life. In Jesus divine love bursts forth with hopes and dreams for a new world. This new world is within our reach if we awaken to the power of love within us as the power to create anew.

> The lover was asked to whom he belonged.
> He answered, "To love."
> "What are you made of?" "Of love."
> "Who gave birth to you?" "Love."
> "Where were you born?" "In love."
> "Who brought you up?" "Love."
> "How do you live?" "By love."

---

[37] Teilhard speaks of the possibility of life being extinguished on earth but continuing elsewhere in the universe. The idea of planetary reflection or socialization, the passage of life to another sphere of the universe, Teilhard writes, is "not an ending of the ultra-human but its accession to some sort of Trans-Human at the ultimate heart of things." Pierre Teilhard de Chardin, *The Future of Man,* trans. Norman Denny (New York: Harper and Row, 1964), 311.

"What is your name?" "Love."
"Where do you come from?" "From love."
"Where are you going?" "To love."
"Where are you now?" "In love."
"Have you anything other than love?"
"Yes, I have faults and wrongs against my
    beloved."
"Is there pardon in your beloved?"
The lover said that in his beloved were mercy
    and justice,
and that he therefore lived between fear and
    hope.

—RAYMOND LULL
The Book of the Lover and the Beloved

Conclusion/Unfinished

An acceptable way to end a book is with a conclusion. I originally planned to follow this protocol until I started walking around a cemetery while on retreat. There I saw rows upon rows of granite stones, each bearing a name and date, some having a memorable saying, others faded with time. Some died early in infancy or childhood, others in mid-life, and still others in old age. I pondered the reality of death with this book in mind. What is this short life we live, this brief span of time in an expanding universe with billions of years before it? We are so accustomed to thinking about death as final, the end of whatever life we have lived. In an evolutionary universe, however, death is integral to the ongoing process of creation. In a universe of unfolding space-time, there are no absolutes, finalities, or fixed essences; rather, life is an unfinished life process toward new creation. Every whole must eventually give way to something more than itself. This has led me to wonder if death is not finality but liminality; finite life is released from its limits to become part of something that is more than itself, a new whole of cosmotheandric life, a new relatedness with God and cosmos that we name the risen Christ. Saint Paul writes: "Where, O death, is your victory? Where, O death, is your sting?" (1 Cor 15:55). Death stings in a fixed universe of absolute limits, but in the unfinished process of evolution, death is the path to new life. Even in death everything is in process of becoming something new. Hence, death appears as final only until we realize it is the only way we can evolve.

We cannot possibly know what any of this means in our high-tech, consumer-driven culture controlled by top-down authoritarian systems. There is little interest in adapting to an evolutionary universe, even though our culture struggles with pluralism, consumerism, and polarization. Technologically, we are being lured

201

into a cyber-platonism that can be deceptively other-worldly and anti-ecological, if we allow ourselves to be controlled by our artifacts. On the whole we are not conscious of evolution; we do not live as creatures in evolution, and we do not act as if our choices can influence the direction of evolution. Yet, after 13.7 billion years life keeps pushing onward toward more complex being, consciousness, and unity. There is an unbearable and unstoppable energy at the heart of the cosmos that is relentless, despite billions of years of cosmic life. This yearning for wholeness is integral to the unfinished process of evolution because it is an ultimate wholeness that exceeds the human grasp. God *is* the unbearable wholeness of being, the unrelenting dynamism of love, pushing through the limits of matter to become God at the heart of this evolutionary universe. Divine love evolves the universe as it leans into an unknown future.

What will it take for us to realize that we are unfinished crea-tures who are in the process of being created? That our world is being created? That our church is being created? That Christ is being formed in us? We cannot consider these questions under the present static structures of church and society. We need to hold the scriptures in one hand and *Scientific American* in the other. The future fullness of life is barely visible on the horizon of transhumanism and global warming. Without taking modern science seriously as revelatory of a living God, and evolution as the way God delights in creating anew, we are aiming to devolve. The good news of Jesus Christ is not so much what happens to us but what must be done by us. The choices we make for the future will create the future. We must reinvent ourselves in love.

In the late 1960s there was a spirit of new life generated af-ter Vatican II, the antiwar sentiment, the love feast of the 1969 Woodstock festival, and the rise of liberation theology. There was a sense of new world community, of brotherhood and sisterhood, of a new future. This sentiment dissipated not simply with new levels of authority in church and society; rather, it dissipated with the rise of the cyber world as well. People began to seek in virtual reality what was not being found in biological reality. Authority became less important as social networking shifted the attention of many people toward a new locus of authority, the cyber com-munity. Technology can bind us together toward ultrahumanity or it can isolate us into little fragments. The oneness that we seek, the love that does justice, must be face to face and heart to heart. To love means not only to discover the other but also to realize the other in his or her boundless depth and indestructibility, precisely as that other is known by God.[1] In this unfinished universe commitment and fidelity hold life together. This means that no matter what happens, you belong to me and I belong to you. Together we make a whole that is more than each of our selves and, if we are open to other wholes, then we can evolve into something more whole and life giving. In the inner freedom to be for another, we can become something new.

We must consciously evolve; we must orient our being toward new life and growth because the unity that we really are, the deep connective tissue of oneness, will not let us rest with separateness. Deep within we yearn to be one, but because we cannot find a way to live as one, we fear the cost of oneness. Too much is at stake now to hide behind our secure walls of separateness, control, and power. We must evolve toward the next level of ultrahumanity or brace ourselves for the breakdown of all systems, including the basic elements of water and air that sustain human life. We must *choose to be whole*, to be attentive to God's ongoing work in our lives. God will not create a new future for us, but God invites us to become more whole within ourselves so that we may become more whole among ourselves. Evolution toward greater wholeness is evolution toward more life and love. This is the basis of contemplative evolution and the emergence of Christ.

We need a revolution of evolution. Eaton suggests that "we ground religious awareness first in the Earth processes, second within the processes of human symbolic consciousness and only third within specific religious traditions."[2] We have abandoned the book of Nature and have lost trust in our inner power to change. The evolution of Christianity requires a return to nature, to the mountains and desert, to find—in the solitude of oneness

---

[1] Renate Wind, *Dorothy Soelle: Mystic and Rebel* (Minneapolis, MN: Fortress Press, 2012).

[2] Heather Eaton, "An Ecological Imaginary: Evolution and Religion in an Ecological Era," in *Ecological Awareness: Exploring Religion, Ethics, and Aesthetics,* ed. Sigurd Bergman and Heather Eaton, Studies in Religion and the Environment series, vol. 3 (Berlin: LIT Verlag, 2011), 16.

with God—our kinship with the earth. The birthing of Christ invites us to trust the power of love, to trust God in the face of defeat, in the midst of failure, when the forces from without want to crush the spirit within. We need to trust the power of God's love in our lives because this love *is* our life. To do so lessens the need to control and manipulate or to acquire greedily the things of the earth that we must justly share. Evolving love is birthing religion anew, but it requires new symbols and images that communicate the reality in which we are immersed. Creativity and imagination are needed as we enter more fully into evolutionary consciousness. Our ecclesial, political, economic, and social systems come out of a "*men*-tal" consciousness, a male, top-down system of analysis based on precise and detailed understanding of parts. In turn, understanding of parts has created concepts and abstract ideas, and while concepts can give rise to new theories, and new theories to new policies, and new policies to new laws, and new laws to new actions, in the end, it is all about parts. We never really understand the whole or the parts within the whole. Integral thinking is thinking the whole and the parts as wholes within the whole. The lines of analysis are not linear but contextual. As we enter a new consciousness of interbeing, we need a new way of knowing, a new subjectivity that is not locked up within itself but conscious of belonging to the whole. Integral knowledge sees things intersubjectively so that knower and known are part of the whole process of knowing. Love does not bypass the mind but deepens it to get to the truth of reality.

If the church can embrace evolution and the wholeness of love within evolution, it can contribute to the emergence of ultrahumanity—the deepening of human consciousness and interrelatedness as the next step of evolution. Transhumanism is alluring, but its basic principles are erroneous. By seeing ourselves as digitized beings, we threaten to depersonalize all of nature. Instead of leading the whole into greater wholeness, transhumanism threatens to disintegrate the whole in the search for personal enhancement. Thus, instead of evolving the whole, transhumanism can devolve us. Technology is a good; in itself it is not the problem. It is what we do with our technologies, what we expect of them, and how we relate to them that are problematic. When people who lose their cell phone say they have lost a part of themselves, we are in trouble. Katherine Losse describes her career at the forefront of Facebook, where she came to realize that social networks can depersonalize and insulate rather than enhance intersubjectivity (or interbeing).[3] Computer technology can augment the integrated wholeness of being if we use it as a means of integrated wholeness rather than as a replacement for wholeness; it can help realize our new, emerging global consciousness where the lines of difference are replaced by a consciousness of oneness. Teilhard's ultrahumanism is knowing we are not enemies to one another but brothers and sisters of the same cosmic family. We need symbols of ultrahumanism that signify the hope of a new global community.

Perhaps what I see most in this new age of integrated wholeness is the urgent need to wake up religion. Christianity is a religion of wholeness; it gathers together, tells the story of the whole, and symbolizes the whole through prayer and worship. Community is what happens when oneness is at the heart of being. Religion brings to light the transcendent nature of the cosmos, the excess of love that lures the whole into more love and a new future. Religious practices should connect inner and outer worlds into a unified whole, so that what fills our inner worlds, our hearts and minds, is expressed in our outer worlds, our actions and decisions. To be catholic is to live in conscious evolution, to be engaged actively in this unfinished universe as co-creators of justice, peace, mercy, and compassion. Catholic is less what we are than what we do; catholicity is a virtue of relatedness, a dynamic energy of wholemaking. Catholic evolution connotes love-energy that unifies humanity and earth together for the new world ahead. It means putting new life into new wineskins. We have a core doctrine of incarnation that expresses integrated wholeness in the Christ; what we lack is the lived expression of this reality. The church still operates out of a Greek metaphysical framework and an Aristotelian philosophy of body and soul. Continuing religious practices and beliefs based on an ancient cosmos is comparable to having a brain lesion. The heart and mind are not connected, and we function with cognitive dissonance; we live religiously in the Middle Ages and culturally in a scientific age.

---

[3] Katherine Losse, *The Boy Kings: A Journey into the Heart of the Social Network* (New York: Free Press, 2012).

Teilhard's greatest frustration was perceiving the power of Christianity to lead evolution into the next level of noogenesis and the resistance of the church to embrace evolution as the human story. He wrote: "There are times when one almost despairs of being able to disentangle Catholic dogmas from the geocentrism in the framework of which they were born."[4] Yet he saw the power of the incarnation to gather the cosmic whole into a greater unity. Christianity tells the story of our divinely imaged lives in a way that allows us to continue the work of Jesus in evolution. Christianity is a religion of evolution, according to Teilhard, and until we can get our heads wrapped around this reality, we are on the way to becoming religious dinosaurs. Liturgy, worship, and the sacramental life have the capacity to orient us toward a new future—the emergence of Christ and the deepening of love in the cosmos. Teilhard said that "a new vision of the universe calls for a new form of worship and a new method of action."[5] To do so, however, we need a cosmology of worship that reflects our universe. Celebrating together the wholeness of love should empower us to go forth with new energy, working together to create new energy fields of compassion, peace, mercy, and forgiveness. Encouraging theologians to think in the context of evolution may help move the church forward in the twenty-first century. Theological education should include Big Bang cosmology, quantum physics, systems biology, consciousness studies, as well as tradition and scripture. Can we theologically educate to evolve through deepened love?

The truth that liberates is not limited to the human person alone; it pertains to the whole of nature. Because we are unfree, nature is unfree; we seek to control and manipulate nature in our quest for freedom. But it cannot continue far into the future. The decentered human person *will* become a new posthuman species and earth will be mechanized too if we do not wake up to the radical disconnect among church, culture, and the future of evolution. Teilhard saw that by not engaging evolution, the church would become enervated from within, weakened by the need to

---

[4] Pierre Teilhard de Chardin, *Christianity and Evolution*, trans. René Hague (New York: Harcourt, 1971), 44.

[5] Pierre Teilhard de Chardin, *Activation of Energy*, trans. René Hague (New York: Harcourt Brace Jovanovich, 1971), 267.

control and maintain order rather than letting go to evolve. But he also saw the power of the gospel to gather humanity into a new whole. Something new broke open in the life of Jesus, a power of love that was reconciling, transformative, and future oriented. Teilhard sought to articulate this newness in the life of Jesus. By doing so, he changed the pattern of religious thinking and challenged us to think anew. God is not the divine mechanic above but the power of love within—the unbearable wholeness of love pushing through the limits of being to become more visible and alive. God beyond us, within us, and around us must return to the center of what we are if we are to evolve toward a new, ultra-humanity. God cannot move mountains, but faith moves mountains and uproots mulberry trees (Mt 17:20; Lk 17:6); faith is trust in the power of love within us to do incredible things because this love is God's unlimited power.

In the end it is love that matters; all else will pass away. We need a thoughtful love, a wisdom that sees and knows more deeply; a faith that trusts in the power of God who lives beneath our wings. Ours is the age of something radically new; it is more than a reformation; it is an evolution in love. It is not simply we humans who are in evolution but God seeks to evolve—to become more being in love, more conscious, more God at the heart of the universe. This is the truth that sets us free, the light that eludes our sight: *we* are the privileged bearers of transcendence. God cannot do for us what we must do for ourselves, empty our lives of the inner clutter and noise so that we may welcome God within. Only when we allow God to be God for us can God save us, because divine love can do no other than make whole. The hubris of our age is thinking that we know enough to control our lives, including the earth, when in fact it is the earth that controls us. Without carbon and oxygen, centered in divine love, we would cease to exist.

God's love is unmanageable and unruly; it is creative, spontaneous, and novel. It slips in between our controlling urges and dwells in the unbearable wholeness of our being. What a cunning God this is who hides in lepers and appears as a poor carpenter-turned-preacher. Prime mover? Divine love is beyond what the human mind can imagine or invent; it is not logical or predictable. It has empowered life from the beginning and promises to stay forever because love is ever new, ever more whole, deepening in the rich creativity of life's playfulness. We all have a part in this unfolding love. We are wholes within wholes, persons within persons, religions within religions. We are one body, and we seek one mind and heart, more personal and unified in love. This urging toward oneness is an invitation to evolve the christic. We must enfold the past into the quantum moment and aim toward the future, for up ahead is the Christ rising from the dead in the darkness of night to become for us the God of the future.

Select Bibliography

Bloom, Howard K. *The Global Brain: The Evolution of Mass Mind from the Big Bang to the Twenty-First Century.* New York: Wiley, 2001.

Bohm, David. *Wholeness and the Implicate Order.* New York: Routledge, 1995.

Bracken, Joseph A. *Subjectivity, Objectivity, and Intersubjectivity: A New Paradigm for Religion and Science.* West Conshohocken, PA: Templeton Foundation Press, 2009.

Brown, Barbara Taylor. *The Luminous Web: Essays on Science and Religion.* Cambridge, MA: Cowley Publications, 2000.

Cannato, Judy. *Radical Amazement.* Notre Dame, IN: Sorin Books, 2006.

Capra, Fritjof. *The Tao of Physics.* 4th ed. Boston: Shambhala, 2000.

———. *The Web of Life: A New Scientific Understanding of Living Systems.* New York: Doubleday, 1996.

Clayton, Phillip. *Mind and Emergence: From Quantum to Consciousness.* New York: Oxford University Press, 2006.

Cousins, Ewert, ed. *Process Theology: Basic Writings.* New York: Newman Press, 1971.

Damasio, Antonio R. *Descartes' Error: Emotion, Reason, and the Human Brain.* New York: Avon Books, 1994.

Deane-Drummond, Celia, ed. *Pierre Teilhard de Chardin on People and Planet.* London: Equinox, 2006.

Delio, Ilia. *The Emergent Christ: Exploring the Meaning of Catholic in an Evolutionary Universe.* Maryknoll, NY: Orbis Books, 2011.

De Lubac, Henri, SJ. *The Eternal Feminine: A Study on the Text of Teilhard de Chardin.* Translated by René Hague. New York: Harper and Row, 1971.

Edwards, Denis. *The God of Evolution: A Trinitarian Theology.* Mahwah, NJ: Paulist Press, 1999.

Ellard, Peter. *The Sacred Cosmos: Theological, Philosophical, and Scientific Conversations in the Twelfth-Century School of Chartres.* Scranton, PA: University of Scranton Press, 2007.

Frank, Adam. *The Constant Fire: Beyond the Science vs. Religion Debate.* Berkeley and Los Angeles: University of California Press, 2009.

Gao, Shan. *God Does Play Dice with the Universe.* Suffolk: Abramis, 2008.

Geis, Jack. *Physics, Metaphysics, and God.* Bloomington, IN: AuthorHouse, 2003.

Grau, Joseph A. *Morality and the Human Future in the Thought of Teilhard de Chardin: A Critical Study.* Lanham, MD: Associated University Press, 1976.

Gray, Donald P. *The One and the Many: Teilhard de Chardin's Vision of Unity.* London: Burns and Oates, 1969.

Hathaway, Mark, and Leonardo Boff. *The Tao of Liberation: Exploring the Ecology of Transformation.* Maryknoll, NY: Orbis Books, 2009.

Haughey, John, SJ. *Where Is Knowing Going: The Horizons of the Knowing Subject.* Washington, DC: Georgetown University Press, 2010.

Hayles, Katherine. *How We Became Posthuman: Virtual Bodies in Cybernetics, Literature, and Informatics.* Chicago: University of Chicago Press, 1999.

Herbert, Nick. *Quantum Reality: Beyond the New Physics.* New York: Anchor Press, 1985.

Herzfeld, Noreen. *Technology and Religion: Remaining Human in a Co-created World.* Conshohocken, PA: Templeton Press, 2009.

Kearney, Richard. *Anatheism.* New York: Columbia University Press, 2010.

Kenny, Henry, SJ. *A Path Through Teilhard's Phenomenon.* Dayton, OH: Pflaum Press, 1970.

King, Thomas M. *Teilhard's Mysticism of Knowing.* New York: Seabury Press, 1981.

King, Ursula, ed. *Pierre Teilhard de Chardin.* Maryknoll, NY: Orbis Books, 2003.

Losse, Katherine. *The Boy Kings: A Journey into the Heart of the Social Network.* New York: Free Press, 2012.

Marshall, David, ed. *Science and Religion: Christian and Muslim Perspectives.* Washington, D.C.: Georgetown University Press, 2012.

Matt, Daniel C. *God and the Big Bang: Discovering Harmony Between Science and Spirituality.* Woodstock, VT: Jewish Lights Publishing, 2001.

McIntyre, Margaret. *The Cosmic Pilgrim: A Spiritual Exploration of the New Story of Science and Religion.* Eugene, OR: Wipf and Stock, 2010.

Merton, Thomas. *Love and Living.* Edited by Naomi Burton Stone and Brother Patrick Hart. New York: Harcourt, 1979.

Moltmann, Jürgen. *God in Creation: A New Theology of Creation and the Spirit of God.* Minneapolis, MN: Fortress Press, 1983.

North, Robert G. *Teilhard and the Creation of the Soul.* Milwaukee, WI: Bruce Publ. Co., 1967.

Oord, Thomas Jay. *Defining Love: A Philosophical, Scientific, and Theological Engagement.* Grand Rapids, MI: Brazo Press, 2010.

Panikkar, Raimon. *Christophany: The Fullness of Man.* Translated by Alfred DiLascia. Maryknoll, NY: Orbis Books, 2004.

———. *The Rhythm of Being: The Gifford Lectures.* Maryknoll, NY: Orbis Books, 2010.

Phipps, Carter. *Evolutionaries: Unlocking the Spiritual and Cultural Potential of Science's Greatest Idea.* New York: Harper, 2012.

Polkinghorne, John, ed. *The Work of Love: Creation as Kenosis.* Grand Rapids, MI: Eerdmans, 2001.

Purcell, Brendan. *From Big Bang to Big Mystery: Human Origins in the Light of Creation and Evolution.* New York: New City Press, 2012.

Rolheiser, Ronald. *The Holy Longing: The Search for a Christian Spirituality.* New York: Doubleday, 1999.

Rubenstein, Richard E. *Aristotle's Children: How Christians, Muslims, and Jews Rediscovered Ancient Wisdom and Illuminated the Middle Ages.* New York: Harcourt Books, 2003.

Shults, F. Leron. *Science and Christology.* Grand Rapids, MI: Eerdmans, 2008.

Swimme, Brian. *The Hidden Heart of the Cosmos.* Maryknoll, NY: Orbis Books, 1996.

Taylor, Mark. *After God.* Chicago: University of Chicago Press, 2007.

Teilhard de Chardin, Pierre. *Activation of Energy.* Translated by René Hague. New York: Harcourt Brace Jovanovich, Inc., 1970.

———. *Christianity and Evolution.* Translated by René Hague. New York: Harcourt, 1971.

———. *The Divine Milieu: An Essay on the Interior Life.* Translated by William Collins. New York: Harper and Row, 1960.

———. *The Future of Man.* Translated by Norman Denny. New York: Harper and Row, 1964.

———. *Human Energy.* Translated by J. M. Cohen. New York: Harcourt Brace Jovanovich, 1969.

———. *The Human Phenomenon.* Translated by Sarah Appleton-Weber. Brighton: Sussex Academic Press, 1999.

———. *The Phenomenon of Man.* Translated by Bernard Wall. New York: Harper and Row, 1959.

———. *Toward the Future.* Translated by René Hague. New York: Harcourt, 1975.

———. *Writings in Time of War.* Translated by René Hague. New York: Harper and Row, 1968.

Tillich, Paul. *Biblical Religion and the Search for Ultimate Realty.* Chicago: University of Chicago, 1955.

———. *Systematic Theology.* Vol. 1. Chicago: University of Chicago Press, 1951.

———. *Theology of Culture.* New York: Oxford University Press, 1959.

Toolan, David. *At Home in the Cosmos.* Maryknoll, NY: Orbis Books, 2003.

Tucker, Mary Evelyn, ed. *Sacred Universe: Earth, Spirituality, and Religion in the Twenty-First Century.* New York: Columbia University Press, 2009.

Turkle, Sherry, *Alone Together: Why We Expect More from Technology and Less from Each Other.* New York: Basic Books, 2011.

Volf, Miroslav. *Exclusion and Embrace: A Theological Exploration of Identity, Otherness, and Reconciliation.* Nashville, TN: Abingdon Press, 1996.

Wilber, Ken. *The Integral Vision.* Boston: Shambhala, 2007.

————. *Sex, Ecology, Spirituality: The Spirit of Evolution.* Boston: Shambhala, 2001.

————. *Up from Eden: A Transpersonal View of Human Evolution.* Wheaton, IL: Quest Books, 1996.

Wildiers, N. Max. *The Theologian and His Universe: Theology and Cosmology from the Middle Ages to the Present.* New York: Seabury Press, 1982.

Index

acosmism, 59
Activation of Energy (Teilhard de Chardin), 8n16
active principles, 11
agape, 41–42
al-'Adawiya, Rabe'a, 106–7
Alexander of Hales, 6
Alexandrian Christology, 122
al-Farid, Ibn, 106, 112–13
Alhazen, 6
alienation, 14, 116
Alone Together (Turkle), 162
altruism, 33, 52–53
American Beauty (dir. Mendes), 188
amorization, 99, 100, 146, 173
anatheism, xxii
anthropocentrism, 14, 145
Antiochene Christology, 121–22
apocalyptic spirit, 155
Aquinas, Thomas, xv, xx, 2, 6, 64, 82, 139
Arguelles, José, 166–67
Aristotle, 5, 6, 67
Arrupe, Pedro, 186–87
Arthur, W. Brian, 159
artificial intelligence, 155–56, 159–60, 165, 167, 174
astronomy, 10
atheism, 14, 59
attraction, 38

Augustine, xx, 1, 62–63, 82, 124
autopoeisis, 31–32
Ayala, Francisco J., 17, 116

Bacon, Francis, 7
Bacon, Roger, 6–7
Baldwin, James, 33, 34
Baldwin effect, of evolutionary change, 33–34
Balthasar, Hans Urs von, 85
baptism, 118, 192
Baronius, Caesar, 3
Bateson, Gregory, 146
Baum, Gregory, 87
beauty, 151, 185–86
becoming, 64–65
being: oriented toward becoming, 64–65; relational nature of, 45; union and, 45
Being Digital (Negroponte), 159–60
Bell, John, 27
Bellarmine, Robert, 3
Benedict XVI, xviii, xx
Bergson, Henri, 96n8
Bertalanffy, Ludwig von, 30
Bible: critical approach to, 96n8; images from, xv; stories of, created for building community, xv

Big Bang, xxii, 5, 23, 124, 128, 178, 179, 180
biogenesis, 170
biology, synthetic, 158–59
biosphere, 169
Black Death, 15, 155
Blondel, Maurice, 96n8
Bohm, David, xxi, 27–29, 41
Bonaventure, xv, 2, 120, 139–41, 193
bonding energy, 38–39
Bonhoeffer, Dietrich, 83–84, 93n1, 181
Bostrom, Nick, 7, 156
Boykin, William G., 190
Broglie, Louis de, 25
Brown, Barbara Taylor, 12
bubonic plague, 15
Bush, George W., 190

Capra, Fritjof, 25–26
Cartesian dualism, 10, 50
Casanova, José, 94, 111
Catholic Church: alienation of, 96–97; intellectual tradition in, 149; responding to modernity, 96; stance toward evolution, xvii–xviii; stance toward science, xvii
catholicity, 149, 150, 185, 188
Catholic Modernism, 96n8
cell phones, 162
centration, 41
centricity, 40, 47–48
centro-genesis, 20
chastity, 50n39
children, violent behavior among, 166
Christ: Adam and, 117; birth of, 136; commonality of, with all creatures, 193; as cosmic Person, 78; creation patterned on, xxii; crucified, significance of, 191–92; emergence of, 175, 176, 203; evolution directed toward, 78; faith in, 131; forming in evolution, 47; making evolution possible, 110; mystery of, and evolution, 194, 196; primacy of, 120; relationship to, 192; significance of, 116; transfiguration of, 193; understanding, 105, 123; universe organically linked to, 98
Christianity: ambivalence of, regarding evolution, 119; beginning with the Big Bang, 124; cognitive dissonance of, living with, 82, 205; divinization of humanity and cosmos, 175; doctrine of, xv; as drama of evolving love, 185; evolution and, xvii, 127–28; evolution of, 203–4; finding new meaning and purpose, xxv; forfeiting its transformative power, 118; fragmenting the whole, 102; losing its core personality, 115; new order from, 128–29; part of larger cosmic phenomenon, 104, 108–9, 118; reclaiming, as religion of unity, 101; as religion of cosmic personalization, 194; as religion of evolution, 108–10, 193, 197, 206; as religion of whole-making, 118; resisting evolution as the human story, 206–7; as return to human personhood, 104; secularity

of, 98; as secular religion, xxii; uniting power of, 105
Christianity and Evolution (Teilhard), 67, 69, 117
Christian life: attentiveness toward connectedness, 196; as evolution in love, 187; about love, 197; structured according to Newton's world, 12
Christian love, demanding thoughtfulness, 137
Christian thought, liberty of, xx
Christians, commitment of, to love, 183
christification, 127, 198
Christogenesis, xxii, xxv, 124–25, 127, 192, 195
Christology, 121–22
Clare of Assisi, 134
Clayton, Philip, 18
coherence, 150–51
Cole-Turner, Ronald, 167–68
collective consciousness, 170, 171, 175, 176
collective mind, 170
complementarity, 25
complexification, 47, 98
complexity, xxi, 20, 21, 30
complexity-consciousness, 73
compression, external, 168–69
computers, invention of, 156
Confessions, The (Augustine), 62–63
connectedness, 196
consciousness, xxi, 102; convergence of, 170, 198; energy of, 38; evolution and, 39, 40; evolving, 39, 40, 43, 54, 173–74; global, 175; human experience of, 38; integral, xxiv, 123; inward turn of, 9;

love intertwining with, 180; maximization of, 170–71; studies of, 38; system of, 178
contemplation, 112, 137
contemplative evolution, 203
control, need for, relinquishing, 186
convergence, xxi, 18, 20, 98, 111–12, 124–25
convergence-complexity, inner law of, 176
cooperation, 33, 52
Cooperation Among Animals (Dugatkin), 33
Copernicus, 3, 8–9
cosmic personalism, 106
cosmic personalization, 47, 49, 51, 101, 127, 194
cosmogenesis, 19–20, 125–26, 127
cosmology, theology and, xix–xx, 4, 12, 58
cosmos: God belonging to, 59; God severed from, 85; hole in, 155; Jesus' death and resurrection and, 192–93; origin of term, 138–39; religion belonging to, 58
cosmotheandric invariant, 66
cosmotheandric process, Trinity and, 102
cosmotheandric union, 102
cosmotheandrism, 65–66, 74
Council of Chalcedon, 121
Council of Ephesus, 121
creation, 95; as book of revelation, 115–16; demonstrating God's boundless love, 81; emerging from trinitarian life, 70–71; gift of, 143; goal of, 1; gratuitous, 69; human persons

at center of, 2; Incarnation and, 120–21; from light, 5; new meaning given to, 73; ordering of, 1–2; as a present becoming, 74–75; reflecting God, 2, 77; violence of, 82

creative union, 67–68, 75; needing Christ, 78; stimuli for, 76

critical realism, 6

cross: as God's passion, 191; mystery of, 85; poverty of, 189–90; significance of, 85–88; theology of, 133; viewing, as a mirror, 134

Crowley, Paul, 152

Crucified God, The (Moltmann), 86

culture, most significant factors affecting, xxiii

Cuomo, Mario, 169

cybergnosticism, 160

cyber life, 160

cybernetics, 146

Damasio, Antonio, 177–78

Dante, 1–2

dark energy, 24

dark matter, 24

dark night, xiii

Darwin, Charles, xvi, 17, 52

Dawkins, Richard, 53

death, 54, 201

deism, 11–12

De Luce (Grosseteste), 5

Descartes, René, 8–9, 11, 12, 142, 177

Descartes' Error: Emotion, Reason, and the Human Brain (Damasio), 177

de Wall, Frans, 52–53

Dewart, Leslie, xx

disconnectedness, 142

disorder, trend toward, 30

divine, supernaturality of, 115

divine crucifixion, 85

divine love, xxiv, xxv, 69, 70, 71–72, 77; creation as kenosis of, 68, 78; dynamic nature of, 197–98; explicit in Jesus as the Christ, 122; fidelity of, 85; freedom of, 74–75; mystery of, 81; perseverance of, 135; power of, 86

Divine Milieu, The (Teilhard), 78–79

divine nature, 121–22

divinization, beginning of, 133

Doming, Daryl, 116

Doom, 166

Dowd, Michael, 106

dualism, Cartesian, 50

Dugatkin, Lee Alan, 33

Durkheim, Emile, 94

dynamics, 10–11

dynamism, 73

Eaton, Heather, 183–84, 203

Eckhart, Meister, 61–62n12, 62, 63, 73

Ecklund, Elaine, 143

education: affecting culture, xxiii; reform of, 145–46

Edwards, Denis, 70–71

ego cogito, 9

Einstein, Albert, 22–23, 24, 25, 26, 27, 197

Ellard, Peter, 138, 139

embrace, phenomenology of, 134–35

emergence, 18

emotions, as part of the brain, 177–78

energy, 24–25; dissipation of, 30; psychic, 171, 172; sexual, 47–50; spiritual, 170; transformative, 182; types of, 38–40

Enlightenment, 7, 9, 14

entanglement, 27

environmental sustainability, xxiii

epistemology, 144, 151

EPR experiment, 26, 27

eros, 42, 46n25, 47

Eros and Agape (Nygren), 41

ethics, new basis for, 195

Ethics, The (Spinoza), 178

Eucharist, 118, 191–92

evil, 54, 95–96, 190

evolution: altruism and, 52–53; baptism and Eucharist as sacraments of, 192; belief in, xviii–xix; biological, 21, 159; catholic, 205; Catholic Church's stance toward, xvii–xviii; Christianity and, xvii, 104, 108–9, 127–28; concept of, xvi –xvii; consciousness and, 39; consciousness of, 203; contemplative, 203; continuing through a consciousness of love, 51; convergence as principal factor in, 124–25; convergent, 20; cosmotheandric process of, 126; cruciform process of, 88; dependent upon healthy sexuality, 51; direction of, 46, 78, 159, 193, 202; disclosing a new God, xxvi; discovery of, 60; as energy becoming aware of itself, 38; faith and reason built into, 148; future of, 159; as Genesis story, 98, 174; giving rise to religion, 98; goal of, 41; God and, xix, 71–72; God of, embracing, 98; as greater unification of the whole, 176; of human morality, 53; as the human story, 19–21; ideological offspring of, xviii; imparting new identity to humans, xx–xxi; imparting new meaning to the Christ, xxii; incarnation continuing in, 109; individualism opposing, 180; of intelligence, 162; as key to secularization, 98; love and, xxiv, 44–45, 55; love's emergence in, 179; love's primacy in, 193; making Christ possible, 110; metanarrative of, xvii, 99; moving forward, xxiv, 40, 159, 176, 194; narrative of unfolding reality, 149; process of, 17–19, 47, 173–75; religious dimension to, xix, 73; requiring new science of complexity, 30; resistance to, roots of, xx; revealing newness to God, 76–77; revolution of, 183–84; rise of, 15, 17; sexuality and, 51; as spiritual process, 173; starting point of Christian phenomenon, 119; technical, 159, 161; as theophany unfolding, 128; thinking as essential to, xxiii; thwarting the direction of, 168; Trinity and, 70–71; unifying influence in process of, 125–26

exclusive secularity, 94n2

existentialism, 168
experimental science, 6
experimentation, 10

faith, 84, 101, 207; belonging
    with thought, 148; built into
    evolution, 148
Falque, Emmanuel, 140
fecundity, 150–51
Fiddes, Paul, 77
Fitzgerald, Connie, xiii–xiv
Foligno, Angela, 81
form, xx
Francis of Assisi, 80–81, 184–85
Frank, Adam, 22, 24
freedom, 2, 99, 133
Freud, Sigmund, 63
fundamentalism, 62, 190
future: openness to, 197; power
    of, 133

Galileo, 3, 12
Garner, Stephen, 160
general systems, theory of, 30
genetics, 33, 53–54, 160, 174
geocentrism, xx, 1, 3
Geraci, Robert, 161
global mind, 40
God: abandoning, 83; absence
    from, 57; action of, 82; ap-
    pearance of, 101; arising
    with the development of con-
    sciousness, 72n41; arising
    within evolution, 71–72, 173;
    arriving at the future, 193;
    becoming remote and distant,
    xiv; being born from within,
    176; being-in-love with, 69;
    belonging to the cosmos, 59;
    as center, 63, 67, 69, 75, 102;
    concept of, detached from

earth, 4; controlling, 112; as
    cosmotheandric invariant,
    58; as cosmotheandric whole
    of life, 90; creating by letting
    go, 79–80; creative energy of,
    coinciding with, 103; death
    of, 9, 60, 103; destiny of, 71;
    as direction of evolution, 76;
    disappearance of, 190; dis-
    placement of, 4; as dynamic
    communion of Persons in
    love, xxiv; embrace of, 135;
    encountering, 194; evolution
    and, xix; evolutive, 75–76; as
    existence, 64; existing in mys-
    tery of persons in commu-
    nion, 70; freedom of, 78; as
    goal of multiplicity, 75; hel-
    lenization of, overturning, 67;
    humility of, 80, 85; knowl-
    edge of, 124; letting go of,
    62; as love, 70, 82, 179; love
    of, 71–72, 82, 87, 207–8;
    love-energy and, 74; matter
    and, 69; misunderstanding,
    59; mutually co-inhering with
    creation, 66; name of, refer-
    ring to divine energy of love,
    74; new, birth of, 60; new
    level of evolution in, 172–73;
    new meaning given to, xxi–
    xxii, 73; Newton's account
    of, 11–12; Omega identified
    with, 41; as omnipotence
    of love, 190–91; opposition
    to, 97; powerlessness of, 94;
    as prime mover, 12, 59, 67;
    removed from history, 60;
    return of, to the world, 104;
    ruling a static universe, 10;
    of Scholasticism, 67; seeking

greater wholeness, 102; self-emptying of, 68, 78, 79–80, 86, 102, 103, 109, 132, 190; self-involvement of, 190; severed from cosmos, 85; suffering and, 81–83; as Super Being, 60; timelessness of, 82; unfolding in evolution, 76; unlimited power of, 207; works of, attributed to science, 7–8. *See also* divine love

God-Omega, xxiv

God-world relationship, 76–77

Gore, Al, 169

Grande, Rutilio, 188

gravity, 23, 37–38

Grosseteste, Robert, 5–6

Haase, Albert, 192

Harris, Eric, 166

Haughey, John, xxiii, 149–51

Hayes, Zachary, xix–xx, 127

Hayles, Katherine, 161–62

Hefner, Philip, 41, 173

Heidegger, Martin, 9, 60, 61, 156

Heim, Michael, 160

heliocentrism, xx, 2–4, 142; atheism and, 14; combined with Cartesian dualism, 10; new cosmology stemming from, 7–8

hellenic complex, xx

Heraclitus, 76–77

Herzfeld, Noreen, 156–57, 165–66

hierarchies, 2

hierarchy, distinguished from holarchy, 35

Higgs Boson particle, 24, 58–59

Hillsum, Etty, 89, 133

holarchy, 34–35, 128

holiness, path to, 139–40

holism, 32

holistic systems, 147–48

holomovement, 28–29

holons, 34–35

hope, 89, 198

Hopkins, Gerard Manley, 100, 104

How I Believe (Teilhard), 126–27

How We Became Posthuman (Hayles), 162

Hugh of St. Victor, 120

human history, theatre of, 95

Humani generis (Pius XII), xvii, xviii n.8, 21n15

humanism, 7, 95, 131

humanity. *See* human persons

human nature, 121–22

human persons: as bearers of transcendence, 90–91; at center of creation, 2; change for, in heliocentric universe, 3–4, 7; as co-creators, 194–96; decentering of, xiv, 14, 163; depersonalized, 102; dispensed with, as image of God, 13–14; distinctiveness of, 20; fatigued brains of, 177; freedom of, 2; gaining mastery, 9; genetic diversity of, 116; higher self-consciousness of, 180; lacking a role in the universe, 13; last arrival in evolutionary story, 180–81; mechanized, 50–51; navigating dualistic lives, 183; new identity for, xx–xxi; as outflow of evolution,

19–21; primary task of, 139; related with the cosmos, 139; renouncing transcendence and immanence, 8; seeking transcendence, 10; surrendering personal autonomy, 9; welfare of, xiv
Human Phenomenon, The (Teilhard de Chardin), 19–20, 47
humility, 80
Huxley, Julian, 20, 157, 171
hyperphysics, 45–46
hyperspace, 22

idolatry, 63
immortality, xxiii
impasse, xiii–xiv
implicate order, xxi, 28–29
incarnation, 79–80, 86, 102–3, 104, 194; as act of creative personalization, 126; continuing in evolution, 109; creation and, 120–21; defense of, 121; doctrine of, 120; making new the universe's powers and forces, 127; mystery of, 122–23
individual, protection of, xiv
individualism, 180–81, 193
infinite, awareness of, 64
information, as basis for reality, 159–60
integral consciousness, 123
integral systems, 35
integral theology, xvii
integral thinking, 204
integral wholeness, 40, 47
integration, 40
intelligence, evolution of, 162
interbeing, xxiv, 45, 204

interdependence, xxi
interrelatedness, 165
Ionians, 138
Irenaeus of Lyons, 103, 120
Islamic mysticism, 106–7

James, William, 96n8
Jami, 107
Jastrow, Robert, 162
Jeans, James, 40
Jesus: changing images of, 123; death and resurrection of, 192–93; emphasizing priority of human values, 130; encounter with the Samaritan woman, 129–30; free in love, 133; greatest evolutionary act of, 131–32; life of, 105, 109, 132, 181, 185, 188; new religious consciousness of, 129–30; ushering in a new humanism, 131; as wholemaker, 131
John XXIII, 97
John Paul II, xvii–xviii, xx
joy, suffering through to, 88
Judeo-Christian tradition, as foundation of modern science, 1, 5
justice, 189
justification, 14

Kabbalists, 107
Kant, Immanuel, 30–31, 143–44
Kasper, Walter, 86, 132, 190–91
Kearney, Richard, xxii, 103–4, 133, 190
Kelly, Kevin, 158–59
kenosis, 77, 109–10, 189, 190. *See also* God, self-emptying of
King, Thomas, 20, 68

Klebold, Dylan, 166
knowing, separating from loving, 142
knowledge, 140–45, 182; consumptive, 153; deepening
  participation in the whole,
  152–53; engaging physical reality, 148; love and, 152–53;
  process of, 149–50; types
  of, 147
Koestler, Arthur, 34
Kosko, Bart, 161
Kracher, Alfred, 167
Kurzweil, Ray, 156–57, 159,
  160, 173
Kvamme, Janet, 70

Laplace, Pierre Simon, 7–8
learning, 137, 139–41
Levada, William, 119
Levertov, Denise, 122–23
life: Christification of, 100; functioning as process rather than
  machine, 196–97; future fullness of, 202; organic nature
  of, 194; partial understanding
  of, 37
light: expansion of, 5; as first
  form of all things, 5
living systems, interdependence
  of, xxi
Loisy, A.F., 96n8
loneliness, 61
Lonergan, Bernard, 149–50
Losse, Katherine, 204–5
Lossky, Vladimir, 80
Louv, Richard, 166
love: call to, 183; commitment
  to, 183; complementing the
  rise of consciousness, 43; conscious, 184; as consciousness

of belonging, xxv; controlling, and the effect on evolution, 196; as cosmological force, 43; embedded in
  the universe's fabric, 44–46;
  emergence of, in evolution,
  179; as end of all knowledge, 46; equated with self-
  gratification, 134; evolution
  and, 55; evolution in, 207;
  flow of, 180; as fundamental
  energy of evolution, xxiv; as
  God's creative secret, 131;
  as intellectual capacity, 82;
  intertwining with consciousness, 180; knowledge and,
  152–53; law of, 128, 135; as
  law of evolution, 184; nature
  of, xxi–xxii; neuroscience
  of, 43–44n20; new spirit of,
  181; oneness of, 108; of a
  parent for a child, 80; reinventing, 183–84; rendered
  a consumer product, 183;
  revolution in, 184–85; risk
  of, 84–85; suffering and, 54,
  190; transformational nature
  of, 186–87; types of, 41–42;
  ultimacy of, 75; wholeness of,
  xxv; as worship, 185. See also
  divine love
love-energy, 44–46, 54, 73, 74,
  205
love-field, 100–101
Lull, Raymond, 198–99
Luther, Martin, 14–15

Malone, Patrick, 84, 89
Mary, as symbol of the cosmos,
  75
materialism, 46, 171

mathematics, 5–6, 10–11
Matt, Daniel, 107
matter, xx, 24–26, 29, 68, 69
Maturana, Humbert, 31–32
McCarthy, John, 155–56
measurement, as public act, 27
mechanics, 11
mechanism, 22, 25, 31, 32, 50–51, 145
mechanistic systems, 147–48
meditation, 137
Meerson, Michael, 69–70
memory, purification of, xiii–xiv, xv
mere secularity, 94n2
Merton, Thomas, 90, 97–98, 99–100, 131, 133, 137–38, 141, 145, 183, 186
metanarratives, xiv, 99
metaphysics, xx, 46
Metz, Johann, 189
Middle Ages, xiv, xv, 7, 14
Milky Way, emergence of, 23–24
Mind, 146
mind-brain-body complex, 178–79
Mir (Muhammad Taqi), 103
modernism, 96
modernity, xiv, 60, 93, 94–95, 96, 142–43, 188, 190
modernization, 94
Moltmann, Jürgen, 86
monasteries, 137–38
Monod, Jacques, 13
monogenism, 116
Mooney, Christopher, 68–69
morality, human, evolution of, 53
Moravec, Hans, 161
morphogenetic fields, 33–34

multiplicity, 75
multiversity, 143
mysticism, 100, 101, 103, 106–7

Nachmanides, 107
narratives, relevance of, xv
natural theology, development of, 11
nature: as blank slate, 166; changes in, observing, 167; cruciform nature of, 88; depth in, 39–40; direction in, 125n23; hierarchies of, 34; incompleteness of, 18; as interlocking network of systems, 32; mindfulness of, 178; new optimism about, 143; quantum potential in, 41; restlessness of, 173; wholeness in, 22, 24, 30–31, 43
negentropy, 39n5
neo-foundationalists, 62
Neoplatonic spirituality, 75
Newton, Isaac, 11, 12, 22, 23
Newtonian worldview, 15, 25, 29–30, 60
Nicholas Copernicus, 3
Nicholas of Cusa, 3
Nietzsche, Friedrich, 9, 60, 94, 103
nihilism, 14
nonlocal behavior, 26–28
noogenesis, 40, 192, 206
noosphere, xxiv, 169–73, 175, 176
novelty, irreducible, 18–19
Nygren, Anders, 41

Ockham, William, 142
Ockham's razor, 142

Old Testament, emphasizing an orderly world, 1
Omega, 40–41, 54, 71, 72, 123; endpoint of evolutionary convergence, 176; finding within, 183
Omega point, 20, 78, 176
Ong, Walter, 14
On Human Nature (Wilson), 52
On the Origin of Species (Darwin), xvi, 17
ontology, 144
ontotheology, 60
Oord, Jay, 42
open systems, 30, 40
order, implicate, 28–29
Origen of Alexandria, 75, 120
original sin, 116–17
otherness, 118

panentheism, 58
Panikkar, Raimon, xix, xxii, 4, 13–14, 58, 65–66, 67, 109
pantheism, 58
Pascendi Dominici gregis (Pius X), 96n8
passion, 49–50, 51
Pelikan, Jaroslav, 123
perscrutator, 140
personalization, 46–47, 49–51, 106
personhood, 122, 188
phenomenology of embrace, 134–35
Phenomenon of Man, The (Huxley), 171
philia, 42
Philosophiae naturalis principia mathematica (Mathematical Principles of Natural Philosophy; Newton), 11

philosophy: in academic silo, 151–52; modern, 95, 96
Phipps, Carter, xix, 161
Pius IX, 97
Pius X, 96n8
Pius XII, xviii n.8, 21n15
planetary reflection, 198n37
planetization, 176
Plato, 138
Platonists, 165
Plotinus, 75
pluralism, xiv
Podolsky, Boris, 26
posthumanism, 160, 161–62
postmodernism, xiv n.3
postmodernity, xiv, xvi, 163
posttheism, 61–62
prayer, 90; evolution and, 112; silent, xiii–xiv
primates, moral behavior in, 53
Principia. See Philosophiae naturalis principia mathematica
printing press, 14, 164
process theology, 77–78n7
progress, law of, 135
Pseudo-Dionysius, 5, 47
psychic energy, 38–39, 171, 172
Public Religions in the Modern World (Casanova), 94
Pythagoras, 138

quantum entanglement, 27–28
quantum physics, 24–27, 29, 60, 147, 178
quantum weirdness, 26

radial energy, 38–40, 46, 102
Rahner, Karl, xxiv, xxv, 74–75, 133
reality, new understanding of, xxi–xxii

redemption, 14
reflection, 20–21
Reformation, 14, 144, 163, 164–65
reign of God, 95, 96
rejection, 84
relatedness, 197
relationality, constitutive, 144
relationships, 133
relativity, Einstein's theories of, 24, 25, 29
religion: affecting culture, xxiii; authority of, humans freed from, 7; becoming anthropocentric, 98; belonging to the cosmos, 58; birth of, 58; as call to wholeness, 106; connecting inner and outer worlds, 205; convergence of, 110; decline of, 93; as dimension of depth, 63–64; estranged from science, 152; evolution of, 111–12; evolution giving rise to, 98; greatest danger of, 113; as heart of evolution, 73; mystical dimension of, 108; needing new symbols and images, 204; not adopting evolution as Genesis story, 174; obstacles to, 62; privatization of, 164; return to, 103; separated from the material, xix; separating from science, 143; spiritual power of, 176; technology and, 174–76; uniting, 175–76, 185; expressing human consciousness, 118
Religion without Revelation (Huxley), 157
religiosity, 113

religious convergence, 111–12
Renaissance, 7
resurrection, 105, 123, 132–33
Rhythm of Being, The (Pannikar), xxii
Richard of Cornwall, 6
righteousness, 14
Rolheiser, Ronald, 48
Rolston, Holmes, 53–54, 88
Romero, Oscar, 188–89
Rosen, Nathan, 26
Roszak, Theodore, 146

Sacred Cosmos, The (Ellard), 138
salvation, xxiii, 15, 69; human subject as object of, 165; personal, 164–65
Schneiders, Sandra, 95–96, 97
Scholasticism, 67
Scholastic theology, 96n8, 139–40, 148
School of Chartres, 138
Schrödinger, Erwin, 27
science: estranged from religion, 10, 143, 152; experimental, 6, 10; foundations of, 1; modern, xiv, xv, xxv, 1, 5, 7, 9, 13–14, 40, 163; source of, 1, 5; value of, 172
Science and Christology (Shults), 122
scientific paradigm, 13
scientific reasoning, 5
Scotus, Duns, xxii, 78, 120
Second Vatican Council, 97
secularism, 93–94
secularist secularity, 94n2
secularity, Christian response to, 102
secularization, 94

self: authenticity of, 100; freedom of, 99; return to, 136; technologies of, 167
self-consciousness, 144
self-fulfillment, 193
self-gift, 193
self-sacrifice, 52
self-transcendence, 64–65, 173
sexuality, 47–50
Sharpe, Kevin, 28–29
Sheldrake, Rupert, 33–34
Shults, F. LeRon, 122
sin, 15, 76, 116, 117–18, 135
Singularity, 157, 180, 181
Sobrino, Jon, 86n28
social imaginary, 94–95
social networks, 174–75, 205
sola scriptura, 14
Sölle, Dorothy, 83
soul, 21n15, 115
space, absolute, 22
space-time, 23
Spe salvi (Benedict XVI), xviii
species, survival of, dependent on love, 54
Specter, Michael, 159
Spinoza, Baruch, 178
spirit, 102
spiritual energy, 170
spirituality, 95, 171
Splangler, David, 35
spooky action at a distance, 26
star, birth of, 37
Stein, Edith, 61
Steps to an Ecology of Mind (Bateson), 146
Stevens, Wallace, 45
structure, 31
subjectivity, 9–10, 61
suffering, 190; God and, 81–83; living joyfully in midst of, 89–90; love and, 54; meanings of, 87
suffering ex abundantia, 87
suffering ex carentia, 87
Summa Fratris Alexandri, 120
superconsciousness, 172
superhumanity, 194
Swimme, Brian, 37
synthetic biology, 158–59
systems, 30; deconstruction of, 163–64; integral, 35; as networks, 34–35; open, 40; organization of, 31–32; resembling organisms, 32–33; self-organizing, 34
systems biology, 30–31

Talbott, Stephen L., xxi, 32
tangential energy, 38–40, 102
Taylor, Charles, 93, 94–95
Taylor, Mark, 8–9, 144, 163–64
technical evolution, 159, 161
Techno sapiens, 158
technocracy, 66
technology, 15; celebration of, 162–63; as destiny, 161–62; dependent upon control, 167; furthering evolution, 173–74; leading to forward movement of spiritual energy, 170–71; losing control of, 165; lure of, 160–61, 165, 167–68, 201–2; mirroring human desires, 156–57; offering a controlled world, 166; pace of, increasing, 159; religion and, xxiii–xxiv, 174–76; rise of, 155, 156; Teilhard's fascination with, 169
Teilhard de Chardin, Pierre, xv–xvi; aware of forces

thwarting direction of evolution, 168–69; calling for embrace of the world, 75; on the Catholic intellectual tradition, 149; on Christianity's power to unite, 105; on Christogenesis, xxii; encouraging Christians to accept evolution, 126–27; on energy, types of, 38–40; envisioning a convergence of religions, 110; on evil, formation of, 54; on evolution, xxi, 19–21, 37, 38, 99, 172, 173–74; fascinated with technology, 169; freeing religion from institutional constraints, 101; on God acting in evolution, 67–69; God's activity, 67–69, 73, 75–76; on the gospel life in evolution, 182; grasping organic nature of life, 194; greatest frustration of, 206; on human decentering following heliocentrism, 8n16; on human distinction, 20; on human persons' role in the cosmos, 90, 194–95; identifying criteria of truth, 150–51; introducing hyperphysics, 45–46; on knowledge, types of, 147; on love, 42–46; on a new understanding of God, xxii; on Omega, 40–41; on original sin, 116–17; placing Christianity within cosmic history, 104, 108–9; portraying evolution as dynamic process of love, 99; positing an intergalactic consciousness, 198; rejecting Scholastic theology, 148; on religion, birth of, 58; on secularization, 98; seeing forward movement in spiritual energy, 170–71; seeing potential of computer technology, xxiv; on sexuality, 47–51; on *Someone* forming in evolution, 47; suggesting that someone was the product of evolution, 124; on thinking undergirding evolution, 146–47; on unsatisfied theism, 111–12

teleology, 144

Teresa of Calcutta, 185–86

theism, 190; new type of, 106; unsatisfied, 111–12

theodicy, 83

theogenesis, 76

theology: in academic silo, 151–52; cosmology and, xix–xx, 4, 12, 58; developing rift with science, 10; evolution and, xix; integral approach to, xvii; purpose of, 140; related to the whole, 66; scientific knowledge in service of, 7

theonomous culture, 65

thermodynamics, laws of, 30, 38–39

thinking, spiritual act of, 146–47

Thomas Aquinas. *See* Aquinas, Thomas

thought experiment, 26n24

Tillich, Paul, xxii, 59, 63–65, 67

time, absolute, 22

Toolan, David, 57
Touber, Tijn, 53
transcendence, 10, 62, 71, 73, 101, 118, 173
transformation, 182
transformism, 19
transhumanism, xxiii, 157–59, 161, 162, 172, 173, 174, 204
tribalism, 175, 181
Trinity, xxiv–xxv, 101–2; evolution and, 70–71; in process of personalization, 125
Turing, Alan, 155
Turkle, Sherry, 162
Tyrrell, George, 96n8

ultimacy, 73, 118
ultrahumanity, xxiv, 171, 172, 204, 205
unification, 47–48
union: creative, 67–68; giving rise to personalization, 46–47, 49–50; significance of, 44–45
unity: conscious love giving birth to, 181; desire for and fear of, 180
universals, 6, 142
universe: age of, 23; christification of, 78, 79; expansion of, 24; mechanistic, 11; multidimensional, 21–22; in a Newtonian world view, 25, 29–30; oneness of, 26; personalization of, 50; in a quantum world view, 25; relational nature of, 45; return to, 182–83; span of, 23
universities, 137–38, 141, 142, 145

University of Oxford, 5
univocity, 65

Vacek, Edward, 42
Vance, Ashlee, 157–58
Varela, Francisco, 31–32
Vatican II. See Second Vatican Council
video games, 165–66
violence: addiction to, 166; as element of human persons, 134
virtual communities, 165
Volf, Miroslav, 134, 191

Ward, Keith, 82
wave-particle duality, 25
Weil, Simone, 61
Where Is Knowing Going? (Haughey), 149
White, Lynn, 164–65
Whitehead, Alfred North, 64, 77n7
whole, sexuality and, 48, 49
wholemaking, 149–51, 188, 191
wholeness, xxi, 28–29, 179; choosing, 203; consciousness of, lacking, 57–58; greater, God seeking, 102; integral, 40, 47; integrated, 70; rediscovery of, 101; religion as call to, 106; salvific nature of, 179–80; science of, 30–31; yearning for, 47, 49–50, 202
Wilber, Ken, xxi, 35, 9–10, 101, 195
Wildiers, N. Max, 98
William of Thierry, 138–39
Wilson, Edward O., 52

wisdom, 139–40, 182
Wolfenstein 3D, 166
word-event, 164
world: renunciation of, 97; varying meanings of, 95–96
worLd, 75

world religions, 111, 175, 176
World Transhumanist Association, 158
World Wide Web, 110, 170
worship, cosmology of, 206
Wright, Robert, 125n23